HOUGHTON MIFFLIN

Reading
A Legacy of Literacy

Grade 3

Horizons

Teacher's Edition

Back to School

Theme 1 **Off to Adventure!**

Theme 2 **Celebrating Traditions**
Focus On **Trickster Tales**

Theme 3 **Incredible Stories**

Theme 4 **Animal Habitats**

▶ **Theme 5** **Voyagers**
Focus On **Biography**

Theme 6 **Smart Solutions**

Senior Authors J. David Cooper, John J. Pikulski

Authors Patricia A. Ackerman, Kathryn H. Au, David J. Chard, Gilbert G. Garcia, Claude N. Goldenberg, Marjorie Y. Lipson, Susan E. Page, Shane Templeton, Sheila W. Valencia, MaryEllen Vogt

Consultants Linda H. Butler, Linnea C. Ehri, Carla B. Ford

HOUGHTON MIFFLIN   BOSTON • MORRIS PLAINS, NJ

California • Colorado • Georgia • Illinois • New Jersey • Texas

Literature Reviewers

Consultants: **Dr. Adela Artola Allen**, Associate Dean, Graduate College, Associate Vice President for Inter-American Relations, University of Arizona, Tucson, Arizona; **Dr. Manley Begay**, Co-director of the Harvard Project on American Indian Economic Development, Director of the National Executive Education Program for Native Americans, Harvard University, John F. Kennedy School of Government, Cambridge, Massachusetts; **Dr. Nicholas Kannellos**, Director, Arte Publico Press, Director, Recovering the U.S. Hispanic Literacy Heritage Project, University of Houston, Texas; **Mildred Lee**, author and former head of Library Services for Sonoma County, Santa Rosa, California; **Dr. Barbara Moy**, Director of the Office of Communication Arts, Detroit Public Schools, Michigan; **Norma Naranjo**, Clark County School District, Las Vegas, Nevada; **Dr. Arlette Ingram Willis**, Associate Professor, Department of Curriculum and Instruction, Division of Language and Literacy, University of Illinois at Urbana-Champaign, Illinois

Teachers: **Suzanne Clark**, C. B. Smith School, Burlington, Vermont; **Leola J. Burton**, Cave Elementary, Vallejo, California; **Kathleen Gousha**, Sharpe School, Camden, New Jersey; **Angie Pink**, St. John's Elementary School, Independence, Iowa; **Anita Pohlman**, St. Mary's Episcopal School; Memphis, Tennessee

Program Reviewers

Supervisors: **Judy Artz**, Middletown Monroe City School District, Ohio; **James Bennett**, Elkhart Schools, Elkhart, Indiana; **Kay Buckner-Seal**, Wayne County, Michigan; **Charlotte Carr**, Seattle School District, Washington; **Sister Marion Christi**, St. Matthews School, Archdiocese of Philadelphia, Pennsylvania; **Alvina Crouse**, Garden Place Elementary, Denver Public Schools, Colorado; **Peggy DeLapp**, Minneapolis, Minnesota; **Carol Erlandson**, Wayne Township Schools, Marion County, Indianapolis; **Brenda Feeney**, North Kansas City School District, Missouri; **Winnie Huebsch**, Sheboygan Area Schools, Wisconsin; **Brenda Mickey**, Winston-Salem/Forsyth County Schools, North Carolina; **Audrey Miller**, Sharpe Elementary School, Camden, New Jersey; **JoAnne Piccolo**, Rocky Mountain Elementary, Adams 12 District, Colorado; **Sarah Rentz**, East Baton Rouge Parish School District, Louisiana; **Kathy Sullivan**, Omaha Public Schools, Nebraska; **Rosie Washington**, Kuny Elementary, Gary, Indiana; **Theresa Wishart**, Knox County Public Schools, Tennessee

Teachers: **Carol Brockhouse**, Madison Schools, Wayne Westland Schools, Michigan; **Eva Jean Conway**, R.C. Hill School, Valley View School District, Illinois; **Carol Daley**, Jane Addams School, Sioux Falls, South Dakota; **Karen Landers**, Watwood Elementary, Talladega County, Alabama; **Barb LeFerrier**, Mullenix Ridge Elementary, South Kitsap District, Port Orchard, Washington; **Loretta Piggee**, Nobel School, Gary, Indiana; **Cheryl Remash**, Webster Elementary School, Manchester, New Hampshire; **Marilynn Rose**, Michigan; **Kathy Scholtz**, Amesbury Elementary School, Amesbury, Massachusetts; **Dottie Thompson**, Erwin Elementary, Jefferson County, Alabama; **Dana Vassar**, Moore Elementary School, Winston-Salem, North Carolina; **Joy Walls**, Ibraham Elementary School, Winston-Salem, North Carolina; **Elaine Warwick**, Fairview Elementary, Williamson County, Tennessee

Student Writing Model Feature

Special thanks to the following teachers whose students' compositions appear as Student Writing Models: **Cindy Cheatwood**, Florida; **Diana Davis**, North Carolina; **Kathy Driscoll**, Massachusetts; **Linda Evers**, Florida; **Heidi Harrison**, Michigan; **Eileen Hoffman**, Massachusetts; **Julia Kraftsow**, Florida; **Bonnie Lewison**, Florida; **Kanetha McCord**, Michigan

Credits

Cover and Theme Opener
Copyright © James Randklev/Tony Stone Images

Photography
The Granger Collection
pp. 167X, 167V

Illustration
Jamichael Henterly, p. 107C; Charles Jordan, p. 139V

Acknowledgments

Grateful acknowledgment is made for permission to reprint copyrighted material as follows:

Theme 5
"Going West: Children on the Oregon Trail," by Helen Wieman Bledsoe, from *Appleseeds'*, the September 1999 issue: Growing Up on the Oregon Trail. Copyright © 1999 by Cobblestone Publishing Company. All Rights Reserved. Reprinted by permission of the publisher.

Excerpt from *Pedro's Journal, A Voyage with Christopher Columbus August 3, 1492 – February 14, 1493,* by Pam Conrad, illustrated by Peter Koeppen. Text copyright © 1991 by Pam Conrad. Illustrations copyright © 1991 by Peter Koeppen. Reprinted by permission of Caroline House, Boyd's Mills Press, Inc., a Highlights Company.

"Sugar: Cross Country Traveler" from *Incredible Animal Adventures,* by Jean Craighead George. Copyright © 1994 by Jean Craighead George. Reprinted by permission of HarperCollins Publishers.

Theme 5

Voyagers

OBJECTIVES

Reading Strategies question; predict/infer; monitor/clarify; phonics/decoding

Comprehension making inferences; predicting outcomes; text organization

Decoding Longer Words suffixes *-less,* and *-ness;* possessives, VCCV pattern; vowel sounds in *tooth* and *cook;* vowel sound in bought; double consonants

Vocabulary dictionary: syllables; analogies; homophones

Spelling vowel sounds in *tooth* and *cook;* vowel sound in *bought;* VCCV pattern

Grammar subject pronouns; sentence combining with subject pronouns; object pronouns; using the correct verb form; possessive pronouns; proofreading for *its* and *it's*

Writing writing a play; using exclamations; writing a message; writing complete information; write a learning log entry; writing dates and times; process writing: description

Listening/Speaking/Viewing oral book report; nonverbal communication skills; group problem solving

Information and Study Skills multimedia report; graphic organizers; time lines

Theme 5

Voyagers
Literature Resources

Teacher Read Aloud
Sugar: Cross-Country Traveler
by Jean Craighead George
page 106A

Get Set to Read
Journey of the Pilgrims
page 108A

Main Selection 1
Across the Wide Dark Sea
historical fiction
by Jean Van Leeuwen
page 110

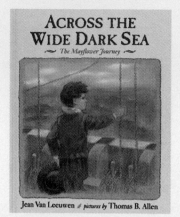

Social Studies Link
Young Voyagers: A Pilgrim Childhood
nonfiction article about life as a Pilgrim child
page 134

Very Easy **Reader's Library**
The Golden Land
by Lee S. Justice
Lesson, page R2

Teacher Read Aloud
Pedro's Journal
by Pam Conrad
page 139S

Get Set to Read
Visiting Another Country
page 140A

Main Selection 2
Yunmi and Halmoni's Trip
realistic fiction
by Sook Nyul Choi
page 142

Art Link
Journeys Through Art
fine art and folk art related to travel
page 164

Very Easy **Reader's Library**
Brothers Are Forever
by Marcy Haber
Lesson, page R4

Teacher Read Aloud
Going West: Children on the Oregon Trail
by Helen Weiman Bledsoe
page 167U

Get Set to Read
Exploring Antarctica
page 168A

Main Selection 3
Trapped by the Ice!
narrative nonfiction
by Michael McCurdy
page 170

Media Link
Shackleton's Real-Life Voyage
photo essay with photos by Frank Hurley
page 202

Very Easy **Reader's Library**
Iceberg Rescue
by Sarah Amada
Lesson, page R6

Theme Writing Process: Description

Student Writing Model

A Trip I Have Taken
a description by Maurice B.
page 138

Reading-Writing Workshop

Description
pages 138–139G

Leveled Books

See Cumulative Listing of Leveled Books.

Reader's Library

Theme Paperbacks

Very Easy

- **The Golden Land**
- **Brothers Are Forever**
- **Iceberg Rescue**

Lessons, pages R2–R7

Easy

The Josefina Story Quilt
by Eleanor Coerr
Lesson, page 139I

On Level

A Child's Glacier Bay
by Kimberly Corral, with Hannah Corral
Lesson, page 139K

Challenge

Balto and the Great Race
by Elizabeth Cody Kimmel
Lesson, page 139M

🎞 Audiotape and Selection Summary Masters

Voyagers
Across the Wide Dark Sea
Yunmi and Halmoni's Trip
Trapped by the Ice!

Houghton Mifflin Classroom Bookshelf

Level 3

SOAR to SUCCESS!

The Intermediate Intervention Program
Level 3

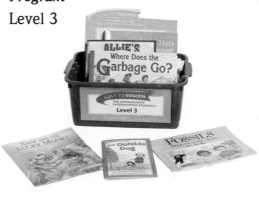

Theme 5

Bibliography

Leveled Books for Independent Reading

Key

 Science

 **Social Studies**

 **Multicultural**

 Music

 Math

 Classic

 Art

Very Easy

Take Off!
by Ryan Ann Hunter
Holiday 2000 (32p)
Takes the reader from the days of the Wright brothers to today's jumbo jets.

Henry the Sailor Cat
by Mary Calhoun
Morrow 1998 (40p) paper
Henry, the Siamese cat, stows away on a sailboat.

My Father's Boat
by Sherry Garland
Scholastic 1998 (40p)
This is a story of three generations of Vietnamese American fishermen.

The Relatives Came
by Cynthia Rylant
Simon 1985 (32p) also paper
When the relatives from Virginia arrive for a summer visit, everyone has a boisterous, affectionate good time.

Easy

Pigs Ahoy
by David McPhail
Penguin 1995 (32p) also paper
Stowaway pigs wreak hilarious havoc on a cruise ship.

Jack's Fantastic Voyage
by Michael Foreman
Harcourt 1992 (32p)
Jack enjoys a fantastic adventure at sea with his grandfather.

Edna
by Robert Burleigh
Orchard 2000 (32p)
Living in Greenwich Village, Edna St. Vincent Millay enjoys riding the Staten Island ferry.

Tulip Sees America
by Cynthia Rylant
Scholastic 1998
(32p)
A young man and his dog, Tulip, marvel at the beauty of the country.

Stringbean's Trip to the Shining Sea
by Vera B. Williams
Scholastic 1990 (48p) also paper
Stringbean Coe describes his trip to the West Coast with his big brother, Fred, and their dog, Potato.

Baby Whale's Journey
by Jonathan London
Chronicle 1999 (32p)
A baby whale is born and begins to learn the ways of the ocean, including its dangers.

On Level

The Sailor's Alphabet
by Michael McCurdy
Houghton 1998
(32p)
A collection of sea chanteys sung by sailors in the 1880s.

The Glorious Flight
by Alice and Martin Provensen
Penguin 1987 (40p) paper
Louis Blériot is determined to fly across the English Channel.

* Annushka's Voyage
by Edith Tarbescu
Clarion 1998
(32p)
Annushka and Tanya sail to America to join their father.

Spray
by Robert Blake
Penguin 1996 (32p)
The true story of Captain Joshua Slocum is woven into this story of a lonely boy.

* How Many Days to America?
by Eve Bunting
Houghton 1990 (32p)
A family from the Caribbean sets sail for America in a small fishing boat.

Racing a Ghost Ship: The Incredible Journey of _Great American II_
by Rich Wilson
Walker 1996 (48p)
Wilson sails from San Francisco to Boston to break a record.

Bluewater Journal: The Voyage of the _Sea Tiger_
by Loretta Krupinski
Harcourt 1995 (32p)
Young Benjamin and his family experience many adventures aboard a clipper ship in 1860.

Duncan's Way
by Ian Wallace
DK 2000 (32p)
When his father can no longer work as a cod fisherman, Duncan tries to find a solution.

* = Included in Houghton Mifflin Classroom Bookshelf, Level 3

Going West
by Jean Van Leeuwen
Puffin 1997 (48p)
Hannah tells of her
family's trip by
covered wagon
from Wisconsin to
Oregon.

Good-bye for today
by Peter and Connie Roop
Atheneum 2000
(48p)
A young girl keeps
a journal as she
sails with her fami-
ly from Japan to
the Arctic.

Challenge

Journey to Ellis Island
by Carol Bierman
Hyperion 1998 (48p) also paper
Young Julius
Weinstein, his moth-
er, and sister sail
from Russia in 1922
to Ellis Island.

**Titanic: The Disaster
That Shook the World**
by Mark Dubowski
DK 1998 (48p)
Photographs and
newspaper articles
help tell the story of
the sinking of the
Titanic, thought to be
unsinkable.

* **Paddle-to-the-Sea**
by Holling C. Holling
Houghton 1976 (64p)
A young Indian boy carves a small
canoe with a figure he calls
Paddle-to-the-Sea and sends it on
a voyage from the Great Lakes to
the Atlantic Ocean.

* = Included in Houghton Mifflin Classroom Bookshelf, Level 3

Back to the *Titanic*
by Beatrice Gormley
Scholastic 1997 (96p) paper
Three children use a time machine
to try to get back to the *Titanic*
and prevent its sinking.

Books for Teacher Read Aloud

 **The Fool of the World
and the Flying Ship**
by Arthur Ransome
Farrar 1976 (48p)
When the Czar promises his
daughter to whoever brings him a
flying ship, the Fool of the World
sets out to do that, meeting many
unusual people along the way.
Available in Spanish as
Tontimundo y el barco volader.

 **The True Adventures
of Daniel Hall**
by Diane Stanley
Penguin 1999 (40p)
Based on fact, this story tells of a
boy who went on a whaling voyage
at age fourteen and found both
excitement and danger.

Follow the Stars
by Kristina Rodanas
Cavendish 1998 (32p)
In this Ojibwa tale, animals travel
across snowbound
land in search of
the Birds of
Summer and the
return of the warm
season.

Technology

Computer Software Resources

- **Get Set for Reading CD-ROM
  Voyagers**
  *Provides background building, vocabulary support, and
  selection summaries in English and Spanish.*

Video Cassettes

- **The Glorious Flight** by Alice and Martin Provensen. *Live
  Oak Media*
- **The Fool of the World and the Flying Ship** by Arthur
  Ransome. *BMG Kidz*

Audio Cassettes

- **The Relatives Came** by Cynthia Rylant. *Live Oak Media*
- **The Glorious Flight** by Alice and Martin Provensen. *Live
  Oak Media*
- **Lily's Crossing** by Patricia Reilly Giff. *Bantam*
- **The Fool and the Flying Ship.** *Rabbit Ears*
- **Audiotapes for *Voyagers.*** *Houghton Mifflin Company*

Technology Resources addresses are on page R28.

Education Place
www.eduplace.com *Log on to Education
Place for more activities relating to* Voyagers.

Book Adventure
www.bookadventure.org *This Internet reading
incentive program provides thousands of titles
for students to read.*

Theme at a Glance

Theme Concept: *No matter where they travel, voyagers have a lot in common.*

	Reading		Word Work
	Comprehension Skills and Strategies	**Information and Study Skills**	**Decoding Longer Words** Structural Analysis/Phonics
Anthology Selection 1: **Across the Wide Dark Sea** Social Studies Link	✓ Making Inferences, *109C, 129, 137A* **Comprehension:** Story Structure, *113*; Making Judgments, *125*; **Writer's Craft:** Vivid Language, *115*; **Genre:** Historical Fiction, *117* **Strategy Focus:** Question, *109B, 116, 124*	How to Read a Diagram, *134* Multimedia Report, *137C*	✓ Structural Analysis: Suffixes *-less* and *-ness*, *137E* **Phonics:** The Vowel Sounds in *tooth* and *cook*, *137F*
Anthology Selection 2: **Yunmi and Halmoni's Trip** Art Link	✓ Predicting Outcomes, *141C, 157, 167A* **Comprehension:** Making Generalizations, *151*; Cause and Effect, *159*; **Visual Literacy:** Picturing the Scene, *155*; Cubism, *166* ✓ **Strategy Focus:** Predict/Infer, *141B, 152, 156*	Using Graphic Organizers, *167C*	✓ Structural Analysis: Possessives, *167E* **Phonics:** The Vowel Sound in *bought*, *167F*
Anthology Selection 3: **Trapped by the Ice!** Media Link	✓ Text Organization, *169C, 187, 205A* **Comprehension:** Sequence of Events, *175*; Topic, Main Idea, Supporting Detail, *177*; How to Read a Photo Essay, *202*; **Writer's Craft:** Setting, *193*; **Genre:** Narrative Nonfiction, *197*; **Visual Literacy:** Photography, *204* **Strategy Focus:** Monitor/Clarify, *169B, 176, 186*	✓ Using a Time Line, *205C*	✓ Structural Analysis: VCCV Pattern, *205E* **Phonics:** Double Consonants, *205F*
Theme Resources	Reteaching: Comprehension, *R8, R10, R12* Challenge/Extension: Comprehension, *R9, R11, R13*		Reteaching: Structural Analysis, *R14, R16, R18*

Special Theme Features

Pacing

- This theme is designed to take approximately 4 to 6 weeks, depending on your students' needs.

Multi–age Classroom

Related themes—

- **Grade 2:** *Nature Walk*
- **Grade 4:** *Journeys*

Technology

Education Place: www.eduplace.com Log on to Education Place for more activities relating to *Voyagers*.
Lesson Planner CD-ROM: Customize your planning for *Voyagers* with the Lesson Planner.

		Writing & Language			Cross-Curricular
Spelling	**Vocabulary Skills, Vocabulary Expansion**	**Grammar, Usage, and Mechanics**	**Writing**	**Listening/ Speaking/Viewing**	**Content Area**
☑ The Vowel Sounds in *tooth* and *cook*, 137G	☑ Dictionary: Syllables, 137I Words for Ship Parts, 137J	☑ Subject Pronouns, 137K	Writing a Play, 137M Using Exclamations, 137N	Present an Oral Book Report, 137O	**Responding:** Math, Vocabulary, Internet, 133 **Theme Resources:** R26–R27
☑ The Vowel Sound in *bought*, 167G	☑ Vocabulary: Analogies, 167I Family Words, 167J	☑ Object Pronouns, 167K	Writing a Message, 167M Writing Complete Information, 167N	How to Look at Fine Art, 164 Develop Nonverbal Communication Skills, 167O	**Responding:** Social Studies, Listening and Speaking, Internet, 163 **Theme Resources:** R26–R27
☑ The VCCV Pattern, 205G	☑ Homophones, 205I Words Used on Ships, 205J	☑ Possessive Pronouns, 205K	Write a Learning Log Entry, 205M ☑ Writing Dates and Times, 205N	Practice Group Problem Solving, 205O	**Responding:** Science, Social Studies, Internet, 201 **Theme Resources:** R26–R27
	Challenge/Extension: Vocabulary Activities, R15, R17, R19	**Reteaching: Grammar,** R20–R22	**Writing Activities,** R23–R25		**Cross-Curricular Activities,** R26–R27

- Teacher's Edition, *139F, 207*
- Practice Book, *78–80, 114–116*

Reading-Writing Workshop: Description

- Anthology: Student Writing Model, *138–139*
- Practice Book, *76, 77*

- Teacher's Edition, *138–139G*
  Writing Process
  Ordering Information
  Using Sensory Language
  Writing Complete Sentences

Planning for Assessment

Use these resources to meet your assessment needs. For additional information, see the *Teacher's Assessment Handbook.*

Diagnostic Planning

Leveled Reading Passages

Lexia Quick Phonics Assessment CD-ROM

- **Leveled Reading Passages** can be used to diagnose students' reading level and knowledge of skills and strategies.
- **Theme Skills Test** can be used as a pretest to determine what skills students know prior to instruction, and to plan levels of support for meeting individual needs.
- **Lexia Quick Phonics Assessment CD-ROM** can be used to identify students who need more help with phonics.

Ongoing Assessment

Comprehension Checks

Selection Tests

Reading-Writing Workshop

Comprehension
- Selection Comprehension Checks, **Practice Book,** pp. 63, 83, 98
- Selection Tests, **Teacher's Resource Book**

Writing
- Reading-Writing Workshop: Description, pp. 138–139G
- Other student writing samples for portfolios

Informal Assessment
- **Diagnostic Checks,** pp. 119, 131, 137B, 137F, 137L, 153, 161, 167B, 167F, 167L, 183, 199, 205B, 205F, 205L, R8, R10, R12, R14, R16, R18, R20, R21, R22, R23
- **Student Self-Assessment,** pp. 133, 139G, 163, 201
- **Reading Fluency,** p. 207A
- Observation Checklist, **Teacher's Resource Book**

End-of-Theme Assessment

Integrated Theme Test

Theme Skills Test

Integrated Theme Test
- Integrated test of reading and writing, matching many state test formats
- Comprehension strategies and skills, word skills, spelling, grammar, and writing

Theme Skills Test
- Tests discrete skills: Comprehension skills, word skills, spelling, grammar, writing, and information and study skills

Periodic Progress Assessment

Benchmark Test

Benchmark Test
- Assesses overall student progress in reading and writing, two to four times a year

National Test Correlation

✓ TESTED SKILLS for *Voyagers*	Teacher's Notes	ITBS	Terra Nova (CTBS)	CAT	SAT	MAT
READING						
Comprehension Strategies and Skills						
• Strategies: Predict/Infer, Monitor/Clarify, Question*		O	O	O	O	O
• Skills: Making Inferences, Predicting Outcomes, Text Organization*, Making Judgments*, Cause and Effect*, Sequence of Events*, Story Structure*, Making Generalizations*, Topic/Main Idea/Detail*		O	O	O	O	
Information and Study Skills						
• Timelines/Schedules			O	O		
WORD WORK						
Structural Analysis						
• Suffixes *-less, -ness*		O	O	O		
• Possessives, including *s'*		O	O		O	
• VCCV Pattern		O	O	O	O	
Spelling						
• VCCV Pattern		O	O	O	O	O
• Vowel Sounds in *tooth* and *cook*		O	O	O	O	O
• Vowel Sound in *bought*		O	O	O	O	O
Vocabulary/Dictionary						
• Syllables						
• Analogies						
• Homophones						O
WRITING & LANGUAGE						
Grammar						
• Pronouns: Subject, Object, Possessive		O	O			
Writing						
• Formats: Writing a Play, Taking Messages, Learning-log Entry		O	O			O
• Writing Dates and Times		O	O		O	O
• Reading-Writing Workshop: Description		O	O		O	O

*These skills are taught, but not tested, in this theme.

KEY
ITBS Iowa Tests of Basic Skills
Terra Nova (CTBS) Comprehensive Tests of Basic Skills
CAT California Achievement Tests
SAT Stanford Achievement Test
MAT Metropolitan Achievement Tests

Theme 5

Meeting Individual Needs

Houghton Mifflin Reading includes a wide variety of resources for meeting the needs of all students. The chart below indicates features and components of the program and the students for whom they are most appropriate.

	On Level Students	English Language Learners	Challenge Students	Extra Support Students	Inclusion/ Special Needs
Anthology					
• Get Set to Read	★	★	○	★	★
• Content Links	★	★	★	★	★
• Education Place	★	○	★	○	★
• Student Writing Model	★	★	○	★	★
• Taking Tests	★	★	○	★	★
Audiotape	○	★		★	★
Teacher's Edition					
• Teacher Read Aloud	★	★	○	★	★
• Meeting Individual Needs notes		★	★	★	★
• Theme Resources	★	★	★	★	★
• Selection Summaries	○	★		★	★
• Theme Project	★	○	★	○	○
• Reading-Writing Workshop	★	★	★	★	★
Practice Book	★	★	★	★	★
Leveled Books					
• Reader's Library *Very Easy*	○	○		★	★
• Theme Paperback *Easy*		★		★	★
• Theme Paperback *On Level*	★		○		
• Theme Paperback *Challenge*	○	○	★		
• Classroom Bookshelf	★	○	★	○	○
Challenge Handbook	○	○	★		
Extra Support Handbook		○		★	★

KEY: ★ = highly appropriate   ○ = appropriate

	On Level Students	English Language Learners	Challenge Students	Extra Support Students	Inclusion/ Special Needs
Language Development Resources		★		○	○
Home/Community Connections	★	★	★	★	★
SOAR to SUCCESS		○		★	★
Phonics Intervention		○		★	★

Technology

	On Level Students	English Language Learners	Challenge Students	Extra Support Students	Inclusion/ Special Needs
Education Place	★	○	★	○	○
Get Set for Reading CD-ROM	★	★	○	★	★
Lexia Quick Phonics Assessment CD-ROM				★	★
Lexia Phonics CD-ROM: Intermediate Intervention				★	★
Published by Sunburst Technology*					
• Tenth Planet™: Vowels: Short and Long	○	○		★	★
• Tenth Planet™: Blends and Digraphs	○	○		★	★
• Word Parts	★	★	○	★	★
• Reading Who? Reading You!	○	○		★	★
• Easy Book Deluxe	★	★		○	○
• Media Weaver™ (Sunburst/Humanities Software)	★	★	★	○	

Theme 5

Launching the Theme
for *Voyagers*

Theme 5

Voyagers

Travellers

Come, let us go a-roaming!
The world is all our own,
And half its paths are still untrod,
And half its joys unknown.

from the poem
by Arthur St. John Adcock

102

103

▶ **Using the Theme Opener**

Read aloud the theme title, the poem title, and the stanza from the poem by Arthur St. John Adcock on Anthology page 102. Then prompt student discussion with questions such as the following:

• What makes someone a *voyager?* (taking a long journey to a distant place)
• Name some *voyagers* that you know about. (Neil Armstrong [the moon], Christopher Columbus [America], friends or relatives that have immigrated from other countries, etc.)
• What do the lines from the poem "Travellers" make you think about? (that there is a lot of the world that I do not know about yet; that it would be exciting to explore more of the world)
• Based on the poem "Travellers" and the picture, what do you think the stories in this theme will be about? (long journeys; explorers; seeing new people and places; learning more about the world)

Multi-age Classroom

Related Themes:

Grade 4 . . . Journeys

Grade 3 . . . Voyagers

Grade 2 . . . Nature Walk

▶ Theme Connections

Introduce **Practice Book** pages 59–60. Have students complete page 59. Then discuss the Selection Connections chart on page 60. Explain that students will return to the chart after reading each selection and at the end of the theme to build their understanding of *Voyagers*.

⭐ **Connecting/Comparing** questions on Responding pages (Anthology pages 132, 162, 200) help students focus on relationships among selections and on how the selections connect to the theme overall.

Writing Project

✏️ **Reflecting** Ask students to write about a time when they traveled a long distance or went to a new place. How did they get there? How long did it take? How did it feel to arrive in a new place? How long did they stay? What did they do there? How did it feel to come back? Have them list events and feelings they might want to include before they begin writing.

What Happened	How I Felt
packed suitcase	excited
flew plane	nervous
arrived in Dallas	

Challenge Have students write a narrative about a voyage someone else has taken. This could be a famous voyage or the voyage of someone they know. Ask students to think about what it might have been like to go on this voyage. Have them make a chart listing what happened on the voyage, and what the voyager might have felt. Finally, tell students to write a story about this voyage from the perspective of their chosen voyager.

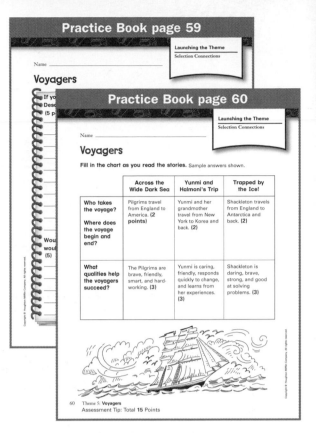

Practice Book page 59

Practice Book page 60

Launching the Theme
Selection Connections

Name _____

Voyagers

Fill in the chart as you read the stories. Sample answers shown.

	Across the Wide Dark Sea	Yunmi and Halmoni's Trip	Trapped by the Ice!
Who takes the voyage? Where does the voyage begin and end?	Pilgrims travel from England to America. **(2 points)**	Yunmi and her grandmother travel from New York to Korea and back. **(2)**	Shackleton travels from England to Antarctica and back. **(2)**
What qualities help the voyagers succeed?	The Pilgrims are brave, friendly, smart, and hard-working. **(3)**	Yunmi is caring, friendly, responds quickly to change, and learns from her experiences. **(3)**	Shackleton is daring, brave, strong, and good at solving problems. **(3)**

60   Theme 5: **Voyagers**
Assessment Tip: Total **15** Points

Education Place

www.eduplace.com

Log on to **Education Place** for more activities relating to *Voyagers*.

Lesson Planner CD-ROM

Customize your planning for *Voyagers* with the Lesson Planner.

Home Connection

Send home the theme letter for *Voyagers* to introduce the theme and suggest home activities. See **Teacher's Resource Blackline Masters.**

Home
Community
Connection

For other suggestions relating to *Voyagers*, see **Home/Community Connections.**

Across the Wide Dark Sea: The Mayflower Journey

Different texts for different purposes

ACROSS THE WIDE DARK SEA

~ The Mayflower Journey ~

Jean Van Leeuwen & pictures by Thomas B. Allen

Anthology: Main Selection

Purposes

- strategy focus: question
- comprehension skill: making inferences
- vocabulary development
- critical thinking, discussion

Genre: Historical Fiction

This fictional story realistically recreates a past time and is based on a true story.

Awards

★ New York Public Library 100 Titles for Reading and Sharing

★ Washington Irving Children's Choice Book Award

Selection Summary

A young boy tells of his voyage on the *Mayflower* and of the settlement of Plymouth once the ship arrives in the new land.

Teacher's Edition: Read Aloud

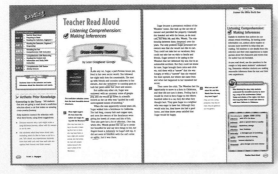

Purposes

- listening comprehension: making inferences
- vocabulary development
- critical thinking, discussion

Anthology: Get Set to Read

Purposes

- background building: Pilgrims
- developing key vocabulary

Anthology: Content Link

Purposes

- content reading: social studies
- skill: how to read a diagram
- critical thinking, discussion

Leveled Books and Resources

See Cumulative Listing of Leveled Books.

Reader's Library

Very Easy

The Golden Land
by Lee S. Justice

(Also available on blackline masters)

Purposes

- fluency practice in below-level text
- alternate reading for students reading significantly below grade level
- strategy application: question
- comprehension skill application: making inferences
- below-level independent reading

Lesson Support

- Guided Reading lesson, page R2
- Alternate application for Comprehension Skill lesson on making inferences, page 137A
- Reteaching for Comprehension Skill: making inferences, page R8

Selection Summary Masters

Audiotape

Across the Wide Dark Sea: The Mayflower Journey
Audiotape for *Voyagers*

Across the Wide Dark Sea: The Mayflower Journey
Teacher's Resource Blackline Masters

Theme Paperbacks

Easy

The Josefina Story Quilt
by Eleanor Coerr

Lesson, TE page 139I

On Level

A Child's Glacier Bay
by Kimberly Corral

Lesson, TE page 139K

Challenge

Balto and the Great Race
by Elizabeth Cody Kimmel

Lesson, TE page 139M

MEETING INDIVIDUAL NEEDS

Inclusion Strategy

Significantly Below-level Readers

Students reading so far below level that they cannot read *Across the Wide Dark Sea: The Mayflower Journey* even with the suggested Extra Support should still participate with the class whenever possible.

- Include them in the Teacher Read Aloud (p. 106A) and Preparing to Read (pp. 108A–109C).
- Have them listen to *Across the Wide Dark Sea: The Mayflower Journey* on the audiotape for *Voyagers* and read the Selection Summary while others read Segment 1 of the selection.
- Have them read "The Golden Land" in the Reader's Library collection for *Voyagers* while others read Segment 2 of *Across the Wide Dark Sea: The Mayflower Journey.*
- Have all students participate in Wrapping Up Segment 2 (p. 131) and Responding (p. 132).

Technology

Get Set for Reading CD-ROM
Across the Wide Dark Sea: The Mayflower Journey

Provides background building, vocabulary support, and selection summaries in English and Spanish.

Education Place
www.eduplace.com
Log on to Education Place for more activities relating to this selection.

Book Adventure
www.bookadventure.org
This Internet reading incentive program provides thousands of titles for students.

Suggested Daily Routines

Instructional Goals	Day 1	Day 2

Reading
 	
Strategy Focus: Question
 	
 Comprehension Skill: Making Inferences
 	
Comprehension Skill Review: Story Structure; Making Judgments
 	
Information and Study Skills: Multimedia Report
	Teacher Read Aloud
	Sugar: Cross-Country Traveler, 106A
	Preparing to Read Across the Wide Dark Sea
	• Get Set: Background and Vocabulary, *108A*
	• Key Vocabulary, *109A*
	  Selection Vocabulary, ***Practice Book,*** *61*
	• Strategy/Skill Preview, *109B*
	  Inference Chart, ***Practice Book,*** *62*
	Reading Segment 1
	Across the Wide Dark Sea, 110–119
	• Supporting Comprehension
	• Strategy Focus, *116*
	Wrapping Up Segment 1, *119*
		Reading Segment 2
		Across the Wide Dark Sea, 120–131
		• Supporting Comprehension
		• Strategy Focus, *124*
		
		Wrapping Up Segment 2, *131*
		
		Responding
		• Comprehension Questions: Think About the Selection, *132*
		• Comprehension Check, ***Practice Book,*** *63*
		
		Revisiting the Text
		• Making Inferences, *129*

Word Work *Spelling:* The Vowel Sounds in *tooth* and *cook* *Decoding Longer Words:* *Structural Analysis:* Suffixes *-less* and *-ness* *Phonics:* Vowel Sounds in *tooth* and *cook* *Vocabulary:* Dictionary: Syllables	**Spelling** • Pretest, *137G* • Instruction: The Vowel Sounds in *tooth* and *cook*, *137G* • Take-Home Word List, ***Practice Book: Handbook***	**Decoding Longer Words Instruction** • Structural Analysis: Suffixes *-less* and *-ness*, *137E* • ***Practice Book,*** *66* **Spelling** • ***Practice Book,*** *67*
Writing & Language *Grammar:* Subject Pronouns *Writing:* Writing a Play; Using Exclamations *Listening/Speaking/Viewing:* Present an Oral Book Report	**Daily Language Practice,** *137L* **Grammar Instruction** • Subject Pronouns, *137K* **Writing** • Journal Writing, *111*	**Daily Language Practice,** *137L* **Grammar Instruction** • Subject Pronouns, ***Practice Book,*** *71* **Writing Instruction** • Writing a Play, *137M* • Journal Writing, *120*

 = tested skills

 **Leveled Books**

See Cumulative Listing of Leveled Books.

Reader's Library
• **Very Easy** *The Golden Land,* Lesson, *R2*

Book Links: Anthology, *106*
Bibliography: Teacher's Edition, *102C*

Theme Paperbacks, Lessons, *139H–139N*
• **Easy** *The Josefina Story Quilt*
• **On Level** *A Child's Glacier Bay*
• **Challenge** *Balto and the Great Race*

Houghton Mifflin Classroom Bookshelf, Level 3

Allow time every day for students to read independently from self-selected books.

Technology

Lesson Planner CD-ROM:
Customize your planning for *Across the Wide Dark Sea* with the Lesson Planner.

Day 3

Revisiting the Text
- Writer's Craft: Vivid Language, *115*
- Genre: Historical Fiction, *117*

Comprehension Skill Instruction
- Making Inferences, *137A*
- *Practice Book,* 64

Phonics Instruction
- Vowel Sounds in *tooth* and *cook, 137F*

Spelling
- *Practice Book,* 68

Daily Language Practice, *137L*

Grammar Instruction
- I Match, It Matches, *137K*

✎ **Writing**
- Responding: Write a Travel Diary, *132*

Day 4

Comprehension Skill Instruction
- Reteaching Making Inferences with Reader's Library, *R8*
- Independent Application, *Practice Book,* 65

Reading the Social Studies Link
- "Young Voyagers: A Pilgrim Childhood," *134–137*

Information and Study Skills Instruction
- Multimedia Report, *137C*

Decoding Longer Words
- Reteaching Structural Analysis: Suffixes -less and -ness, *R14*
- Challenge/Extension Activities, *R15*

Spelling
- *Practice Book,* 69

Vocabulary Skill Instruction
- Dictionary: Syllables, *137I*
- *Practice Book,* 70

Daily Language Practice, *137L*

Grammar
- Reteaching, *R20*
- I Match; It Matches, *Practice Book,* 72

✎ **Writing**
- Using Exclamations, *137N*

Listening/Speaking/Viewing
- Present an Oral Book Report, *137O*

Day 5

Revisiting the Text: Comprehension Review Skill Instruction
- Story Structure, *113*
- Making Judgments, *125*

Rereading for Fluency
Across the Wide Dark Sea, 110–131

Activity Choices
- Responding Activities, *133*
- Challenge/Extension Activities, *R9*
- Cross-Curricular Activities, *R26*

Vocabulary Expansion
- Words for Ship Parts, *137J*

Spelling
- Posttest, *137H*

Daily Language Practice, *137L*

Grammar
- Sentence Combining with Subject Pronouns, *137L*
- *Practice Book,* 73

✎ **Writing**
- Sentence Combining with Subject Pronouns, *137L*
- Writing Activities, *R23*
- Sharing Students' Writing: Author's Chair

 ## Reading-Writing Workshop: Description

Based on the **Student Writing Model** in the Anthology, this workshop guides students through the writing process and includes skill lessons on—

- Ordering Information
- Using Sensory Language   See Teacher's Edition, *pages 138–139G.*
- Writing Complete Sentences

Allow time every day for students to write independently on self-selected topics.

Reading Instruction

DAY 1	• Teacher Read Aloud • Preparing to Read • Reading the Selection, Segment 1
DAY 2	• Reading the Selection, Segment 2 • Responding
DAY 3	• Revisiting the Text • Comprehension Skill Instruction
DAY 4	• Comprehension Skill Reteaching • Reading the Content Link • Information and Study Skills Instruction
DAY 5	• Comprehension Skill Review • Activity Choices

OBJECTIVES

Students listen to the selection and make inferences about the characters and events.

▶ **Activate Prior Knowledge**

Connecting to the Theme Tell students that you are going to read aloud a nonfiction selection about a cat that makes an amazing cross-country journey.

Help students connect the selection with what they know, using these suggestions:

■ Discuss reasons why a pet might make a long-distance journey, either with its owners or on its own.

■ Ask students what they know about cats, including what it's like to have a cat for a pet. Talk about any experiences students have had with cats and how well cats recognize their homes and their owners.

Teacher Read Aloud

Listening Comprehension:
☑ Making Inferences

Sugar
Cross-Country Traveler

by Jean Craighead George

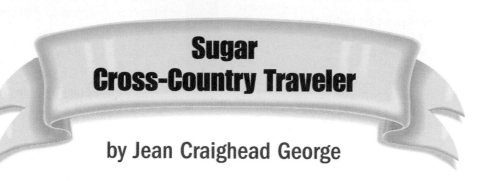

from
Incredible Animal Adventures

This nonfiction selection comes from the book Incredible Animal Adventures.

1 What might Sugar's life have been like before she began living with the Woodses? (She may have been living in the wild or traveling from farm to farm; she may have fallen or had a fight with another animal; she had probably lived with people before because she wasn't afraid of the Woodses.)

Like any cat, Sugar, a part-Persian house pet, lived in her own secret world. She followed her night trails into the countryside. She met up with friends and enemies unknown to her owners. And she <u>withdrew</u> to sunning spots to tuck her paws under her chest and snooze.

But unlike any other cat, Sugar was <u>endowed</u> with an <u>uncanny</u> sense of geography, and she would go down in scientific records as the cat who was "guided by a still unrecognized means of knowing."

When she was apparently several years old, Sugar walked into a farmhouse in California. She had long, creamy hair and copper eyes, and soon the owners of the farmhouse were **1** giving her bowls of cream and bits of fish. They also gave her a lot of <u>affection</u>. One day, when Mrs. Woods picked the cat up to stroke her beautiful fur and say nice things to her, her fingers found a <u>deformity</u> in Sugar's left hip. It did not seem to interfere with the cat's stride or <u>agility</u>, but it was there.

Sugar became a permanent resident of the Woodses' home. She took up the cat role of mouser and patrolled the property. Gradually she bonded not with the house, as do most cats, but with Mr. and Mrs. Woods. The relationship between them deepened over the years. The only problem Sugar presented her owners was that she would not ride in cars. They could not take her on vacations; they could not take her on visits to family and friends. Sugar seemed to be saying to the Woodses that her deformed hip was due to an automobile accident. But they could not know for sure. Sugar brought them mice and crickets, told them with a "meow" that she was hungry, or with a "merow" that she wanted the door opened, but where she came from and what had happened to her remained her secret.

2 Then came the crisis. The Woodses had the opportunity to move to a farm in Oklahoma, and they did not turn it down. Feeling that it would be cruel to force Sugar to ride fifteen hundred miles in a car, they did what they thought best. They gave Sugar to a neighbor who was eager to have her. Although they would miss her, they knew she had a good home, and they drove away satisfied that Sugar would be happy.

2 What can you tell about Mr. and Mrs. Woods from the way they treat Sugar?

(They are kind, caring, protective; they like animals; they are generous and thoughtful.)

Listening Comprehension: Making Inferences

Explain to students that authors do not always reveal everything. By leaving some information out, authors allow readers to become more involved in what they are reading. Tell students to use details from this selection and their own experiences to make guesses about the characters and events that the author has not included.

As you read aloud, use the questions in the margin to help assess students' understanding. Determine whether students are making reasonable inferences from the text and their own experiences.

MEETING INDIVIDUAL NEEDS

English Language Learners

After finishing the story, help students understand the incredible journey by showing a map of the southwestern United States and photos of the region. Ask them how long they think it would take them to walk from California to Oklahoma.

Vocabulary (pages 106A–107A)

withdrew: went off to be alone

endowed: given a special talent or quality

uncanny: mysterious; strange

affection: love; fondness

deformity: a damaged part of something

agility: quickness; ease in moving

bonded: became attached to

deepened: grew stronger and more intense

(Teacher Read Aloud, *continued***)**

3 How do you think Mrs. Woods feels when the cat lands on her shoulder? (Frightened at first, then surprised and shocked; she can't believe that it's Sugar until she runs her fingers over the cat's hip and finds the deformity.)

Two weeks after the Woodses left California, Sugar disappeared.

3 Fourteen months later, Mrs. Woods was in her barn working when a part-Persian cat leaped through the window and landed softly on her shoulder.

Mrs. Woods took her in her arms. She saw the cream-colored fur and the copper eyes. Then she ran her fingers over the hip.

"Sugar," she said. "It's you!"

Mrs. Woods called her friend in California. "Yes," she said, "Sugar did run away."

No one had given her a ride; no one had reported seeing her. Sugar had crossed fifteen hundred miles of deserts and mountains. She had passed through or around towns. She had eaten well, avoided cars, and had somehow found the Woodses on their new farm in Oklahoma. Sugar's story would be hard to believe if Mr. and Mrs. Woods hadn't known that they had left Sugar in California and that she had arrived a year and two months later on their Oklahoma farm.

Even now, scientists at Duke University wonder what signals from the earth Sugar listened to in her long journey across the southwestern United States.

Sugar kept these secrets to herself, too.

4 How is the author able to give so many details about Sugar's journey even though she doesn't know how Sugar did it? (She knows what the geography is like between California and Oklahoma where Sugar traveled; she knows Sugar wasn't injured or weak or sick when she found the Woodses, so she must have been eating well and avoiding other dangers, such as cars.)

▶ **Discussion**

Summarize After reading, discuss what students found most surprising about Sugar's journey. Then have them summarize the selection.

Listening Comprehension:
☑ **Making Inferences** Reread the second paragraph of the selection to students. Explain that when the author writes that Sugar had "an uncanny sense of geography," she is using her own knowledge and the information she has about Sugar to make an inference about Sugar's abilities. Then ask students to tell what they think Sugar is like. Write their responses on the board. After writing, ask students to explain what details they used from the selection and what they used from their own knowledge to make each guess about Sugar. As they respond, write their answers beneath each inference. List selection details in one column and students' own knowledge in another.

Personal Response Have students tell how they think Sugar "knew" where to find the Woodses. Ask them to describe any similar stories they know about other animals finding their owners after a long time apart.

★ **Connecting/Comparing** Ask students what qualities Sugar has that make her a voyager. Would they call any animal or person that makes a long journey a voyager? Why or why not?

Anthology

ACROSS THE WIDE DARK SEA
~ The Mayflower Journey ~

Jean Van Leeuwen *pictures by* Thomas B. Allen

Technology

Get Set for Reading CD-ROM

Across the Wide Dark Sea

Provides background building, vocabulary support, and selection summaries in English and Spanish.

Preparing to Read

▶ Using *Get Set* for Background and Vocabulary

Connecting to the Theme Tell students that they will meet a variety of travelers in the theme called *Voyagers*. The first story, *Across the Wide Dark Sea*, tells about a boy traveling on the *Mayflower*.

Discuss what students know about the Pilgrims' journey on the *Mayflower* in 1620. Then use the Get Set to Read on pages 108–109 to introduce some of the challenges they faced.

■ Have someone read aloud "Journey of the Pilgrims."

■ Have students take turns reading the captions and describing the photos.

■ Ask students to explain the meaning of the Key Vocabulary in color: *journey, cramped, seeping, weary, anchor, survive,* and *settlement*.

Get Set to Read

Across the Wide Dark Sea

Background and Vocabulary

Journey of the Pilgrims

It's hard to imagine making a long **journey** across stormy seas on a **cramped** and crowded ship. But in 1620, that's exactly what the Pilgrims did. They traveled all the way across the Atlantic Ocean from England to America on a ship called the *Mayflower*.

The sea was rough, and water was constantly **seeping** through the walls of the ship. After sixty-six days, the **weary** travelers reached America and dropped the ship's **anchor**. Only one Pilgrim did not **survive** the trip.

After exploring the area, the Pilgrims built a **settlement** and named it Plymouth. In *Across the Wide Dark Sea*, you will read about the incredible journey the Pilgrims made and their struggle to build a new home.

This cradle belonged to the family of Peregrine White, the first Pilgrim child born in America.

Mayflower II, a full-size, rebuilt version of what the first *Mayflower* may have looked like, now floats in Plymouth Harbor in Massachusetts.

A cooking pot was one of the most useful things families brought on the *Mayflower*. This one belonged to the Standish family.

108

109

English Language Learners

After reading Get Set, ask: Who were some of the first immigrants to America? Why did they come? What were some of the challenges they faced? Who lived here before the Pilgrims? Focus on words such as *clung, fair, seasick, vast, hauling, leak, worship, faith, streamed, shelter,* and *seldom*.

▶ Developing Key Vocabulary

Use **Transparency 5–1** to introduce the Key Vocabulary words from *Across the Wide Dark Sea*.

- ■ Cover the words and their definitions at the bottom of the transparency.

- ■ Based on the other words in first item, model how to figure out the meaning of the underlined Key Vocabulary word.

- ■ Uncover the first definition, and compare it to the meaning you gave.

- ■ For each remaining item, have a student give the meaning of the underlined word. Then follow the same procedure.

Remind students that it's helpful to use the Phonics/Decoding Strategy when they read. For students who need more help with decoding, use the review below.

Practice/Homework Practice Book page 61.

Strategy Review
Phonics/Decoding

Modeling Write this sentence from *Across the Wide Dark Sea* on the board, and point to *hunched*.

> *Pale yellow sand and dark <u>hunched</u> trees were all we saw.*

Think Aloud

When I look at this word, the first part reminds me of the word fun *except it starts with the letter h. It must be /huhn/. Next I see a c-h, and I know that those two letters make one sound, /ch/. Finally I see the -ed ending. When I put all the sounds together, I say, /HUHN•chehd/. That's not a word I know. I'll try saying it as one syllable instead, /HUHNCHT/. I've heard that word before. If people hunch their shoulders, they bend them up and forward. Maybe the trees are bent forward too. That would make sense.*

Skill Finder • Decoding Longer Words, pp. 137E–137F

Key Concept
the Pilgrims' journey

Key Vocabulary

anchor: a heavy metal hook attached to a ship and dropped overboard to hold the ship in place

cramped: crowded; not enough room to move about

journey: a trip from one place to another

seeping: slowly leaking; oozing

settlement: a small community in a new place

survive: to stay alive; to hold up or withstand

weary: tired; needing rest

See Vocabulary notes on pages 112, 114, 116, 118, 120, 122, 124, 126, and 130.

Practice Book page 61

Name

Tale

On the li
the corr

► heav
► crow
► trip
► passi
► small
► stay
► tired

1. In 16
Ame

2. With

3. Wate
passi

4. Whe
heav

5. The

6. Even
mana

7. After
small

Transparency 5–1

Pilgrim Words

iron, weight, <u>anchor</u>
crowded, tight, squishy, <u>cramped</u>
trip, journey, voyage
<u>seeping</u>, oozing, leaking
village, town, <u>settlement</u>
live, hold up, <u>survive</u>, pull through
tired, <u>weary</u>, unrested, worn-out

<u>anchor</u>: a heavy metal hook attached to a ship and dropped overboard to hold the ship in place
<u>cramped</u>: crowded; not enough room to move about
<u>journey</u>: a trip
<u>seeping</u>: slowly leaking; oozing
<u>settlement</u>: a small community in a new place
<u>survive</u>: to stay alive; to hold up or pull through
<u>weary</u>: tired; needing rest

VOYAGERS *Across the Wide Dark Sea*
Key Vocabulary

TRANSPARENCY 5–1
TEACHER'S EDITION PAGE T109A

Reading

Strategy/Skill Preview

▶ **Strategy Focus:**
Question

Strategy Focus

As you read this story of one boy's journey across the sea, think of **questions** about the Pilgrims and their struggle for survival.

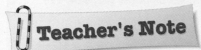

Teacher's Note

Strategy/Skill Connection For a better understanding of *Across the Wide Dark Sea* students can use the

• Question Strategy

• Making Inferences Comprehension Skill

Asking questions to check their understanding of the story will help students become active readers who are better able to make inferences.

As students fill in their Inference Chart (**Transparency 5–2** and **Practice Book** page 62), they can consider how their prior knowledge combines with text information to extend their understanding of characters and events.

Have students turn to page 111 as you read the title and author of the selection. Ask someone to read the Strategy Focus. Have students read the first three paragraphs on page 113, keeping in mind the Strategy Focus. Then ask what questions students can think of based on what they've read. Record their questions.

Teacher Modeling Review how to figure out good questions about the text. (Read carefully and then think of questions that test a reader's knowledge about it.) Then model the strategy.

Think Aloud

On page 113 I learned that a boy and his father are traveling on a sailing ship that is moving out to sea. They're beginning a journey to a new land. One good question I might ask is: Why are the boy and his father traveling to the new land?

Have students think of other questions they might ask and then record both the questions and answers in their journals. Remind students to keep their questions in mind as they read the story. Also be sure to remind them to use their other reading strategies too.

Comprehension Skill Focus:
Making Inferences

Inference Chart Explain that as students read *Across the Wide Dark Sea*, they will focus on making inferences, or reasonable guesses based on story information and their personal experiences. To develop the skill, students will record information on an inference chart. Display **Transparency 5–2**, and explain how to use this graphic organizer.

■ Begin by asking someone to read aloud the first three paragraphs on page 113.

■ Read the first question and point out the boxes below it. Then explain that students will gather information for each box to help them answer the question.

■ Begin by having students identify story details that tell about the boy's feelings. Write them in the first box. Point out that you know travel by sailing ship was very dangerous. Add that detail in the box labeled *What I Know*.

■ Have students write those details in the same places on their chart on **Practice Book** page 62.

■ Explain that as students read, they should list information in the boxes that helps them to figure out the answer to each question.

■ Monitor their work, or have students check each other's charts.

Graphic Organizer: Inference Chart (Responses will vary.)

1. How does the boy feel when the journey begins?

Story Clues (pages 113–115)	What I Know
He looks ahead at the wide dark sea. He stands close to his father and clings to his father's hand.	Children stay close to their parents and hold their hands when they're afraid. Sailing on a ship to an unknown place can be dangerous.

My Inference The boy is sad and afraid.

2. How does the boy feel after six weeks at sea?

Story Clues (pages 116–119)	What I Know
The ship is crowded, cramped, cold, and wet. They must eat hard, dry biscuits and cheese. The ship is helpless in the storms.	It is uncomfortable to be crowded, cold, and wet. It is unpleasant and boring to eat only dried biscuits and cheese. Not knowing what is to happen can be scary.

My Inference He is bored, uncomfortable, hungry, and worried about the future.

Reading

Beginning of Segment 1: pages 110–119

Options for Reading

▶ **Reading in Segments** Students can read *Across the Wide Dark Sea* in two segments (pages 110–119 and 120–131) or in its entirety.

▶ **Deciding About Support** Rich description and exciting events make *Across the Wide Dark Sea* a suspenseful book that will hold the interest of most students.

■ Because of the familiar story events and first-person narration, most students should be able to follow On Level reading instruction.

■ Students who might have difficulty making inferences about story characters and events will benefit from Extra Support.

■ Significantly below-level readers can listen to the Audiotape and read the Selection Summary for *Across the Wide Dark Sea*, and then read "The Golden Land" in the **Reader's Library**.

▶ **Meeting Individual Needs** Use the notes at the bottom of the pages.

MEET THE AUTHOR
Jean Van Leeuwen

MEET THE ILLUSTRATOR
Thomas B. Allen

For Jean Van Leeuwen, getting lost in a good book is great fun. As a child, she would get so interested in a book that when anyone called her name she would look up wondering where she was! Now Van Leeuwen writes books too. Sometimes an idea just strikes her like lightning. As she says, "For me, each book begins with a thunderbolt from the sky."

Other books:
A Fourth of July on the Plains, Nothing Here But Trees, The Strange Adventures of Blue Dog

Thomas B. Allen likes to mix and match his tools when he draws. For this book he used charcoal, pastels, and colored pencils on rough, bumpy paper to give him just the look he wanted. Allen also illustrated *Going West,* another book by Jean Van Leeuwen.

Other books:
Climbing Kansas Mountains (by George Shannon)
Good-bye, Charles Lindbergh (by Louise Borden)
A Green Horn Blowing (by David F. Birchman)

Visit Education Place to discover more about Jean Van Leeuwen and Thomas B. Allen.
www.eduplace.com/kids

110

Classroom Management

On Level
Reading Cards 2–3

While Reading: Inference Chart (**Practice Book** page 62); Literature Discussion (p.118, Reading Card 2); Making Judgments (p. 125, Reading Card 3); generate questions

After Reading: Literature Discussion (page 130); Wrapping Up Segment 1 (page 119) and Segment 2 (page 131)

Challenge
Reading Cards 1–3

While Reading: Inference Chart (**Practice Book** p. 62); Problem Solving (p. 113, Card 1); Literature Discussion (p.118, Card 2); Making Judgments (p. 125, Card 3);

After Reading: Literature Discussion (p. 130); Wrapping Up Segment 1 (p. 119) and Segment 2 (p. 131)

English Language Learners

Intermediate and Advanced Fluency Students should try to complete the story and exercises individually. Assign a certain number of pages to be completed either in class or at home.

For English language learners at other proficiency levels, see **Language Development Resources.**

Selection 1

ACROSS THE WIDE DARK SEA
~ The Mayflower Journey ~

Jean Van Leeuwen & pictures by Thomas B. Allen

Strategy Focus

As you read this story of one boy's journey across the sea, think of **questions** about the Pilgrims and their struggle for survival.

111

Reading Segment 1
pages 110–119

Purpose Setting After a brief preview of the selection, have students describe what they recall about the Pilgrims. Then ask them to predict what the story will tell them about the journey on the *Mayflower.* Have students read to confirm or change their predictions as the story unfolds.

Journal Writing Students can use their journals to record their original predictions and questions to ask their classmates. Also ask students to evaluate how well the author describes the hardships of the voyage.

Reinforcing Comprehension and Strategies

- Remind students to use Question and other strategies as they read and to add to their Inference Chart (**Practice Book** page 62).

- Use the Strategy Focus notes on pages 116 and 124 to reinforce the Question strategy.

- Use Supporting Comprehension questions beginning on page 112 to help students develop higher-level understanding of the text.

Extra Support: Previewing the Text

Before each segment, preview the text, using the notes below and on page 120. **While** reading, model strategies (pages 115, 122, and 123). **After** reading, review each segment (pages 118 and 130) before students join the Wrapping Up discussion.

pages 112–113 A young boy and his family set sail on the *Mayflower.* They are jammed tightly below deck and are traveling to an unknown land. How do you think they feel as they sail away from England?

pages 114–117 As the journey goes on, one day seems the same as the next, unless they are hit by storms. Then the ship is helpless in the winds and waves. What is happening to the man on page 117?

pages 118–119 After many weeks, some men talk of turning back. The ship is leaking badly, and people are sick and scared. One leak is fixed with a tool that can raise heavy things. How might it help?

▶ Supporting Comprehension

1 How do you think the boy feels as they begin their journey? How do you know? (anxious, fearful; He clings to his father's hand and looks ahead *at the wide dark sea.*)

2 Why must the travelers bring everything they need with them aboard the ship? (In the new land across the sea, there won't be a way of buying what they need.)

Vocabulary *(page 113)*

anchor: a heavy metal hook attached to a ship that is dropped overboard to hold the ship in place

journey: a trip

cramped: crowded; not enough room to move about

112

 English Language Learners

Students have learned to take notes in outline and key detail form (answering *who, what, where, when,* and *why*). Review summary notes. Read the first page of the story aloud. Then on the board write brief summary notes of what you've read. Read the second page together as a class and ask volunteers to help you write notes on the board.

I stood close to my father as the <u>anchor</u> was pulled dripping from the sea. Above us, white sails rose against a bright blue sky. They fluttered, then filled with wind. Our ship began to move.

My father was waving to friends on shore. I looked back at their faces growing smaller and smaller, and ahead at the wide dark sea. And I clung to my father's hand.

1

We were off on a <u>journey</u> to an unknown land.

The ship was packed tight with people — near a hundred, my father said. We were crowded below deck in a space so low that my father could barely stand upright, and so <u>cramped</u> that we could scarcely stretch out to sleep.

Packed in tight, too, was everything we would need in the new land: tools for building and planting, goods for trading, guns for hunting. Food, furniture, clothing, books. A few crates of chickens, two dogs, and a striped orange cat.

2

Our family was luckier than most. We had a corner out of the damp and cold. Some had to sleep in the ship's small work boat.

113

Challenge

Reading Card 1

Problem Solving

Draw students' attention to the list of everything the Pilgrims needed to live in the new land. Then challenge pairs of students to write a more complete list of items they think the Pilgrims must have brought. Have them star the ones they consider to be the most important to the Pilgrims' survival.

Revisiting the Text

Review/Maintain

Comprehension Skill Lesson
Story Structure

OBJECTIVES

Students identify the main elements of the story structure.

Remind students of the main elements that make up story structure:

■ characters—the main people (or animals) in a story

■ plot—the sequence of story events, which often includes a problem (at the beginning) and how the problem is solved (at the end)

■ setting—where and when the story takes place

Ask students to identify the main story characters and the setting. (the boy, his father; aboard the *Mayflower*) Then discuss the elements of the plot. In particular, ask what the story problem is. (how to survive the journey to a new land) Next, help students identify the story narrator by using text clues and the illustration. (the young boy; from the words *my father* and seeing the boy standing next to the man at the rail) Also have students explain why he is the main character. (The story is told from his perspective.)

Point out how the author's choice of the main character as the narrator affects the interpretation of story events. Discuss how changing the main character would change parts of the plot. Suggest that students consider how a sailor or the captain might tell the story.

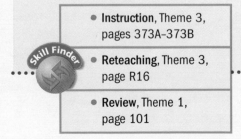

Skill Finder

● **Instruction**, Theme 3, pages 373A–373B

● **Reteaching**, Theme 3, page R16

● **Review**, Theme 1, page 101

Reading

▶ Supporting Comprehension

3 Why do you think the boy believes that a sailor's life is a fine one? (The sailors are doing interesting work and climb and move around, while he can't; he's impressed with what they know and how brave they are.)

4 Why do you think the author uses such vivid words to describe the storm? (to help readers experience what the Pilgrims did)

5 How well do you think the author has described the voyagers' feelings during the storm? (Answers will vary. Example: She makes the travelers' fearful reactions seem realistic by comparing the small, helpless ship to the powerful storm.)

Vocabulary *(page 115)*

rigging: all the ropes, chains, and pulleys used to control the masts and sails of a ship

furl: to roll up and fasten

shuddered: trembled or shivered suddenly

huddled: crowded close together

114

 English Language Learners

Because this is a long selection, remind students to take a few minutes at the end of each session to write summary notes. Then before they begin reading again, they can review the notes to remind themselves what they know so far.

The first days were fair, with a stiff wind.

My mother and brother were seasick down below. But I stood on deck and watched the sailors hauling on ropes, climbing in the rigging, and perched at the very top of the mast, looking out to sea.

What a fine life it must be, I thought, to be a sailor.

3

One day clouds piled up in the sky. Birds with black wings circled the ship, and the choppy sea seemed angry.

"Storm's coming," I heard a sailor say. We were all sent below as the sailors raced to furl the sails.

Then the storm broke. Wind howled and waves crashed. The ship shuddered as it rose and fell in seas as high as mountains. Some people were crying, others praying. I huddled next to my father, afraid in the dark.

4

How could a ship so small and helpless ever cross the vast ocean?

5

115

Writer's Craft Lesson
Vivid Language

OBJECTIVES

Students identify vivid words the author uses to accurately describe story details.

Read aloud the passage on page 115 that describes the storm.

Then the storm broke. Wind howled and waves crashed. The ship shuddered as it rose and fell in seas as high as mountains.

Ask students what they pictured in their minds as you read. Point out that the author's use of words helps paint a picture of the storm, making readers feel as if they were there too. Then have students identify the words that created the image. (*broke, howled, crashed, shuddered, rose and fell; high as mountains*)

Ask students to identify other examples of the author's use of vivid language in the story.

MEETING INDIVIDUAL NEEDS **Extra Support**

Strategy Modeling

Question If students are having trouble modeling the strategy, use this example to model it for them.

On page 115, I read that people are crying and praying during the storm. Also, the boy is huddling next to his father, afraid in the dark. To help me understand the characters better, a good question to ask might be: Why are the people so afraid during the storm?

▶ Strategy Focus: Question

Teacher/Student Modeling Have students identify important story details in the first three paragraphs on page 116. List them on the board.

Ask students to take turns picking a detail and turning it into a question for other students to answer. Then ask students to think of questions that require using personal knowledge as well as story details to form an answer. (Examples: Why do the passengers eat only salt pork, beans, and bread? Why must the boy keep out of the sailors' way?)

▶ Supporting Comprehension

6 What does the boy think about his trip so far? How do you know? (He's tired of it because there is nothing for him to do; from the words *each day like the last.*)

7 Why does the author include the story of the man who is swept overboard? (to add suspense; to show how dangerous the voyage is)

Vocabulary *(page 116)*

<u>overboard:</u> over the side of the boat

<u>desparate:</u> driven by a great need

<u>miraculously:</u> amazingly, like a miracle

<u>plucked:</u> snatched, pulled out

The sun came out. We walked on deck and dried our clothes. But just when my shoes felt dry at last, more clouds gathered.

"Storm's coming," I told my father.

So the days passed, each one like the last. There was nothing to do but eat our meals of salt pork, beans, and bread, tidy up our cramped space, sleep when we could, and try to keep dry. When it was not too stormy, we climbed on deck to stretch our legs. But even then we had to keep out of the sailors' way.

6 How I longed to run and jump and climb!

Once during a storm a man was swept <u>overboard</u>. Reaching out with <u>desperate</u> hands, he caught hold of a rope and clung to it.

Down he went under the raging foaming water.

Then, <u>miraculously</u>, up he came.

Sailors rushed to the side of the ship. Hauling on the rope, they brought him in close and with a boat hook <u>plucked</u> him out

7 of the sea. And his life was saved.

116

Cross-Curricular Connection

Social Studies In 1620 the Pilgrims set out on the *Mayflower* to start a settlement in the New World. William Bradford, a governor of the colony, recorded his experiences, which is why so much is known about the journey and the settlement. Some thirty children traveled aboard the ship, including nine-year-old Love Brewster, the child who serves as "narrator" of this story.

117

Revisiting the Text

Genre Lesson
Historical Fiction

 OBJECTIVES

Students identify historical facts and fictional elements in the story.

Explain that *Across the Wide Dark Sea* is historical fiction. The main events are real events; the *Mayflower* journey and the Pilgrims' settlement of Plymouth actually happened. The author, however, adds many realistic details, such as story characters' words and thoughts, to make the events come alive for readers. Historical fiction weaves details made up by the author with historical facts, which makes history interesting and lively.

Explain that the incident about the man who fell overboard actually happened. The description of his *desperate hands* and the sailors who *rushed to the side of the ship* are ones that Jean Van Leeuwen, the author, has added for drama. Not having witnessed the event, she has no way of knowing exactly what happened.

Discuss other parts of the story with students, identifying facts and fictional details. Summarize the discussion with a chart similar to the one below. Then ask students to share details about other historical fiction stories they've read.

Element	Real	Fictional
characters	✔	
setting	✔	
events	✔	
dialogue		✔
descriptions		✔

Reading

▶ Supporting Comprehension

8 What does the gathering in the captain's cabin suggest about the way the Pilgrims handle their decisions? (They try to come to an agreement about such an important decision; they "brainstorm" to figure out a way to fix the cracked beam.)

9 What decision would you have made about turning back or sailing on? Explain. (Example: Turn back; the ship is damaged and the passengers fear for their lives. Sail on; land will be sighted soon.)

10 Why do you think the passengers left their safe homes to go on this dangerous journey? (They're looking for a better life, for more freedom, for adventure, or for an escape from a troubled past.)

Vocabulary *(page 119)*

survive: to stay alive; to hold up or withstand

jack: a mechanical tool used to raise or move heavy objects, such as a car or house

seeping: leaking slowly; oozing

118

 Extra Support

Segment 1: Review

Before students join the whole class for Wrapping Up on page 119, have them

- check predictions
- take turns modeling Question and other strategies they used
- add to **Transparency 5–2,** check and revise their Inference Chart on **Practice Book** page 62, and use it to Summarize

 On Level / Challenge

Reading Card 2

Literature Discussion

In mixed-ability groups of five or six, students can discuss their own questions and the discussion prompts on Reading Card 2.

- How might the sailors have felt about taking the Pilgrims to settle in the new land?
- Besides the cracked beam, what other problems might the people on the ship need to solve?

Storm followed storm. The pounding of wind and waves caused one of the main beams to crack, and our ship began to leak.

8 Worried, the men gathered in the captain's cabin to talk of what to do. Could our ship <u>survive</u> another storm? Or must we turn back?

They talked for two days, but could not agree.

Then someone thought of the iron <u>jack</u> for raising houses that they were taking to the new land. Using it to lift the cracked beam, the sailors set a new post underneath, tight and firm, and patched all the leaks.

9 And our ship sailed on.

For six weeks we had traveled, and still there was no land in sight. Now we were always cold and wet. Water <u>seeping</u> in from above put out my mother's cooking fire, and there was nothing to eat but hard dry biscuits and cheese. My brother was sick, and many others too.

10 And some began to ask why we had left our safe homes to go on this endless journey to an unknown land.

End of Segment 1:
pages 110–119

Wrapping Up Segment 1
pages 110–119

First, provide Extra Support for students who need it (page 118). Then bring all students together.

■ **Review Predictions/Purpose** Discuss which predictions were accurate and which needed to be revised. Record any changes and new predictions.

■ **Model Strategies** Refer students to the **Strategies Poster** and have them take turns modeling Question and other strategies they used as they read. Provide models if needed (page 115).

■ **Share Group Discussions** Have students share their questions and literature discussions.

■ **Summarize** Help students use **Transparency 5–2** and their Inference Chart to summarize what has happened in the story so far.

Comprehension/Critical Thinking

1 How are the conditions aboard the ship changing? (They're getting worse: the passengers are always cold and wet; the food is worse; more people are sick.) **Noting Details**

2 What sights, sounds, and smells might the boy have experienced aboard ship that are not described in the text? (Examples: *sights*—ocean everywhere, sighting fish and whales, frightened men; *sounds*—singing, the captain shouting orders, the creaking of the rigging; *smells*—stale food, smoke from the cooking fires, salty air) **Making Inferences**

Diagnostic Check

If . . .	You can . . .
students have successfully completed the Extra Support Activities on page 118,	have them read Segment 2 cooperatively or independently.

Reading Segment 2

pages 120–131

Purpose Setting Have students summarize the story so far. Then have someone read aloud the last two paragraphs on page 119. Ask students to predict what else the boy and his family will experience during and after the voyage. Then ask students to read pages 120–131 to check their predictions.

Journal Writing Students can record any revisions they made to their predictions and explain why they changed their minds. Also ask students to tell how the boy's descriptions compare with their own knowledge of the Pilgrims' journey.

Vocabulary *(page 120)*

worship: to take part in a religious ceremony

faith: trust or belief, even without proof

Why? I also asked the question of my father that night.

"We are searching for a place to live where we can <u>worship</u> God in our own way," he said quietly. "It is this freedom we seek in a new land. And I have <u>faith</u> that we will find it."

Looking at my father, so calm and sure, suddenly I too had faith that we would find it.

Still the wide dark sea went on and on. Eight weeks. Nine.

Then one day a sailor, sniffing the air, said, "Land's ahead." We dared not believe him. But soon bits of seaweed floated by. Then a tree branch. And a feather from a land bird.

Two days later at dawn I heard the lookout shout, "Land ho!"

Everyone who was well enough to stand crowded on deck. And there through the gray mist we saw it: a low dark outline between sea and sky. Land!

Tears streamed down my mother's face, yet she was smiling. Then everyone fell to their knees while my father said a prayer of thanksgiving.

Our long journey was over.

120

Extra Support: Previewing the Text

Before Segment 2, preview the text, using the notes below. **While** reading, model strategies (pages 122 and 123). **After** reading, review the segment (page 130) before students join the Wrapping Up discussion.

pages 120–123 The father explains how they hope to worship in freedom in a new land. After nine weeks, land is finally sighted. How do the travelers feel about that? Now they must search for the right place to build homes. Why might that be?

pages 124–127 When they finally start building their homes, winter has come, and people fall ill. About half die. Why do you think the boy remembers it is as a long, terrible winter?

pages 128–131 In spring the Pilgrims see more Indians and begin to fear them. Then one talks to them in English. Another teaches them how to plant and catch fish. How will this help the Pilgrims? How do the people feel as the *Mayflower* sails back to England?

121

English Language Learners

Pause after reading page 120, and ask: How long have they been at sea? Have a student point to the two references to the period of time: *Eight weeks. Nine.* Then ask: How did they know that land was near? What signs did they see in the water?

▶ Supporting Comprehension

11 Why is the small party's report so important to the Pilgrims? (They have to decide whether to look there for a place to build their homes or to sail to a better spot.)

12 What are some possible good and bad points to the land features they find? (Examples: good points—firewood for cooking and for building houses; ponds for drinking water; rich soil for crops; bad points—sand hills and swamps where food can't grow and mosquitoes can breed)

13 Why do you think the author includes the detail about finding clams and mussels?
(to show that the settlers can find fresh food so they won't starve)

Vocabulary (page 122)

lurked: stayed hidden

shelter: something that protects or covers

swamps: areas of spongy, muddy land that are often filled with water

---

The ship dropped anchor in a quiet bay, circled by land. Pale yellow sand and dark hunched trees were all we saw. And all we heard was silence.

What <u>lurked</u> among those trees? Wild beasts? Wild men? Would there be food and water, a place to take <u>shelter</u>?

What waited for us in this new land?

11 A small party of men in a small boat set off to find out. All day I watched on deck for their return.

When at last they rowed into sight, they brought armfuls of firewood and tales of what they had seen: forests of fine trees, rolling hills of sand, <u>swamps</u> and ponds and rich black **12** earth. But no houses or wild beasts or wild men.

So all of us went ashore.

My mother washed the clothes we had worn for weeks beside a shallow pond, while my brother and I raced up and down the beach.

We watched whales spouting in the sparkling blue bay and helped search for firewood. And we found clams and mussels, **13** the first fresh food we had tasted in two months. I ate so many I was sick.

122

Extra Support

Strategy Modeling

Question Use this example to model the strategy.

On page 122, I read that the small party of men set out to explore the new land. When they return, their report is enough to allow everyone to go ashore after many weeks at sea. So, good questions to ask about this part might be the following: Why do the small party of men set off? What do they find? What do the Pilgrims do as a result?

123

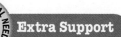
Extra Support

Strategy Modeling

Phonics/Decoding Use this example to model the strategy.

When I look at the word s-p-o-u-t-i-n-g, *I recognize the* s-p *cluster from words such as* spring *and* spell. *Next I see the shorter word* out *and the* -ing *ending. When I blend all the sounds together I'll say,* /SPOWT•ihng/. *I know a spout is the hole on top of a whale's head. Maybe it's called* spouting *when whales blow water out of that hole. That would make sense in this sentence.*

Reading Fluency

- **Rereading for Fluency:** Have students choose a favorite part of the story to reread to a partner, or suggest that they read page 122. Encourage students to read with feeling and expression.

- **Assessing Fluency** See guidelines in the Theme Assessment Wrap-Up, pages 206–207A.

Reading

▶ Strategy Focus: Question

Student Modeling Have students take turns modeling the Question strategy. If necessary, use the following prompt:

Why is the place the men find a good place to build a settlement? What does the answer tell you about their future plans?

▶ Supporting Comprehension

14 What does the boy's father mean by saying that they must find a place before winter comes? (Their survival may depend on having safe homes for the winter; they can't stay on the ship, because it might be wrecked in a storm.)

15 Why do you think the author includes the detail that half of all the people died? (to show the hardships the people faced)

Vocabulary *(page 124)*

settlement: a small community in a new place

weary: tired

rough: built in a hurry; not completely finished

Day after day the small party set out from the ship, looking for just the right place to build our <u>settlement</u>.

The days grew cold. Snowflakes danced in the wind. The cold and damp made many sick again. Drawing his coat tightly around him, my father looked worried.

14 "We must find a place," he said, "before winter comes."

One afternoon the <u>weary</u> men returned with good news. They had found the right spot at last.

When my father saw it, he smiled. It was high on a hill, with a safe harbor and fields cleared for planting and brooks running with sweet water. We named it after the town from which we had sailed, across the sea.

It was December now, icy cold and stormy. The men went ashore to build houses, while the rest of us stayed on board ship. Every fine day they worked. But as the houses of our settlement began to rise, more and more of our people fell sick. And some of them died.

It was a long and terrible winter.

We had houses now, small and <u>rough</u>. Yet the storms and sickness went on. And outside the settlement, Indians waited, seldom seen but watching us.

15 My father and mother nursed the sick, and my father led prayers for them. But more and more died. Of all the people who had sailed for the new land, only half were left.

124

English Language Learners

Pause after reading page 124 to review the plot. Ask: Why are the pilgrims coming to a new world? What problems do they have on the voyage? What problems do they have with the new settlement? Do you think they will survive? Why or why not?

125

Revisiting the Text ·············· Review/Maintain

Comprehension Skill Lesson
Making Judgments

OBJECTIVES

Students make judgments about the story characters' actions.

Review the process of making judgments:

■ Ask questions such as, "Is this fair? Is this a wise decision?"

■ Use story facts and personal experience to think about each side of the issue.

■ Decide whether to agree with what the characters do.

Have students reread the sentence that describes the building site: *It was high on a hill, with a safe harbor and fields cleared for planting and brooks running with sweet water.*

Discuss whether students think the Pilgrims made the right choice for their building site. To help students make a sound judgment, use a chart like the one below to record their ideas about each side of the issue. On the *Yes* side, list all the good things about the site. On the *No* side, list the bad things about the site.

Do you think the Pilgrims made a wise choice for their building site?	
Yes	No

On Level **Challenge**

Reading Card
3

Making Judgments

Have students imagine themselves to be living in England in 1620. Ask: Is it wise to travel on the *Mayflower* with the Pilgrims? Have students discuss the question, listing good and bad points for each side of the issue. Then ask students to write an explanation of their opinions.

Skill Finder

● **Instruction,** Theme 4, pages 99A–99B

● **Reteaching,** Theme 4, page R12

● **Review,** Theme 1, p. 65; Theme 6, p. 323

▶ Supporting Comprehension

16 What does the author mean by *the smell of new-split wood filled the air*? (The settlers are once again at work building their settlement.)

17 Why do you think the Indians are watching the settlers? (The settlers are unfamiliar people with new ways and tools and may be a threat to the Indians.)

18 How do you think the Indian knows English? (He may have met English-speaking explorers or pirates and learned English from them.)

Vocabulary *(page 127)*

defend: to protect from attack

cannons: heavy guns set onto wheels

126

One morning in March, as I was gathering firewood, I heard a strange sweet sound. Looking up, I saw birds singing in a white birch tree.

Could it be that spring had come at last?

All that day the sun shone warm, melting the snow. The sick rose from their beds. And once more the sound of axes and the smell of new-split wood filled the air. **16**

"We have done it," my father said. "We have survived the winter."

But now the Indians came closer. We found their arrows, and traces of their old houses. We caught sight of them among the trees. Our men met to talk of this new danger. How could so small a settlement <u>defend</u> itself? **17**

<u>Cannons</u> were mounted on top of the hill, and the men took turns standing guard. Then one day an Indian walked into the settlement. Speaking to us in our own language, he said, "Welcome." **18**

127

▶ Supporting Comprehension

19 Why do the Indians help the settlers? (They want to show they're sincere about peace; they learn to like the settlers, they know how hard it's been for the settlers to survive.)

20 Why have the Pilgrims brought seeds from England to plant? (to be sure they have seeds so they can grow crops they know are food, or in the case of the herbs, medicine)

21 How does the scene with the boy's mother reveal her thoughts? (She's probably been doubting that the settlement can succeed and now feels some hope.)

19 Our Indian friend came back and brought his chief. We all agreed to live in peace.

And one of the Indians stayed with us, teaching us where to find fish in the bubbling brooks, and how to catch them in traps, and how to plant Indian corn so that next winter we would have enough to eat.

My father and I worked side by side, clearing the fields, planting barley and peas and hills of corn.

20 Afterward I dug a garden next to our house. In it we planted the seeds we had brought from home: carrots and cabbages and onions and my mother's favorite herbs, parsley, sage, chamomile, and mint.

Each day I watched, until something green pushed up from the dark earth. My mother laughed when she saw it.

21 "Perhaps we may yet make a home in this new land," she said.

128

MEETING INDIVIDUAL NEEDS — English Language Learners

Have students find the names of all of the foods mentioned on page 128. Make a list on the board. If possible, show examples of Indian corn. Say that today we use it to decorate in the fall.

129

Tested Skill

Comprehension Skill Lesson
Making Inferences

OBJECTIVES
◎

Students make inferences about story characters and events.

Tell students that authors don't always explain everything in a story. Active readers often use clues in the story as well as personal knowledge to make reasonable guesses about the story characters and events.

Draw attention to the statement about the Indian walking into the settlement on page 127. Model how to infer how the Pilgrims must have felt. Point out how surprised and relieved they probably felt when someone they feared as a possible enemy welcomed them instead.

Ask small groups of students to make inferences to answer the questions below. Also have them list the text information and personal knowledge they used to make sensible guesses.

■ Why does their Indian friend bring his chief to meet with the Pilgrim leaders?

■ Why do the Pilgrims want to learn from the Indian?

Skill Finder

• **Instruction,** pp. 137A–137B; Th. 1, pp. 91A–91B

• **Reteaching,** page R8; Theme 1, page R10

• **Review,** Th. 2, p. 175; Th. 3, p. 305; Th 6, p. 251

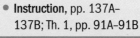

▶ Supporting Comprehension

22 How does the end of the story compare to the beginning? (Example: The descriptions of the ship are similar as it sails into the wide dark sea, but at the end the ship leaves the Pilgrims behind. Both times the Pilgrims' future is uncertain.)

23 How has the family's outlook changed since the beginning of the story? (They've survived the journey and first winter and know what to expect, so they feel surer of their success.)

Vocabulary *(page 131)*

sprouting: beginning to grow as new plants

thatch-roofed: a roof covered with straw or reeds

On a morning early in April our ship sailed back across the sea. We gathered on shore to watch it go. The great white sails filled with wind, then slowly the ship turned and headed out into the wide dark sea.

22 I watched it growing smaller and smaller, and suddenly there were tears in my eyes. We were all alone now.

Then I felt a hand on my shoulder.

130

 Extra Support

Segment 2 Review

Before students join the whole class for Wrapping Up on page 131, have them:

- check predictions
- take turns modeling the reading strategies they used
- help you complete **Transparency 5–2** and their Inference Charts
- summarize the whole story

 On Level **Challenge**

Literature Discussion

Have small groups of students discuss the story using their own questions or the questions in Think About the Selection on page 132.

"Look," my father said, pointing up the hill.

Spread out above us in the soft spring sunshine was our settlement: the fields sprouting with green, the thatch-roofed houses and neatly fenced gardens, the streets laid out almost like a town.

"Come," my father said. "We have work to do."

With his hand on my shoulder we walked back up the hill.

23

End of Segment 2:
pages 120–131

Wrapping Up Segment 2
pages 120–131

First, provide Extra Support for students who need it (page 130). Then bring all students together.

- **Review Predictions/Purpose** Discuss reasons why students' predictions were or were not accurate.

- **Model Strategies** Have students tell how they used the Question strategy, and then have them take turns modeling it. Ask what other strategies they found helpful while reading.

- **Share Group Discussion** Have students share their reactions to the story of the sea journey and the building of a settlement.

- **Summarize** Ask students to summarize the story, using their Inference Chart.

Comprehension/Critical Thinking

1 Why do you think the author has named the story *Across the Wide Dark Sea?* (to describe the Pilgrims' destination and also the uncertain future they faced) **Main Idea**

2 What inferences can you make about people's desire to find freedom and a better way of life? (People will endure many hardships to reach their goal.) **Making Inferences**

English Language Learners

When students have completed reading the story, ask summary questions: How old do you think the narrator is? How can you tell? What problems did the Pilgrims have? How did they survive? Who helped them?

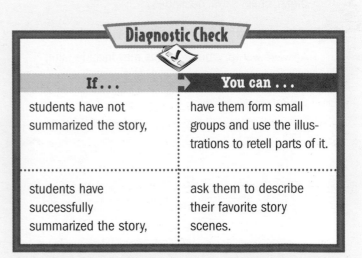

Diagnostic Check

If . . .	You can . . .
students have not summarized the story,	have them form small groups and use the illustrations to retell parts of it.
students have successfully summarized the story,	ask them to describe their favorite story scenes.

Responding

▶ Think About the Selection

Discuss or Write Have students discuss or write their answers. Sample answers are provided; accept reasonable responses that are supported with evidence from the story.

① **Noting Details** They want the freedom to worship the way they wish and hope to find a settlement where their lives will be better.

② **Compare and Contrast** At first he thinks the sailors' lives are exciting because they handle the rigging and climb the masts. Then he realizes how small and helpless the ship is in storms, and he tires of the cold, dampness, and poor food.

③ **Making Inferences** They wish to honor and remember their previous home; they want to think of their new settlement as "home."

④ **Making Generalizations** enduring the terrible storms and living in damp and crowded conditions; weathering each storm and sighting land after nine weeks at sea.

⑤ **Problem Solving** Answers will vary. Examples: tractors, plows, chain saws, backhoes.

⑥ **Connecting/Comparing** Making Inferences Answers will vary, but qualities may include faith, courage, confidence, and stamina.

Responding

Think About the Selection

1. Why do the people in this story travel to an unknown land? In what ways do they hope their lives will be different?

2. How do you think the boy's feelings about a sailor's life change during the voyage?

3. Why do you think the settlers name their new town after the one they sailed from?

4. What would you find most difficult and most exciting about the voyage the boy makes?

5. What tools and machines that we have today would have been most useful to the settlers?

6. **Connecting/Comparing** What qualities do the settlers have that help them succeed on their voyage?

Write a Travel Diary

Choose one part of the story, such as the voyage, the first winter in the new land, or the first spring. Write an entry for a travel diary that summarizes the important events during that time.

Tips
- To get started, brainstorm a list of events or make a story web.
- Include descriptive details.
- Keep your summary short.

132

English Language Learners

Beginning/Preproduction Ask students to draw a scene from the journey. Then ask students to describe what they have drawn.

Early Production/Speech Emergence Students can make a picture quiz by writing words and drawing pictures. They can ask a partner to match the words and pictures.

Intermediate and Advanced Fluency Ask students to write a five-question quiz. Then have them exchange questions with a classmate and respond.

Math

Calculate Amounts

If a person on the *Mayflower* ate one pound of salt pork, one cup of beans, half a pound of cheese, and three biscuits each day, how much of each of those foods would a person eat in one week? Try drawing a picture to help you find the answer.

Bonus The journey lasted sixty-six days. How much would one traveler have eaten during the entire trip?

Vocabulary

Make a Picture Dictionary

With a partner, write all the words from the story about ships and sailing on separate pieces of paper. Look up each word in a dictionary, write down its meaning, and draw a picture of it. Staple your pages together in alphabetical order to make a book.

Build a Model of the Mayflower

Find instructions on how to build your own paper sailing ship when you connect to Education Place. **www.eduplace.com/kids**

133

English Language Learners

Ask students to predict what will happen after the end of the story. List students' ideas on the board. Then challenge them to write their travel diary about a scene in the story or their own ideas of what will happen after the story ends.

Personal Response

Invite volunteers to share their personal responses to *Across the Wide Dark Sea*. As an alternative, ask students to write in their journals or to respond in their own way.

► Comprehension Check

Assign **Practice Book** page 63 to assess students' understanding of the selection.

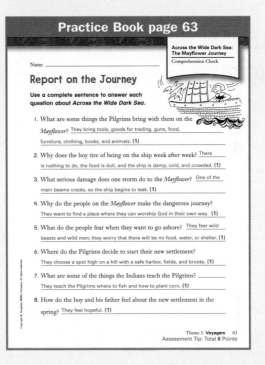

Practice Book page 63

Name

Report on the Journey

Use a complete sentence to answer each question about *Across the Wide Dark Sea.*

1. What are some things the Pilgrims bring with them on the *Mayflower*? They bring tools, goods for trading, guns, food, furniture, clothing, books, and animals. **(1)**

2. Why does the boy tire of being on the ship week after week? There is nothing to do, the food is dull, and the ship is damp, cold, and crowded. **(1)**

3. What serious damage does one storm do to the *Mayflower*? One of the main beams cracks, so the ship begins to leak. **(1)**

4. Why do the people on the *Mayflower* make the dangerous journey? They want to find a place where they can worship God in their own way. **(1)**

5. What do the people fear when they want to go ashore? They fear wild beasts and wild men; they worry that there will be no food, water, or shelter. **(1)**

6. Where do the Pilgrims decide to start their new settlement? They choose a spot high on a hill with a safe harbor, fields, and brooks. **(1)**

7. What are some of the things the Indians teach the Pilgrims? They teach the Pilgrims where to fish and how to plant corn. **(1)**

8. How do the boy and his father feel about the new settlement in the spring? They feel hopeful. **(1)**

Theme 5: **Voyagers**   63
Assessment Tip: Total **8 Points**

End-of-Selection Assessment

Selection Test Use the test in the **Teacher's Resource Blackline Masters** to assess selection comprehension and vocabulary.

Student Self-Assessment Have students assess their reading with additional questions such as

• What parts of this selection were difficult for me? Why?

• What strategies helped me understand the story?

• Would I recommend this story to my friends? Why?

Social Studies Link

pages 134–137

. . . .

▶ Skill: How to Read a Diagram

Read aloud the title and point out that "Young Voyagers: A Pilgrim Childhood" is a nonfiction social studies article. Tell students that the article contains a diagram—a graphic with labels and a legend, or key, that describes something. Tell them that diagrams can help explain the text, and that sometimes diagrams work better than words to convey information. Have students read and discuss each step in the box in the left column on page 134.

■ **Identify** what the diagram is describing. Next, have them predict how the diagram might be useful in understanding the text.

■ Have students **find** the labels on the diagram and understand how they each **match** information corresponding to them in the key.

■ As they read, ask students to **look back** at the diagram. Instruct them to think about how the diagram helps them understand the text.

Vocabulary *(pages 134–135)*

cargo: goods carried by a ship

hardships: things that cause suffering

relieved: not afraid anymore

Social Studies Link

Skill: How to Read a Diagram

❶ **Identify** what the diagram shows.

❷ **Find** the labels on the diagram. The labels will often be letters or numbers.

❸ **Match** each label with one in the key.

❹ **Read** the description of each labeled part.

❺ As you read, **look back** at the diagram to see how it helps you.

Young Voyagers
A Pilgrim Childhood

What was life like for the twenty-eight children aboard the *Mayflower*? How did they live once they settled in America? Read on to find out.

On Board the Mayflower

The *Mayflower* was built to carry cargo, not people. Passengers lived in the 'tween decks — the dark, cramped space between the hold and the main deck.

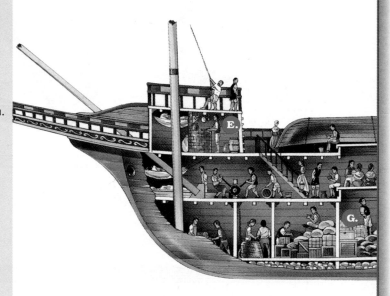

134

Classroom Management

All Students

Reading the Article Involve all students in the activities under How To Read a Diagram, Ship's Diagram, Compare and Contrast, and Comprehension Check. For students needing extra reading support, pair them with more proficient partners to read the article. Remind them to get as much information as they can from the illustrations. After they have studied the diagram, consider having students write a short paragraph describing the diagram. Ask them which best describes what the *Mayflower* looked like inside: their paragraphs or the diagram.

In good weather, children might have read, played games, or exercised on deck. Much of the time, however, the passengers had to stay below deck because of stormy weather. They were often seasick, and the ship's motion — up and down, side to side — made their cramped living space dangerous.

The voyage was filled with <u>hardships</u>, but there were joyful events as well. One baby was born during the voyage and named Oceanus. (Can you guess why his parents gave him that name?) Another child, Peregrine White, was born in Cape Cod Harbor. His first name means "traveler."

After sixty-six days at sea, the Pilgrims were happy and <u>relieved</u> to finally reach their new home.

Parts of the Ship

A. The **Round House** was where the ship's route was planned, using maps and other charts.

B. The **Ship's Bell** was rung during emergencies or to show the passage of time.

C. The **Great Cabin** was where the commander of the ship lived.

D. The **Whipstaff** was a long lever used to steer the ship.

E. The **Cook-room** was where meals were prepared for the crew.

F. The **'tween decks** was where the passengers lived.

G. The **Hold** was where most of the food, tools, and supplies were kept.

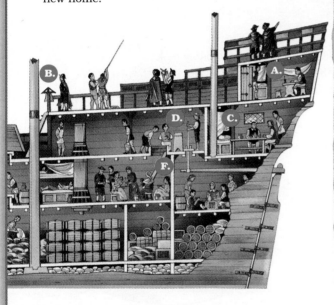

135

▶ Ship's Diagram

Draw a simple cross-section of the *Mayflower* on the board, with lines to indicate its many rooms and sections. Invite students to suggest other criteria for categorizing and classifying the ship's layout. (Possibilities include names of the decks and masts; rooms designated for cargo, living, recreation, and working.) Then have students study the diagram in their books and help you assign numbered labels to the rooms and write the legend accordingly.

Ask students how this diagram compares with the diagram in the book. How is it the same? (It has labels and a legend, and gives information about the ship.) How is it different? (The labels are numbers, not letters, and they appear more than once on the diagram; the diagram is based on judgment, not fact.)

Purpose Setting Have students read "Young Voyagers: A Pilgrim Childhood" to learn more about life as a Pilgrim. Remind them to identify the main ideas and supporting details in the paragraphs and use Question and other strategies as they read.

MEETING INDIVIDUAL NEEDS

Extra Support

Inferring the Main Idea

To help students understand the content on these pages, point out that they sometimes have to "read between the lines" to understand the main idea. Have them read the paragraph on page 134 under the heading "On Board the *Mayflower*." While the main idea is stated, students need to think further about it. What the author doesn't state is that the families on the *Mayflower* were living in spaces meant for cargo, not people. Discuss what the effects might have been.

Living in New Plymouth

What was life like in Plymouth? At Plimoth Plantation in Massachusetts, where these photos were taken, people dress up and show visitors what Pilgrim life may have been like. The facts may surprise you!

Children spent most of the day working! Their chores included <u>fetching</u> water, gathering firewood, herding animals, and gathering berries. They also helped their parents cook, clean, plant and <u>harvest</u> crops, and care for younger children.

Children and adults probably took baths only a few times a year. They thought bathing was unhealthy.

Pilgrim children still had time to play. They probably played marbles, ball games, board games, and running games.

136

 English Language Learners

Before reading, ask students to look at the pictures and label them using stick-on tabs (*ship, toys, cooking pot,* etc.). Then read aloud, referring to the pictures frequently. After you have read through once, ask: Where did people stay on the ship? Where did children play? After they arrived in Plymouth, what chores did children do? What games did they play? Who served dinners?

Vocabulary *(pages 136–137)*

fetching: getting

harvest: to gather

hearth: area in front of a fireplace

At seven years old, children began dressing like their parents. Before that, both boys and girls wore gowns.

There was no school in the early years of New Plymouth. Children learned to read and write from their parents or from neighbors.

Children were expected to serve meals to their parents. Children ate only after their parents had been served. They often ate on stools near the <u>hearth</u>.

137

▶ Comprehension Check

Comprehension/Critical Thinking Ask students to read aloud the parts of the selection that support their answers.

1 Do you think Pilgrim children had as much fun as children today? Explain. (Answers will vary.) **Making Judgments**

2 According to the Parts of the Ship key, where would the most important person on the ship have lived? How is this labeled on the diagram? (The captain lived in the Great Cabin, marked as C.) **Making Inferences/Text Organization**

3 What things did Pilgrim children learn that would be helpful today? Explain why. (From work, they learned valuable skills and responsibility; by serving their parents and eating last, they learned to respect and honor their parents.) **Making Generalizations**

4 **Connecting/Comparing** What are the differences between the descriptions of the sea voyage in *Across the Wide Dark Sea* and in the article? Why are they different? (The boy describes the voyage in more detail. They differ because the story description is fiction and is from the boy's perspective; the article is nonfiction and includes only known facts.) **Compare and Contrast**

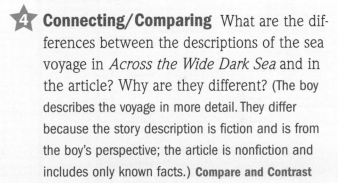

MEETING INDIVIDUAL NEEDS

Challenge

Research Skills

Have students research the *Mayflower* voyage and life as a Pilgrim by providing age-appropriate books, encyclopedias, Web site URLs, and other materials to help students locate information. Invite them to prepare a short report for the class on the *Mayflower* or the New Plymouth settlement. Challenge them to create a diagram, complete with labels and a legend, that shows the route of the ship, the layout of the settlement, or other relevant information.

Comprehension Skills

 Making Inferences

Transparency 5–2

Inference Chart

1. How does the boy feel when the journey begins?

Story Clues (pages 113–115)	What I Know
He looks ahead at the wide dark sea.	

My Inference

2. How does the boy feel after six weeks at sea?

Story Clues (pages 116–119)	What I Know

My Inference

3. How do the people react to the report of the new land?

Story Clues (pages 122-124)	What I Know

My Inference

TRANSPARENCY 5–2
TEACHER'S EDITION PAGES T169A AND T137A

VOYAGERS *Across the Wide Dark Sea*
Graphic Organizer Inference Chart

Practice Book page 62

Name _____

Across the Wide Dark Sea: The Mayflower Journey
Graphic Organizer Inference Chart

Inference Chart
Responses will vary. Examples are given.

1. How does the boy feel when the journey begins?

Story Clues (pages 113–115)	What I Know
He looks ahead at the wide dark sea. He stands close to his father and clings to his father's hand. **(1)**	Children stay close to their parents and hold their hands when children are afraid. **(1 point)**

My Inference The boy is sad and afraid. **(2)**

2. How does the boy feel after six weeks at sea?

Story Clues (pages 116–119)	What I Know
The ship is crowded, cramped, cold, and wet. **(1)**	It is uncomfortable to be crowded, cold, and wet. **(1)**

My Inference He is bored, uncomfortable and worried about the future. **(2)**

3. How do the people react to the report of the new land?

Story Clues (pages 122-124)	What I Know
The search party finds fine trees, ponds, and rich black earth. **(1)**	The materials are good for new homes and growing crops **(1)**

My Inference They are relieved and happy to hear the good news. **(2)**

62 Theme 5: **Voyagers**
Assessment Tip: Total 12 Points

> ## Teach

Use **Transparency 5–2** to review the inferences that students made for *Across the Wide Dark Sea*. Allow students to refer to the selection and revise their work on **Practice Book** page 62. As you discuss their work, explain more about the inferencing process.

■ Authors do not explain in words everything in a story.

■ Readers must use story clues and personal knowledge to make inferences, or reasonable guesses, about characters and events.

■ Readers should monitor and change their inferences based on new story information.

Graphic Organizer: Inference Chart (Responses will vary.)

1. How does the boy feel when the journey begins?

Story Clues (pages 113–115)	What I Know
He looks ahead at the wide dark sea. He stands close to his father and clings to his father's hand.	Children stay close to their parents and hold their hands when they're afraid. Sailing on a ship to an unknown place can be dangerous.

My Inference The boy is sad and afraid.

2. How does the boy feel after six weeks at sea?

Story Clues (pages 116–119)	What I Know
The ship is crowded, cramped, cold, and wet. They must eat hard, dry biscuits and cheese. The ship is helpless in the storms.	It is uncomfortable to be crowded, cold, and wet. It is unpleasant and boring to eat only dried biscuits and cheese. Not knowing what is to happen can be scary.

My Inference He is bored, uncomfortable, hungry, and worried about the future.

Modeling Explain that sometimes students might think of a question that can't be answered by the text alone. For example: What does the character think or feel? Why does he do what he does? How is this event related to what has already happened? To find the answers, students will need to make inferences. Have students reread the last half of page 120, beginning with the words *Still the wide dark sea* .... Then have them consider how the Pilgrims might feel when land is sighted at last. Model the inferencing process.

Think Aloud

The story says that when the lookout shouts, "Land ho!" everyone who isn't sick rushes up on deck. The boy's mother is crying and smiling, and they fall to their knees in thanks. I know that after weeks of worrying about the ship sinking in a storm, I'd feel happy, thankful, and relieved to see land. I can infer that the Pilgrims feel the same way when they see land at last.

Emphasize that readers must monitor their inferences based on new story information. Have students reread page 122 up to the next to last paragraph. Point out that some readers might expect all the Pilgrims to rush ashore right away. Instead they send out a small search party to see if they can safely land. Discuss why the Pilgrims might be worried about their safety.

▶ Practice

Have students think up questions that cannot be answered directly from the text, similar to the ones below. List them on the board. Then have students work in small groups to answer two of the questions, noting the story details and personal knowledge they used for help. Suggest that the groups record their work on a chart similar to the transparency.

Meeting Individual Needs — Extra Support

- Reteaching, page R8
- **Reader's Library:** *Voyagers*
  Selection 1, "The Golden Land"

■ How does the sailor realize that land is ahead before he sees it?

■ How does the boy feel when he hears birds singing in the trees?

■ What do the sprouting seedlings mean to the boy's mother?

■ How do the Pilgrims feel when the ship sails away?

■ How do the Pilgrims feel about their new settlement?

▶ Apply

Use **Practice Book** pages 64–65 to diagnose whether students need Reteaching. Students who do not need Reteaching may work on Challenge/Extension Activities, page R9. Students who need easier text to apply the skill may use "The Golden Land," Selection 1 of the **Reader's Library,** and its Responding activity.

Diagnostic Check

If...	You can...
students need extra help making inferences in the story,	use the Reteaching Lesson on page R8.
students have successfully met the lesson objectives,	have them do the Challenge/Extension Activities on page R9.

• Revisiting, p. 129	• Review, Th. 2, p. 175; Th. 3, p. 305; Th. 6, p. 251	• Reteaching, p. R8

Information & Study Skills

Multimedia Report

 Teach

Explain to students that a multimedia report is a report that contains several kinds of media. Instead of having only written materials, it may also contain one or more of the following:

- photographs or other art

- taped interviews

- music

- maps

- Internet presentations

- CD-ROM, or other computer displays

- videotape

- charts, graphs, or other visual aids

Including any combination of these materials can help bring valuable information to a presentation, as well as help make it much more interesting and lively to others. When creating a multimedia report, students must research a topic to learn something about it. This will help them decide what kinds of media to include in their reports. Then, using the library, the Internet, or other electronic resources, they can find appropriate media, decide how to present it, and practice using it, if necessary.

Modeling Direct attention to "Young Voyagers" on page 134 to demonstrate for students how to plan a multimedia report.

Think Aloud

If I wanted to present this as a multimedia report about life aboard the Mayflower or at New Plymouth, I would start by making a list of the different kinds of media that I could include. I might want a photograph of the Mayflower or of Plimoth Plantation; I'd look for pictures of daily life at the plantation; perhaps I could find an illustration of children doing chores. I'd like to find some sound effects of the ocean or some songs of the sea. I would also look for filmstrips or videos. After I learned what media was available from speaking with a librarian, I would select what I wanted to use. It's important that any media I decide to include should serve a definite purpose and be clearly tied to the topic of my report. Then I would decide how to put everything together in an organized way. I would write a script that included what I would say and where exactly I would include media. Then I would practice my report until I could present it smoothly. Using small note cards might be a good way to do this.

▶ Practice

Have students work in groups to brainstorm different types of media that might be appropriate for a report on early sea voyages, the Pilgrims, or some other general topic. Have them tell where they might find this media and how they would present it. Without actually doing the research, have them draw up a general script, or plan.

▶ Apply

Tell students to work in pairs to create brief multimedia reports either on topics that interest them or on topics that they are studying in other classes. You may wish to have selected students extend their Practice exercises by having them pick up where they left off.

Word Work

Decoding Longer Words

 Structural Analysis:
Suffixes -less and -ness

	Word Work Instruction
DAY 1	• Spelling Pretest • Spelling Instruction
DAY 2	• Structural Analysis Instruction • Spelling Practice
DAY 3	• Phonics Instruction • Spelling Practice
DAY 4	• Structural Analysis Reteaching • Vocabulary Skill Instruction • Spelling Game
DAY 5	• Expanding Your Vocabulary • Spelling Test

OBJECTIVES

Students

- read words with the suffixes *-less* and *–ness*

- read words and syllables with the vowel sounds in *tooth* and *cook*

- use the Phonics/Decoding strategy to decode longer words

▶ Teach

Write these sentences on the board and circle the suffix in each underlined word: *How could a ship so small and underline{helpless} ever cross the vast ocean? Yet the storms and underline{sickness} went on.* Explain that each of the underlined words is made up of a *base word* and a *suffix.* Explain that in *helpless,* the suffix *-less* adds the meaning "without." *Helpless* means "without help." Have students give examples of other words that are formed by adding *-less* to a word. (careless, hopeless, worthless) Explain that the suffix *-ness* often changes a describing word (an adjective) into a noun. The word *sickness* means the "condition of being sick." Pick students to give examples of other words that are formed by adding *-ness* to a word. (darkness, happiness, fairness, kindness) Have students review the Phonics/Decoding strategy.

Modeling Use the following sentence to model how to decode *endless: And some began to ask why we had left our safe homes to go on this underline{endless} journey to an unknown land.*

Think Aloud

I see the word end *and the ending* -less. *When I put these together I say* /EHND•lehs/. *I know the suffix* -less *means "without," so* endless *must mean "without an end." It makes sense that some of the passengers would wonder why they had left their safe homes to go on a trip that seemed to never end.*

▶ Practice

Write these sentences on the board and have students copy the underlined words: *One big problem on the ship was the underline{dampness}. After so many days at sea, we began to feel underline{hopeless}. The Indians showed great underline{kindness} toward the settlers.* Have students work in pairs. Tell students to circle the *-ness* and *-less* ending of each word, decode the word, and give its meaning.

Apply

Have students complete **Practice Book** page 66.

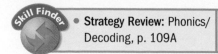

Skill Finder	
• Strategy Review: Phonics/ Decoding, p. 109A	• Reteaching, p. R14

Phonics: Vowel Sounds in tooth and cook

▶ Teach

Tell students that understanding the vowel sounds in *tooth* and *cook* can help them use the Phonics/Decoding strategy to decode unfamiliar words. Explain that

■ the spelling patterns *oo* and *ew* can have the /o͞o/ sound as in *tooth*

■ the spelling pattern *oo* can also have the /o͝o/ sound as in *cook*

Modeling Display this sentence and model how to decode *afternoon*:

> One *afternoon* the weary men returned with good news.

Think Aloud

When I look at this word, I recognize the shorter word after. Next I see the letter n followed by the oo spelling pattern and another n. I know the oo pattern can make the /u/ sound as in cook, but /af•tur•NUN/ doesn't sound right. I know the oo spelling pattern can also have the /oo/ sound as in tooth. I'll try that. /af•tur•NOON/ I know that word, and it makes sense.

▶ Practice

Write these sentences on the board and have students copy the underlined words: *I stood by my father. We grew weary during the long trip. I heard the lookout shout.* Tell students to circle the *oo* spelling in each word, pronounce the word, and see if it makes sense. Call on individuals to come to the board to model the strategy for the class.

▶ Apply

Tell the students to decode the following words from *Across the Wide Dark Sea* and discuss their meanings: *tools, goods, food, books,* page 113; *firewood,* page 122; *brooks,* page 124; *thatch-roofed,* page 131.

Practice Book page 66

Across the Wide Dark Sea: The Mayflower Journey

Structural Analysis Suffixes *-less* and *-ness*

Name _____

Riddled with Suffixes

Each word below contains a base word and a suffix. Write each base word. Put only one letter on each line. To solve the riddle, write each numbered letter on the line with the matching number below.

1. darkness — d a r k (1 point)
2. kindness — k i n d (1)
3. sunless — s u n (1)
4. careless — c a r e (1)
5. hopeless — h o p e (1)
6. worthless — w o r t h (1)
7. goodness — g o o d (1)
8. emptiness — e m p t y (1)
9. priceless — p r i c e (1)
10. fearless — f e a r (1)

Native Americans shared more than their food with the settlers. They also shared their language. Solve the puzzle to learn one Native American word we use in English.

w o o d c h u c k

66 Theme 5: **Voyagers**
Assessment Tip: Total 10 Points

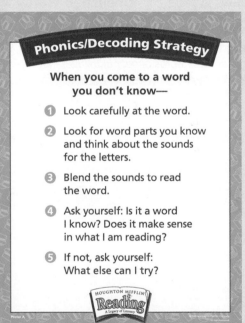

Phonics/Decoding Strategy

When you come to a word you don't know—

1 Look carefully at the word.

2 Look for word parts you know and think about the sounds for the letters.

3 Blend the sounds to read the word.

4 Ask yourself: Is it a word I know? Does it make sense in what I am reading?

5 If not, ask yourself: What else can I try?

HOUGHTON MIFFLIN
Reading
A Legacy of Literacy

Diagnostic Check

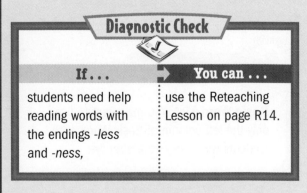

If . . .	You can . . .
students need help reading words with the endings *-less* and *-ness*,	use the Reteaching Lesson on page R14.

Word Work

OBJECTIVES

Students write spelling words that have the vowel sounds in *tooth* and *cook*.

Spelling Words

Basic Words

tooth	boot
chew	flew
grew*	shook
cook*	balloon
shoe*	drew
blue*	spoon

Review Words

good*
soon*

Challenge Words

loose
brook*

Forms of these words appear in the literature.

Extra Support

Basic Word List You may want to use only the left column of Basic Words with students who need extra support.

Spelling

✔ *The Vowel Sounds in* tooth *and* cook

Day 1 | Teaching the Principle

Pretest Use the Day 5 Test sentences. Say each underlined word, read the sentence, and then repeat the word. Have students write only the underlined word.

Teach Write *tooth* and *chew* on the board. Point to and say each word and have students repeat it. Ask students to name the vowel sound in each word. (/ $\overline{oo}$ /) Underline the *oo* and *ew* patterns and explain that *oo* and *ew* are two spellings for the / $\overline{oo}$ / sound.

Write *shoe* and *blue* on the board, say them, and have students repeat them. Underline the *oe* and *ue* patterns. Tell students that these are less common ways of spelling the / $\overline{oo}$ / sound.

Add *cook* to the board, say it, and ask students to repeat it. Ask students to name the vowel sound in *cook*. (/ $\overline{oo}$ /) Underline the *oo* pattern and point out that the / $\overline{oo}$ / sound is often spelled *oo*.

Write the rest of the Basic Words on the board, saying each word and asking students to repeat it. Call on students to underline the / $\overline{oo}$ / and / $\overline{oo}$ / patterns in the words.

Practice/Homework Assign **Practice Book** page 184. Tell students to use this Take-Home Word List to study the words they missed on the Pretest.

Day 2 | Reviewing the Principle

Practice/Homework Review the spelling principle and assign **Practice Book** page 67.

Day 3 | Vocabulary

Exact Words Have students work in small groups. Assign one of these words to each group: *cook, flew, shoe.* Ask each group to brainstorm and list more exact words that could be used in place of their assigned word. Encourage students to use a thesaurus. Groups can meet to pool their exact words and share the final lists with the class. (Responses will vary.)

Technology

Spelling Spree!™

Students may use the **Spelling Spree!™** for extra practice with the spelling principles taught in this lesson.

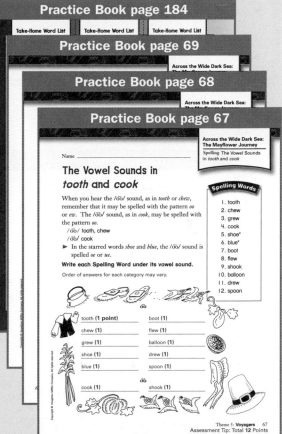

Practice Book page 184

Practice Book page 69

Practice Book page 68

Practice Book page 67

Across the Wide Dark Sea: The Mayflower Journey
Spelling The Vowel Sounds in *tooth* and *cook*

Name _____

The Vowel Sounds in *tooth* and *cook*

When you hear the /o͞o/ sound, as in *tooth* or *chew*, remember that it may be spelled with the pattern *oo* or *ew*. The /o͝o/ sound, as in *cook*, may be spelled with the pattern *oo*.
/o͞o/ tooth, chew
/o͝o/ cook
► In the starred words *shoe* and *blue*, the /o͞o/ sound is spelled *oe* or *ue*.
Write each Spelling Word under its vowel sound.

Order of answers for each category may vary.

Spelling Words
1. tooth
2. chew
3. grew
4. cook
5. shoe*
6. blue*
7. boot
8. flew
9. shook
10. balloon
11. drew
12. spoon

o͞o
tooth (1 point)   boot (1)
chew (1)   flew (1)
grew (1)   balloon (1)
shoe (1)   drew (1)
blue (1)   spoon (1)

o͝o
cook (1)   shook (1)

Theme 5: **Voyagers** 67
Assessment Tip: Total **12** Points

⋯ **Houghton Mifflin Spelling and Vocabulary** ⋯
Correlated instruction and practice

Day 3 *continued ...*

Next, list the Basic Words on the board. Have students use each word orally in a sentence. (Sentences will vary.)

Practice/Homework For spelling practice, assign **Practice Book** page 68.

Day 4 Climb the Mast

Ask students to work in groups of three: two players and a caller. Give each group a long stick (perhaps a yardstick or broom handle) to serve as a "mast." Also give the caller a list of Basic and Review Words. Then explain the game rules. The caller says a list word. If Player 1 spells it correctly, he or she grabs the bottom of the mast with one hand. If Player 2 spells the next word correctly, he or she grabs the mast just above Player 1's hand. As players spell words, they move their hands one over the other up the mast. If they misspell a word, they cannot move. The player who reaches the top of the mast first wins.

Practice/Homework For proofreading and writing practice, assign **Practice Book** page 69.

Day 5 Spelling Assessment

Test Say each underlined word, read the sentence, and then repeat the word. Have students write only the underlined word.

Basic Words

1. I lost a baby <u>tooth</u>.
2. My dog will <u>chew</u> this bone.
3. The corn <u>grew</u> tall.
4. The <u>cook</u> needed a big pot.
5. I have to tie my <u>shoe</u>.
6. The sky is very <u>blue</u>.
7. Some snow got inside my <u>boot</u>.
8. A plane <u>flew</u> over my house.
9. We <u>shook</u> hands when we met.
10. I want a green <u>balloon</u>.
11. Who <u>drew</u> this picture?
12. There is a <u>spoon</u> on the table.

Challenge Words

13. The old rope is <u>loose</u>.
14. Shall we wade in the <u>brook</u>?

Challenge

Challenge Word Practice Students can use the Challenge Words to write sentences about the adventures of the settlers from the story.

OBJECTIVES

Students

- identify the part of a dictionary entry that shows syllabication
- break words into syllables

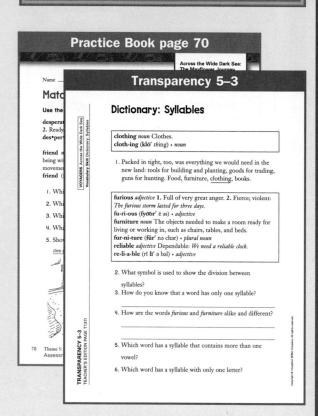

Practice Book page 70

Transparency 5–3

Vocabulary Skills

 ## *Dictionary:* Syllables

··

▶ **Teach**

Display **Transparency 5–3**, blocking out all but the dictionary entries for *clothing*.

---

clothing *noun* Clothes.
cloth•ing (klō´ *th*ing) ♦ *noun*

Review the features of a dictionary entry. Explain that

■ The base, or root, form of a word is shown, along with its part of speech, one or more definitions, and pronunciation.

■ The word is divided into syllables somewhere in the entry.

■ Large dots usually show where the syllables break.

Remind students that a syllable is a word or word part that contains a single vowel sound. If two vowels stand for one sound, they will be part of the same syllable. Knowing how to divide words into syllables can help readers to spell words. It also helps them to know where to insert a hyphen if the word must be broken at the end of a line.

Modeling Display these sentences from page 113 of *Across the Wide Dark Sea*:

Packed in tight, too, was everything we would need in the new land: tools for building and planting, goods for trading, guns for hunting. Food, furniture, clothing, books.

Then model how to use the dictionary syllabication feature to figure out how to divide the word *clothing* into two syllables.

> **Think Aloud**
>
> *If I look at* clothing *and say it out loud, I see that it has two vowel sounds, an o and an i. So* clothing *must have two syllables. Let me try to find where the syllables break. It sounds as if the break might come after* clo-. *However, when I look in the dictionary, I see that the syllable break comes after* cloth-.

▶ Practice

Uncover the remaining dictionary entries on the transparency. In pairs or small groups, have students answer questions 2 through 6. Ask groups to share their answers with the class.

▶ Apply

Have students complete **Practice Book** page 70.

Expanding Your Vocabulary
Words for Ship Parts

The selection contains a number of terms that describe parts of a ship. Have students identify as many of these terms as possible and begin a word cluster similar to the following:

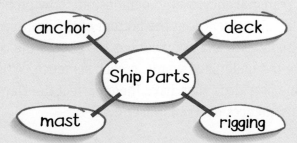

Have students work with partners to find additional words that describe parts of ships. Add the additional words to the cluster.

**Challenge/Extension
Activities, p. R15**

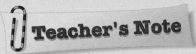

The *Mayflower* was named after a real species of flower that grows in England. A mayflower is the blossom of a flowering hawthorn tree. Since the flowers were used as decorations on May Day, a spring holiday that has survived since ancient times, they were called mayflowers.

····· **Houghton Mifflin Spelling and Vocabulary** ·····
Correlated instruction and practice

	Writing and Language Instruction
DAY 1	• Daily Language Practice • Grammar Instruction • Journal Writing
DAY 2	• Daily Language Practice • Write a Play • Journal Writing • Grammar Practice
DAY 3	• Daily Language Practice • Grammar Instruction • Write a Travel Diary
DAY 4	• Daily Language Practice • Listening/Speaking/Viewing • Writing: Improving Your Writing • Grammar Practice
DAY 5	• Daily Language Practice • Grammar: Improving Your Writing

OBJECTIVES

Students

- identify subject pronouns

- use subject pronouns

- proofread and correct sentences with grammar and spelling errors

- combine sentences with subject pronouns to improve writing

Wacky Web Tales

Students may use the **Wacky Web Tales** floppy disk to create humorous stories and review parts of speech.

Grammar Skills

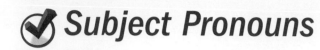

✓ Subject Pronouns

Day 1

Display the paragraph at the top of **Transparency 5–4**.

Have a volunteer read the paragraph aloud. Discuss why the paragraph seems monotonous. Students should notice that the repetition of *the storm* is not interesting. Then display the second paragraph and have a volunteer read it aloud.

Have students identify the difference between the two paragraphs. In the second paragraph *the storm* is replaced with *it*. Explain that *it* is a pronoun. Then go over the following definitions and rules:

■ A pronoun takes the place of one or more nouns.

■ The pronouns *I, you, he, she, it, we,* and *they* are subject pronouns. Pronouns can be singular or plural.

■ Add *-s* or *-es* to a verb when the subject is *he, she,* or *it.*

■ Do not add *-s* or *-es* to a verb when the subject is *I, you, we,* or *they.*

Use the chart on **Transparency 5–4** to demonstrate how pronouns can replace nouns. Then display the sentences at the bottom of the Transparency. Have students read the sentences, and ask volunteers to choose the correct subject pronoun to replace the underlined words in each sentence. Write the subject pronoun on the line provided. Then have them correct the Day 1 Daily Language Practice sentences on **Transparency 5–6**.

Day 2

Practice/Homework Have students correct the Day 2 Daily Language Practice sentences. Then assign **Practice Book** page 71.

Day 3   I Matches; It Matches

Have students write the subject pronouns *I, you, he, she, it, we,* and *they* on note cards. Then have students write several verbs in present time. For each verb, students should write one card that shows the verb without *s* or *es* and one card that shows the verb with *s* or *es.*

Students can create cards using the chart below, or choose verbs of their own.

sail	go	climb
sails	goes	climbs
build	see	hope
builds	sees	hopes
watch	feel	point
watches	feels	points

Students put the pronoun cards in one stack and the verb cards in another. They then take turns selecting one subject pronoun and one verb. If the verb form matches the pronoun, the student writes a sentence using the words and takes the cards. If the pronoun and verb do not match, the student puts the cards in a discard pile. Shuffle the discarded cards before using them again. The student with the most cards at the end of the game is the winner. Then have students correct the Day 3 Daily Language Practice sentences.

Day 4

Practice/Homework Have students correct the Day 4 Daily Language Practice sentences. Then assign **Practice Book** page 72.

Day 5 Improving Your Writing

Sentence Combining with Subject Pronouns Display the two sentences at the top of **Transparency 5–5**.

Ask students how the sentences are similar. They should recognize that the action is the same, but the subjects are different. Show the next sentence on **Transparency 5–5**, and point out that you can combine the sentences using the word *and*. Display the next sentences to model combining sentences using *or*. Then have students combine the remaining sentences, using the word in parentheses.

Then have students review a piece of their own writing to see if they can improve it by using subject pronouns.

Practice/Homework Have students correct the Day 5 Daily Language Practice sentences. Then assign **Practice Book** page 73.

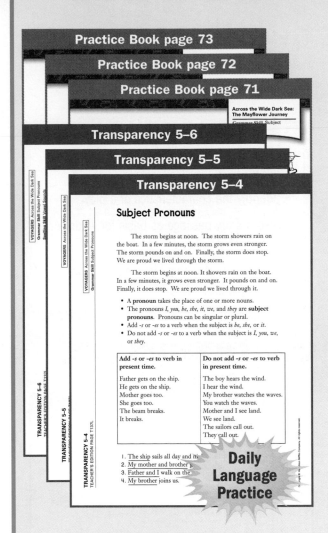

Practice Book page 73
Practice Book page 72
Practice Book page 71
Transparency 5–6
Transparency 5–5
Transparency 5–4

Subject Pronouns

The storm begins at noon. The storm showers rain on the boat. In a few minutes, the storm grows even stronger. The storm pounds on and on. Finally, the storm does stop. We are proud we lived through the storm.

The storm begins at noon. It showers rain on the boat. In a few minutes, it grows even stronger. It pounds on and on. Finally, it does stop. We are proud we lived through it.

• A **pronoun** takes the place of one or more nouns.
• The pronouns *I, you, he, she, it, we,* and *they* are **subject pronouns**. Pronouns can be singular or plural.
• Add *-s* or *-es* to a verb when the subject is *he, she,* or *it.*
• Do not add *-s* or *-es* to a verb when the subject is *I, you, we,* or *they.*

Add *-s* or *-es* to verb in present time.	Do not add *-s* or *-es* to verb in present time.
Father gets on the ship.	The boy hears the wind.
He gets on the ship.	I hear the wind.
Mother goes too.	My brother watches the waves.
She goes too.	You watch the waves.
The beam breaks.	Mother and I see land.
It breaks.	We see land.
	The sailors call out.
	They call out.

1. The ship sails all day and n...
2. My mother and brother ...
3. Father and I walk on the...
4. My brother joins us.

Daily Language Practice

.... **Houghton Mifflin English** ....
Correlated instruction and practice

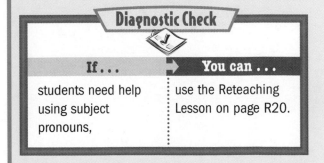

Diagnostic Check

If . . .	You can . . .
students need help using subject pronouns,	use the Reteaching Lesson on page R20.

Writing Skills
Writing a Play

Students

- identify the characteristics of a play
- use a story passage as basis for writing play dialogue
- improve their writing by using exclamation points correctly

---

Transparency 5–8

Using Exclamation Points Correctly

Transparency 5–7

A Play

Title: The Wide Dark Sea

Scene 1: **Time:** October 1620
Place: The crowded passenger area on the sailing ship *Mayflower*

Characters
Father — a Pilgrim leader; a strong, calm man about 40 years old
Son — a boy about 8 years old

(Sounds of a storm are heard. Thunder and loud winds)

Son *(Wakes up with a start. Looks scared. Reaches over and shakes his sleeping father awake.):* Father, Father! Please wake up. I'm so frightened.

Father *(Wakes up. Sees that the boy is trembling.):* Don't be afraid, son. It's just another storm. We've had several since we sailed from England.

Son: I'm afraid the lightning will hit the ship. Or the waves will pull us under. I'm tired of being cold and wet.

Father: I understand. But we must be brave. We are on a long, hard journey to a new home. We must trust that we will get there safely.

Son: Why are we going to this new land? I wish we had never left England.

Father *(Looks calm and sure of what he says. Speaks quietly but strongly.):* We are searching for a place to live where we can worship in our own way. It is this freedom we seek in a new land. And I have faith that we will find it.

Son *(Settles back to sleep.):* I have faith too, Father.

[Curtain]

▶ Teach

Ask students how a play is different from a story. Explain that a play is a story that is written to be acted out for an audience. You may wish to discuss some similarities and differences. A story and a play both have a setting—the time and place where the action happens. They both have characters. The events that happen to the characters are called the plot. A story is meant to be read. The setting, characters, and events are described by a narrator. The characters speak to each other in dialogue, or conversation. A play is meant to be acted out. It is made up of action and dialogue. The dialogue shows what the characters are like and what is happening to them. The stage directions tell the actors what to do. They tell how characters sound and move. They are meant to be followed rather than read aloud.

▶ Practice

Display **Transparency 5–7**. Tell students that this short play is based on the story *Across the Wide Dark Sea*. Have students read the play. Ask:

■ Where and when does the play take place? (On the passenger area of the *Mayflower*, October 1620) How do you know? (It says so in the script.)

■ Who are the characters? (Father, a pilgrim leader, and Son)

■ What is happening to them? (They're sailing in a storm.) How do they feel about it? (The boy is scared. The father is concerned about the boy.)

■ Find the stage directions. What do they tell the actors to do? (They tell the actors how to look and act, for example: *Wakes up with a start. Looks scared.*)

Guidelines for
Writing a Play

- Write the title of the play. Then list the setting and the characters.
- Use the dialogue and the characters' actions to tell the story.
- Each time a different character speaks, write the character's name in capital letters, a colon, and then the words that the character speaks.
- Write stage directions in parentheses to tell the characters how to speak and move.

▶ Apply

Assign **Practice Book** page 74 to help students plan and organize their writing. Have students use it to write several lines of dialogue in play format. Begin by having volunteers read aloud the last two paragraphs on page 123 of *Across the Wide Dark Sea.* Then have volunteers read **Practice Book** page 74 aloud. Discuss with students how the two boys must feel on the beach after months cooped up in the ship. Have students work with a partner and each take the character of one brother. Next, have them playact what each boy might say to the other. Remind them that what the boys say must fit what is happening in the scene and how they feel. Have students take notes as they act out the scenes with their partners. Then have them write their play scenes and share them with the class.

Improving Your Writing
Using Exclamations

Teach Remind students that end punctuation tells how a sentence should be read out loud. Explain that exclamation points have these purposes:

- An exclamation point shows strong feeling.

- An exclamation point may be used at the end of a command to do something.

- An exclamation point is used at the end of a warning.

Practice To model the use of exclamation points, display **Transparency 5–8**. Have a volunteer read the rules for when to use an exclamation point. Then have volunteers read aloud the first example of using an exclamation point to show strong feeling. Next have students read the second example, which includes commands and warnings. Ask students to identify the commands the Captain gives to the drowning man and to the sailors. Then ask them to identify the warnings the Captain gives to the sailors. Invite volunteers to read these commands and warnings with the appropriate tone of voice. Finally, have students find the exclamation points in the scene and explain why they were used.

Apply Assign **Practice Book** page 75. Then have students review their play scenes and add exclamation points where necessary.

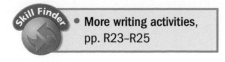
Skill Finder • More writing activities, pp. R23–R25

Technology

Type to Learn™

Students may use **Type to Learn™** to learn proper keyboarding technique. ©*Sunburst Technology Corporation, a Houghton Mifflin Company. All Rights Reserved.*

···· **Houghton Mifflin English** ····
: *Correlated instruction and practice* :

Portfolio Opportunity

Save students' play scenes as samples of their writing skills development.

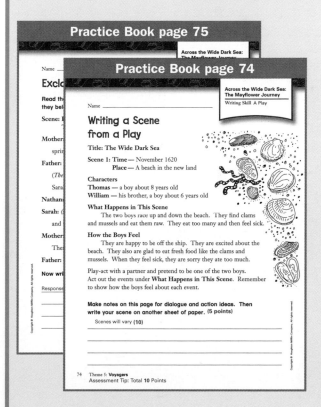

Practice Book page 75

Across the Wide Dark Sea: The Mayflower Journey

Name _____

Exclo...

Practice Book page 74

Across the Wide Dark Sea: The Mayflower Journey
Writing Skill A Play

Name _____

Writing a Scene from a Play

Title: The Wide Dark Sea

Scene 1: Time — November 1620
Place — A beach in the new land

Characters
Thomas — a boy about 8 years old
William — his brother, a boy about 6 years old

What Happens in This Scene
The two boys race up and down the beach. They find clams and mussels and eat them raw. They eat too many and then feel sick.

How the Boys Feel
They are happy to be off the ship. They are excited about the beach. They also are glad to eat fresh food like the clams and mussels. When they feel sick, they are sorry they ate too much.

Play-act with a partner and pretend to be one of the two boys. Act out the events under **What Happens in This Scene**. Remember to show how the boys feel about each event.

Make notes on this page for dialogue and action ideas. Then write your scene on another sheet of paper. (5 points)
Scenes will vary **(10)**

_____
_____
_____

74 Theme 5: **Voyagers**
Assessment Tip: Total **10** Points

Listening/Speaking/Viewing

Present an Oral Book Report

▶ Teach

Explain to students that an oral book report is an oral response to a book that the speaker has read. Speakers may like or dislike their books; however, they should give reasons or other details to support their responses. Identify one or two literary elements that a good report might discuss, such as the characters, the descriptions, or even the illustrations. Have students suggest other elements. Finally, hold a group discussion about the features that all oral book reports should have. Guide students to include at least the following:

- the name and author of the book
- a brief description or summary of the book
- the speaker's response to the book
- reasons to support the response, such as quotations or other details

Remind students that when they give any oral report, they should look at the audience and speak slowly, loudly, and clearly. Since this is a book report, they might also display the book's cover or illustrations.

▶ Practice

Divide students into pairs. Have pairs work together to prepare a short report on a single element of *Across the Wide Dark Sea*. Have the students include at least one reason for their response, such as an example or a direct quotation. Have partners practice delivering their report to one another. Have the listening partner check that the report contains all the elements listed above and provide feedback on how the report was presented.

Apply

Have students select a book or story that they have read recently and either liked or disliked a lot. Have them prepare and deliver an oral book report on it.

Improving Presentation Skills

Have students brainstorm tips to get the audience more involved in their book reports. Guide them to include tips such as the following:

- Invite comments from the audience. For example, if others have read the same book, they might want to add something everyone would be interested in. Or, perhaps someone has read another book by the same author or about the same topic and would like to tell a bit about it.

- Use visuals. If you don't have the book to show, present your own drawing.

- If you enjoy reading aloud dramatically, you might want to read a very short passage from the book to give your audience a quick idea of what it is like.

- If you really liked the book, recommend it to your audience and encourage them to read it. You might even want to recommend other similar books, books by the same author, or books on the same topic.

- Tell enough about your book to keep the audience interested, but don't give everything away—especially the ending. Keep them in suspense!

- Tell the audience where they can get the book if they are interested.

Description

What Makes a Great Description? Review with students these characteristics of a description.

A description is a picture in words that helps the reader see, hear, taste, smell, or feel something that the writer has experienced.

When you write a description, remember to

- begin by telling what you are describing
- start with a high-interest beginning that makes your reader want to find out more
- create vivid pictures in your reader's mind, using sensory language
- use full sentences
- list details in a way that adds meaning to the description
- wrap up the description at the end

Have students read the Student Writing Model. Then discuss with them what the student writer did to make his writing interesting to read.

Student Writing Model

A Description

A description is a picture in words that helps the reader. Use this student's writing as a model when you write a description of your own.

A Trip I Have Taken

> **The opening sentences introduce the topic.**

I love going on trips. It was the end of summer, and my family was planning to go on a picnic. I was very excited because picnics are fun and I get to see a lot of interesting things on our way to the park.

It was a rainy day, and the highway looked all smoky as the cars went swishing by. At times the cars beside us splashed water on our car, and I would dodge for cover, not remembering that the water could not come inside. We kept hoping there would be sun where the picnic was.

> **Sense words create pictures in the reader's mind.**

It was a very busy highway with a lot of big trucks. I am scared of the trucks, especially when they have to blow their horns. It reminds me of thunder, and I always cover my ears. One special thing I wanted to see was the big bridge that went over the huge river. The water is always blue and

138

Theme Writing Skills	Theme Grammar Skills
• Using Exclamation Points, p. 137N	• Sentence Combining with Subject Pronouns, p. 137L
• Writing Complete Information, p. 167N	• Using the Correct Pronoun, p. 167L
• Writing Dates and Times, p. 205N	• Proofreading for *its* and *it's*, p. 205L

looks so beautiful with all the boats with their different colors. Today, even though the water was gray, the boats were still beautiful when we went over the bridge.

Finally we reached the park, and I couldn't wait to get out and have a good stretch. The rain was falling lightly now, and I stuck my tongue out to see if I could taste the rain, but it had no taste. There was a fresh smell in the air, and I took long deep breaths. Then, suddenly, the sun came out! It was time for another fun part of the trip, eating and playing games.

I didn't see much of the journey going back because I was so tired, after a fun day at the picnic, that I fell asleep right away.

Comparisons help the reader create pictures too.

Good writers present details in the **order** in which they happen.

A good **ending** wraps up a description.

Meet the Author

Maurice B.
Grade: three
State: New York
Hobbies: swimming and biking
What he'd like to be when he grows up: a police officer

139

Reading as a Writer

1 How does the writer get right to the point of bringing up the topic of his description? (He says, "I love going on trips" at the outset.)

2 What sights, smells, feelings, tastes, and sounds does the author describe? Find at least one example of each category. (Sample response: sights: the bridge, the water; smells: fresh air; feelings: fear of trucks; tastes: rain; sounds: truck horns, splashes)

3 What sensory words does the writer use to describe the rain on the highway? (swishing, splash, smoky)

4 How does the ending express a sense of satisfaction for the writer? (He fell asleep right away, implying that he had done everything he'd wanted to do and had nothing else left to do.)

Skill Finder

Theme Spelling Skills	**Workshop Focus Skills**
• The Vowel Sounds in *tooth* and *cook,* p. 137G	• Ordering Information, p. 139C
• The Vowel Sound in *bought,* p. 167G	• Using Sensory Language, p. 139D
• The VCCV Pattern, p. 205G	• Writing Complete Sentences, p. 139E

Description, *continued*

·········· **Houghton Mifflin English** ··········

Correlated instruction and practice

Technology

Type to Learn™

Students may use **Type to Learn™** to learn proper keyboarding technique.

©Sunburst Technology Corporation, a Houghton Mifflin Company. All Rights Reserved.

Choosing a Topic

Tell students they are going to write their own description of a person, place, or thing that they know about. Have students answer these questions, either in a writing journal or on a sheet of paper:

■ Who is your audience: friends? people who are interested in your topic? users of a web site?

■ What will be your purpose for writing: to inform people about something that is important to you? to persuade? to entertain?

■ How will you publish your description: in a magazine? as a video or audio presentation? as an illustrated booklet?

Have students generate three or more ideas for their descriptions. Offer the following prompts if students are having trouble getting started.

■ Who is the most fascinating person you know?

■ What was the most interesting or unusual place you visited this year?

■ What was the best new invention or idea you've seen this year?

Have students work with a partner or in small groups to decide which topic would be the best one to write about.

Tips for
Getting Started

- Look through travel guides and maps for interesting places.
- Browse through the biography section of the library to learn about interesting people.
- Look through magazines to find interesting products.
- Imagine your description is to become a magazine article. What pictures or photographs would accompany the article?

Organizing and Planning

Tell students that a good description uses vivid words and key details to give the reader a sharp view of a person, place, or thing. A good writer makes a list of the details that will be described, and may organize them in a number of different ways. Go over these tips for organizing a description.

■ Focus on the person, place, or thing that you are describing. For each detail you include, ask yourself: *Does this describe my topic?* If not, leave the detail out.

■ See things in terms of the "big picture" first. Describe the big, obvious qualities of your topic first. Then work your way to the smaller, less noticeable qualities.

■ Use your eyes like a camera and your ears like a tape recorder to record sights and sounds. Take in other senses in a similar way. Then "play back" the data you took in and translate it into sensory language.

Display **Transparency RWW5–1.** Have students discuss the details listed. Can they think of other sights, smells, feelings, sounds, and tastes at a ball game? Encourage students to use a similar chart to organize their own descriptions.

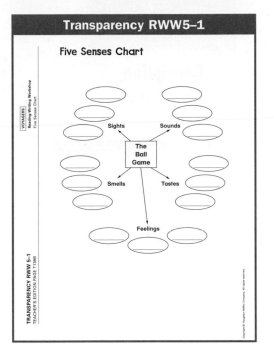

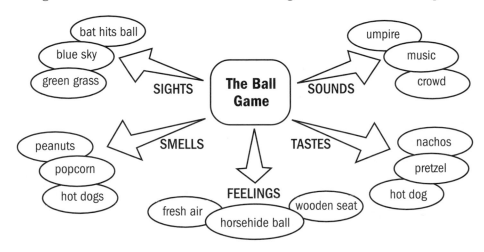

Tips for
Organizing a Description

- Focus on your topic.
- Pay attention to the "big picture" first.
- Then make a list of details, based on your senses.

Reading-Writing Workshop

Description, *continued*

Focus Skill

Ordering Information

Remind students that in a good description, details need to be organized and ordered so that they make sense. Ordering details helps the reader get a clear picture of the subject and also helps to focus the reader's attention on important features of what is being described.

Tell students that there are many ways to order details. They can order according to importance, size, position, number, color, and so on. Examples of ordering schemes include most important to least, general to specific, oldest to newest, biggest to smallest, best to worst, slowest to fastest, right to left, least to most, and so on.

Display **Transparency RWW5–2.** Go over the example for each ordering category given. Then have students complete the categories.

Have students think about which way of ordering the information will work best for their descriptions.

Transparency RWW5–2

Order Words

Size Order	Position Order	Importance Order	Quality Order	Number Order	Time Order
Biggest	Top/bottom	Most important	Best		

Tips for
Ordering Information

- Think of what you are trying to communicate.
- Order the details in a way that makes sense.
- Order according to such things as importance, position, size, number, color, and so on.

Using Sensory Language

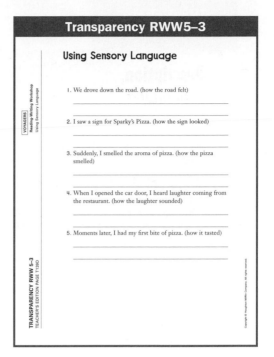

Using Sensory Language

1. We drove down the road. (how the road felt)
   _____

2. I saw a sign for Sparky's Pizza. (how the sign looked)
   _____

3. Suddenly, I smelled the aroma of pizza. (how the pizza smelled)
   _____

4. When I opened the car door, I heard laughter coming from the restaurant. (how the laughter sounded)
   _____

5. Moments later, I had my first bite of pizza. (how it tasted)
   _____

Tell students that the details in a description should appeal to all five senses. Sensory words help the reader experience what is being described. Sensory words must be chosen carefully to give an accurate representation of what the author sees, feels, tastes, touches, and smells.

Display **Transparency RWW5–3,** and read the first sentences aloud. Then ask the students to come up with words that describe how it might feel to drive in a car. Read the sample answer. Then field suggestions from the class and have students come up with their own sentences.

Have students work in pairs to complete the rest of Transparency RWW5–3. Invite volunteers to read their sentences in class. Encourage students to use the Five Senses Chart on Transparency RWW5–1 to help them provide sensory language in their descriptions.

Tips for
Using Sensory Language

- Imagine your eyes are a camera. Use your camera to record visual impressions.
- Try to make the reader see, feel, hear, touch, and taste what you have experienced.
- Use sensory words to liven up your description.

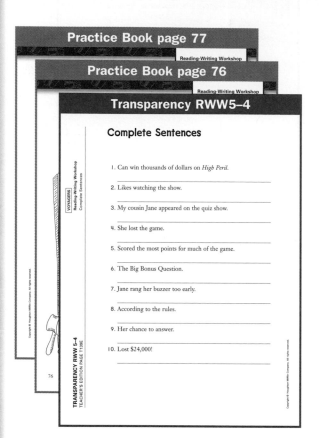

Revising

Once students have finished their drafts, have them evaluate them, using Evaluating Your Description on **Practice Book** page 76. Students may want to evaluate their drafts with a partner in a Writing Conference.

Once students have evaluated and discussed their drafts, have them go back and revise any parts they feel still need work.

Improving Your Writing
GRAMMAR LINK Writing Complete Sentences

Tell students that good writers write in complete sentences. Review the characteristics of a complete sentence:

■ A complete sentence expresses a complete thought.

■ A complete sentence has a subject and a predicate.

■ The subject is the person, place, or thing that the sentence is about. Example: My cousin Bill ran home. (subject: Bill)

■ The predicate has a **verb,** or action word. Example: My cousin Bill ran home. (verb: ran)

■ Some verbs are verbs of being rather than action. Example: Bill is my cousin. (verb of being: is)

Use **Transparency RWW5–4** to model using complete sentences for students. Read the first two sentences aloud. Show that the first sentence is complete because it has both a subject (Jane) and a verb (appeared). Then show that the second sentence is not complete because it does not have a subject. Read the suggested answer. Then have students suggest other acceptable answers. Have students complete Transparency RWW5–4.

Assign **Practice Book** page 77. Then encourage students to examine their own descriptions to make sure that they use only complete sentences.

Proofreading

Have students proofread their papers carefully to correct any capitalization, punctuation, and spelling errors. Students can use the chart on **Practice Book** page 193 to help them with their proofreading marks.

Practice Book
Spelling Practice: pp. 78–80
Take-Home Word List: p. 185

5-Day Spelling Plan
See p. 137G

Improving Your Writing

Spelling · Connection Frequently Misspelled Words

Write the Spelling Words on the board or distribute the Take-Home Word List on **Practice Book** page 185. Read the words aloud, and have students repeat them. Help students identify the part of the word likely to be misspelled.

Spelling Assessment

Pretest

1. Come <u>down</u> to Camp Pogo.
2. <u>How</u> much fun will you have?
3. Camp Pogo has <u>its</u> own lake.
4. I'm <u>coming</u> for six weeks.
5. My brother <u>stopped</u> coming.
6. I <u>started</u> coming last year.
7. I <u>wrote</u> a letter from camp.
8. We went <u>swimming</u> in the frog pond.
9. People come to the camp <u>from</u> far away.
10. Everyone should <u>write</u> home once a week.
11. <u>Writing</u> is my quiet time.
12. I <u>brought</u> some souvenirs home.

Test: Use the Pretest sentences.

Challenge Words

13. Water-skiing is my <u>favorite</u> camp activity.
14. You are <u>sure</u> to get wet.
15. Leave your <u>clothes</u> in the boat.
16. I've <u>heard</u> some good camp tales.

Challenge Word Practice

Have students use the Challenge Words in a fictional postcard that they would write home from camp.

Spelling Words

down	write
how	writing
its	brought
coming	
stopped	**Challenge Words**
started	favorite
wrote	sure
swimming	clothes
from	heard

··· **Houghton Mifflin Spelling and Vocabulary** ···
Correlated instruction and practice

Description,
continued

Publishing and Evaluating

Have students make a final copy of their descriptions. Then have students look back at the publishing ideas note they made when they were choosing a topic for their descriptions. Tell them to decide if that's still the way they want to share their writing. If students need help deciding how to share what they have written, here are some ideas:

■ Submit your description to a magazine.

■ Turn your description into a large greeting card that includes an illustration.

The Scoring Rubric is based on the criteria in this workshop. It reflects the criteria students used to evaluate their own work in Evaluating Your Description on **Practice Book** page 76. A six-point rubric can be found in the **Teacher's Assessment Handbook.**

Portfolio Opportunity

Save students' final copies of their descriptions as examples of the development of their writing skills.

Student Self-Assessment

- What is the most effective part of your description?

- How clear of a picture did your description make in your readers' mind?

- How well did you use sensory language in your description? What was your best use of sensory language?

- How well did you handle details in your description? Was your method of ordering details effective? Explain.

- What did you learn about writing from this description? How can you use what you learned in the next thing you write?

Scoring Rubric

4

The description meets all the evaluation criteria. The description paints an accurate and interesting picture of its topic. Descriptive and sensory language in the work is fresh, imaginative, and accurate. Details are ordered in a way that enhances the impact of the description. There are almost no usage, mechanics, or spelling errors.

3

The description is adequate but lacks cohesion and other elements that would have made it stronger. The writer orders details well in some instances but not all. The writer shows proficiency in handling descriptive and sensory language only in some cases. There are places in which complete sentences are not used. There are still some usage, mechanics, and spelling errors.

2

The work meets the standards only minimally. Details in the description are ordered in a confusing way. The work lacks sensory language. The description contains many sentence fragments. There are many usage, mechanics, and spelling errors.

1

The work does not meet the standards for a description. There are few sentences. The paper has little or no sense of organization and few details. Many mistakes interfere with comprehension.

Using Leveled Books

Paperbacks for *Voyagers*

Leveled **Theme Paperbacks** provide varying levels of reading difficulty—Easy, On Level, and Challenge—to meet all students' needs.

Options for Reading

Students may

- begin reading the Theme Paperbacks at the start of the theme, after the class has read the first Anthology selection, or at any point in the theme;

- read the books at their levels independently or with appropriate teacher support;

- finish an Easy or On Level book before the completion of the theme and move on to the next difficulty level;

- move to an easier book if appropriate, based on your observation. If a student is struggling with the Easy book, have that student read the Very Easy Reader's Library book for this theme.

Theme Paperbacks

Easy   **On Level**   **Challenge**

See **Cumulative Listing of Leveled Books.**

Reader's Library Very Easy

Reader's Library books offer stories related by skill and topic to the Anthology stories at a difficulty level approximately two grades below grade level.

Reader's Library

Houghton Mifflin Classroom Bookshelf

The **Houghton Mifflin Classroom Bookshelf** provides theme-related books for independent reading.

Houghton Mifflin Classroom Bookshelf

The Josefina Story Quilt
by Eleanor Coerr

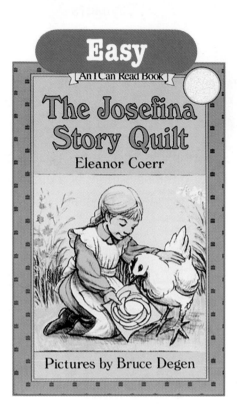

Easy

An I Can Read Book

The Josefina Story Quilt

Eleanor Coerr

Pictures by Bruce Degen

Selection Summary

Set in the 1850s, this historical fiction book tells the story of Faith and her pet hen, Josefina, as they travel with Faith's family to California by wagon train. Only because of Faith's pleading has Josefina, an old and useless hen, been allowed to come along. But she proves valuable during the long, hard journey. And she gives Faith memories that will endure through her story quilt.

Key Vocabulary

calico, p. 27: brightly patterned cotton cloth

bellowed, p. 33: gave a loud roar

pesky, p. 33: troublesome; annoying

stampede, p. 34: a sudden rush of startled animals

current, p. 41: a mass of liquid in motion

▶ Preparing to Read

Building Background Briefly discuss the historical setting with students. Begin by reading the author's note on pages 63–64. Ask students about different ways people keep memories alive for future generations. Explain that quilts, with their patchwork squares, began as a way to tell and preserve stories. Remind students to use their strategies as they read *The Josefina Story Quilt.*

Developing Key Vocabulary Before students read the book or book part, preview with them the Key Vocabulary words. Have volunteers read and define the words. Ask students how these words might be used in a book about settling the West.

▶ Guided Preview

Read *The Josefina Story Quilt* in its entirety or in two segments, pages 5–36 and pages 37–62. Have students preview the book by reading the chapter titles and looking at the illustrations. Then have students view the cover. What is the square that Faith is holding? Have students predict what will happen to Josefina. Will she be allowed to go on the trip?

▶ Guiding the Reading

pages 5–36

■ Why won't Pa let Faith bring Josefina? (There isn't much room, and Josefina is old and useless.)

■ Does Pa have good reasons for telling Faith that her hen can't go West? Explain why or why not. (Answers will vary. Some students may think Pa doesn't realize that just being a pet is an important use for an animal.)

■ Based on what you've read about Faith so far, what inferences can you make about her character? (She is loyal and very persistent. She is also smart to realize the stampede was the dog's fault, and brave for saying so.)

■ What does the author mean when she says, "They understood one another as true friends do"? (Answers will vary.)

pages 37–62

■ Ask volunteers to share how they used reading strategies to figure out the meaning of *humdinger* on page 54. (Since Josefina has just saved the family from robbers, Pa must think she is a great "watchdog." So *humdinger* must mean "very good" or "fantastic.")

■ After Josefina dies, what finally makes Faith begin to feel better? (She decides to make a pine tree patch for her quilt so she can remember her hen.)

■ Do you think Faith will continue to make quilts in the future? Why or why not? (Answers will vary. Some students may think Faith will make many quilts because her experience has shown her how important they are.)

■ Why does the author end the story by saying, "And every night Faith felt warm and happy under the Josefina story quilt"? (The quilt keeps Faith physically warm, while the memories the quilt bring about give her emotional warmth.)

▶ Responding

Have students summarize the main events in *The Josefina Story Quilt*. Ask them to share their latest predictions and discuss which were accurate. Then have them make a paper quilt by first brainstorming class memories or stories, and then representing each in a pattern drawn in a large square. Help students cut out the squares and tape them together to make a class story quilt.

MEETING INDIVIDUAL NEEDS

English Language Learners

Some students may not know that the buffalo (page 48) was crucial to American Indians' survival in many ways, providing meat for food, hide for clothes and tents, and bone for tools and weapons.

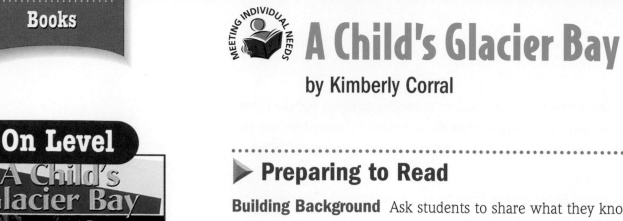

A Child's Glacier Bay

by Kimberly Corral

On Level

Selection Summary

This nonfiction narrative presents the wild habitat of Alaska's Glacier Bay through the eyes of young Hannah Corral. During a three-week family trip along the coastline, Hannah learns to take on the challenges of the wilderness and appreciate its beauty.

Key Vocabulary

kayaks, p. 12: Eskimo canoes made of skins stretched over wooden frames

molting, p. 13: shedding outer skin, feathers, or hair, and replacing with new growth

flukes, p. 13: flaps of a whale's tail

endangered, p. 14: faced with extinction

swells, p. 17: long, rolling waves

wake, p. 25: the track or path of waves, ripples, or foam left by a moving boat

dramatically, p. 31: with a striking or forceful effect

▶ Preparing to Read

Building Background Ask students to share what they know about Alaska, inviting volunteers to indicate this state on a map. Explain that *A Child's Glacier Bay* tells the real story of one family's trip through the Alaskan wilderness. Note that a *glacier* is a huge mass of ice and the more familiar *iceberg* is a piece that has broken off a glacier. Tell students that this book is a narrative told through the eyes of Hannah, a young girl, but that it also contains many facts about the environment. Ask what reading strategies might be helpful for this type of book. Remind students to use these strategies as they read *A Child's Glacier Bay*.

Developing Key Vocabulary Before students read the book or book part, preview with them the Key Vocabulary words. Have volunteers read and define the words. Ask students which words might help describe certain animals. Which might describe an ocean or bay?

▶ Guided Preview

Read *A Child's Glacier Bay* in its entirety or in two segments, pages 9–21 and pages 22–36. Have students preview the book by looking at the cover and inside photographs. Point out the map on page 7, indicating Bartlett Cove, where the Corrals begin and end their trip. Then have students predict what the family might encounter during their journey. What animals will they see? What dangers will they face?

▶ Guiding the Reading

pages 9–21

- Is the kayak trip up the West Arm too dangerous for small children? Explain. (Answers will vary. Some students may think that the children are safe because they're with their parents, who seem to be experienced kayakers.)

- Use what you've learned so far about Hannah's dad to make inferences about what he's like. (Since he's already been to Glacier Bay, he must love the wilderness. He seems to know a lot about the animals. And he's a good photographer.)

- Have students share and evaluate the predictions they made before reading. Then have them make new predictions about what the family will encounter in the next section. Will they complete their trip safely?

pages 22–36

- What challenge does Hannah face while crossing the West Arm? (She has to help land her kayak in big crashing waves.)

- Why have Ben and his dad fallen behind? (Ben is only six and can't paddle very fast.)

- Help students pronounce *lichens* (LI-kens) on page 28 and explain that these plants are made up of fungus and algae growing together. Lichens look like scaly growths on rocks or tree trunks.

- Will Hannah go on future wilderness trips? Explain. (Answers will vary. Most students may think that Hannah will go on future trips because she enjoyed her experience at Glacier Bay.)

- What does the author mean when she writes, "It's clear to me that wilderness is the real treasure at Glacier Bay"? (Since so many places have become overcrowded, a place that is still in its natural state is very valuable.)

▶ Responding

Ask students to share their use of strategies while reading *A Child's Glacier Bay*. Ask for examples of how they used the Monitor/Clarify strategy to help them follow the narrative and understand the information presented during the story. Then have them share and evaluate their latest predictions. Finally, have students share their reactions to *A Child's Glacier Bay*.

English Language Learners

Some students may not understand why Hannah believes seeing a bald eagle on July 4 before a treacherous journey might be a good sign (pages 24–25). Explain that the bald eagle is the national symbol of the United States and that July 4 is our Independence Day.

Balto and the Great Race

by Elizabeth Cody Kimmel

Challenge

▶ Preparing to Read

Building Background Ask students to share what they know about mushers or sled dogs. Tell them that the book they are about to read tells the true story of a famous sled dog and the race that made him so well known. Explain that the race is not a competition but a race against time to save lives. Be sure students are aware of the harsh weather conditions and isolation experienced by people living in Alaska. Ask what reading strategies might be helpful to use with this type of book. Remind students to use these strategies as they read *Balto and the Great Race.*

Developing Key Vocabulary Before students read the book or book part, preview with them the Key Vocabulary words. Have volunteers read and define the words. Ask students how the words might relate to a sled dog race.

▶ Guided Preview

Balto and the Great Race may be read in its entirety or in three segments, pages 1–26, pages 27–62, and pages 63–97. Have students preview the book by looking at the cover, the chapter titles, and the illustrations. Point out the map of Alaska at the front of the book, indicating Nome, Bluff, and Nenana. Then have students predict what dangers a musher and a team of sled dogs might encounter during their journey.

▶ Guiding the Reading

pages 1–26

■ What does the author mean when she says that a musher "could look at a dog and know in an instant if he was a natural for a team"? (The author means that an experienced musher can easily recognize the qualities that make a good sled dog.)

■ Why are the workers for the Northern Commercial mail system so willing to try to get the serum to Nome? (They want to try to help save lives. They understand that people who live in such an unforgiving climate have to help each other as much as possible.)

■ Have students share and evaluate the predictions they made before reading. Then have them make new predictions about what Balto's role will be in delivering the serum.

pages 27–62

- Why are mushers concerned about the effect of ice on the dogs' feet? (The bitter cold can make the ice crystals as sharp as glass; the ice can cut the dogs' feet, and the cuts can become infected.)

- Point out the word *anchor* on page 52 and explain that it refers to the way the musher positions himself on the sled. Discuss the other meaning of *anchor:* a weight used to hold a ship in place.

- Why does the author write that Balto "remembered what they had left behind in [Nome] and why they needed to return"? (The author wants to show that Balto seems to understand the importance of the journey they are about to begin.)

pages 63–97

- How does Kassen's team become lost? (The lead dog can't tell where the trail is because of the high winds and blowing snow of the blizzard.)

- How is Balto able to follow the trail? (He relies on his sense of smell and his memory of the feel of the land.)

- What information is given in the afterword on pages 96–97? Why is this information in a separate section? (The section explains that the Iditarod is run in memory of the efforts that brought the serum to Nome. This separate section gives information that is not central to Balto's story.)

▶ **Responding**

Ask students to share their use of strategies while reading *Balto and the Great Race.* Have them give examples of how they used the Predict/Infer strategy to help them understand story events. Then have them share and evaluate their latest predictions. Finally, ask students to define the characteristics of a hero and explain whether Balto fits that definition.

 English Language Learners

Be sure students understand that the sentence "Seppala had not made the decision to cross the sound lightly" on page 47 means that Seppala had thought carefully about his decision. Point out the multiple-meaning words *sound* and *light* in the sentence and discuss the meanings with which students are familiar.

Yunmi and Halmoni's Trip
Different texts for different purposes

Anthology: Main Selection

Purposes

- strategy focus: predict/infer
- comprehension skill: predicting outcomes
- vocabulary development
- critical thinking, discussion

Genre: Realistic Fiction

Realistic characters and events come to life in a fictional plot.

Selection Summary

During their trip to Korea, Yunmi sees how happy Halmoni is to see her relatives. She worries that Halmoni will not want to return to New York. When Halmoni reassures her, Yunmi learns how lucky she is to belong to two families.

Teacher's Edition: Read Aloud

Purposes
- listening comprehension: predicting outcomes
- vocabulary development
- critical thinking, discussion

Anthology: Get Set to Read

Purposes
- background building: traveling
- developing key vocabulary

Anthology: Content Link

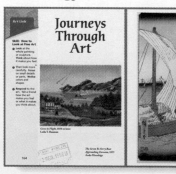

Purposes
- content reading: art
- skill: how to look at fine art
- critical thinking, discussion

Leveled Books and Resources

See Cumulative Listing of Leveled Books.

Reader's Library

Very Easy

Brothers Are Forever
by Marcy Haber

(Also available on blackline masters)

Purposes

- fluency practice in below-level text
- alternate reading for students reading significantly below grade level
- strategy application: predict/infer
- comprehension skill application: predicting outcomes
- below-level independent reading

Lesson Support

- Guided Reading lesson, page R4
- Alternate application for Comprehension Skill lesson on predicting outcomes, page 167A
- Reteaching for Comprehension Skill: predicting outcomes, page R10

Selection Summary Masters

Yunmi and Halmoni's Trip
Teacher's Resource Blackline Masters

Audiotape

Yunmi and Halmoni's Trip
Audiotape for *Voyagers*

 Inclusion Strategy

Significantly Below-level Readers

Students reading so far below level that they cannot read *Yunmi and Halmoni's Trip* even with the suggested Extra Support should still participate with the class whenever possible.

- Include them in the Teacher Read Aloud (p. 139S) and Preparing to Read (pp. 140A–141C).
- Have them listen to *Yunmi and Halmoni's Trip* on the audiotape for *Voyagers* and read the Selection Summary while others read Segment 1 of the selection.
- Have them read "Brothers Are Forever" in the Reader's Library collection for *Voyagers* while others read Segment 2 of *Yunmi and Halmoni's Trip*.
- Have all students participate in Wrapping Up Segment 2 (p. 161) and Responding (p. 162).

Theme Paperbacks

Easy

The Josefina Story Quilt
by Eleanor Coerr

Lesson, TE page 139I

On Level

A Child's Glacier Bay
by Kimberly Corral

Lesson, TE page 139K

Challenge

Balto and the Great Race
by Elizabeth Cody Kimmel

Lesson, TE page 139M

Technology

Get Set for Reading CD-ROM
Yunmi and Halmoni's Trip

Provides background building, vocabulary support, and selection summaries in English and Spanish.

Education Place
www.eduplace.com
Log on to Education Place for more activities relating to *Yunmi and Halmoni's Trip.*

Book Adventure
www.bookadventure.org
This Internet reading incentive program provides thousands of titles for students.

Suggested Daily Routines

Instructional Goals	Day 1	Day 2
Reading ☑ *Strategy Focus:* Predict/Infer ☑ *Comprehension Skill:* Predicting Outcomes *Comprehension Skill Review:* Making Generalizations; Cause and Effect *Information and Study Skills:* Using Graphic Organizers	**Teacher Read Aloud** Pedro's Journal, *139S* **Preparing to Read *Yunmi and Halmoni's Trip*** • Get Set: Background and Vocabulary, *140A* • Key Vocabulary, *141A* Selection Vocabulary, ***Practice Book, 81*** • Strategy/Skill Preview, *141B* Character Chart, ***Practice Book, 82*** **Reading Segment 1** *Yunmi and Halmoni's Trip, 142–153* • Supporting Comprehension • Strategy Focus, *152* **Wrapping Up Segment 1,** *153*	**Reading Segment 2** *Yunmi and Halmoni's Trip, 154–161* • Supporting Comprehension • Strategy Focus, *156* **Wrapping Up Segment 2,** *161* **Responding** • Comprehension Questions: Think About the Selection, *162* • Comprehension Check, ***Practice Book, 83*** **Revisiting the Text** • Comprehension: Predicting Outcomes, *157*
Word Work ☑ *Spelling:* The Vowel Sound in *bought* *Decoding Longer Words:* ☑ *Structural Analysis:* Possessives *Phonics:* The Vowel Sound in *bought* ☑ *Vocabulary:* Analogies	**Spelling** • Pretest, *167G* • Instruction: The Vowel Sounds in *bought*, *167G* • Take-Home Word List, ***Practice Book: Handbook***	**Decoding Longer Words Instruction** • Structural Analysis: Possessives, *167E* • *Practice Book, 86* **Spelling** • *Practice Book, 87*
Writing & Language ☑ *Grammar:* Object Pronouns ☑ *Writing:* Writing a Message; Writing Complete Information *Listening/Speaking/Viewing:* Develop Nonverbal Communication Skills	**Daily Language Practice,** *167L* **Grammar Instruction** • Object Pronouns, *167K* **Writing** • Journal Writing, *143*	**Daily Language Practice,** *167L* **Grammar Instruction** • Object Pronouns, *Practice Book, 91* **Writing Instruction** • Writing a Message, *167M* • Journal Writing, *154*

 = tested skills

 Leveled Books

See Cumulative Listing of Leveled Books.

Reader's Library
• **Very Easy** *Brothers Are Forever,* Lesson, *R4*
Book Links: Anthology, *106*
Bibliography: Teacher's Edition, *102C*

Houghton Mifflin Classroom Bookshelf, Level 3

Theme Paperbacks, Lessons, *139H–139N*
• **Easy** *The Josefina Story Quilt*
• **On Level** *A Child's Glacier Bay*
• **Challenge** *Balto and the Great Race*

Allow time every day for students to read independently from self-selected books.

Lesson Planner CD-ROM:
Customize your planning for *Yunmi and Halmoni's Trip* with the Lesson Planner.

Day 3

Revisiting the Text
• Visual Literacy: Picturing the Scene, *155*

Comprehension Skill Instruction
• Predicting Outcomes, *167A*
• *Practice Book, 84*

Phonics Instruction
• The Vowel Sound in *bought, 167F*

Spelling
• *Practice Book, 88*

Daily Language Practice, *167L*

Grammar Instruction
• The Object Comes After, *167K*

Writing
• Responding: Write a Personal Narrative, *162*

Day 4

Comprehension Skill Instruction
• Reteaching Predicting Outcomes with Reader's Library, *R10*
• Independent Application, *Practice Book, 85*

Reading the Art Link
• "Journeys Through Art," *164–167*
• Visual Literacy: Cubism, *166*

Information and Study Skills Instruction
• Using Graphic Organizers, *167C*

Decoding Longer Words
• Reteaching Structural Analysis: Possessives, *R16*
• Challenge/Extension Activities, *R17*

Spelling
• *Practice Book, 89*

Vocabulary Skill Instruction
• Analogies, *167I*
• *Practice Book, 90*

Daily Language Practice, *167L*

Grammar
• Reteaching, *R21*
• The Object Comes After, *Practice Book, 92*

Writing
• Writing Complete Information, *167N*

Listening/Speaking/Viewing
• Develop Nonverbal Communication Skills, *167O*

Day 5

Revisiting the Text: Comprehension Review Skill Instruction
• Making Generalizations, *151*
• Cause and Effect, *159*

Rereading for Fluency
Yunmi and Halmoni's Trip, 141–161

Activity Choices
• Responding Activities, *163*
• Challenge/Extension Activities, *R11*
• Cross-Curricular Activities, *R26*

Vocabulary Expansion
• Family Words, *167J*

Spelling
• Posttest, *167H*

Daily Language Practice, *167L*

Grammar
• Using the Correct Verb Form, *167L*
• *Practice Book, 93*

Writing
• Using the Correct Verb Form, *167L*
• Writing Activities, *R23*
• Sharing Students' Writing: Author's Chair

Reading-Writing Workshop: Description

Based on the **Student Writing Model** in the Anthology, this workshop guides students through the writing process and includes skill lessons on—

• Ordering Information
• Using Sensory Language
• Writing Complete Sentences

See Teacher's Edition, *pages 138–139G.*

Allow time every day for students to write independently on self-selected topics.

Teacher Read Aloud

Listening Comprehension:
✓ Predicting Outcomes

Pedro's Journal
A Voyage with Christopher Columbus
August 3, 1492–February 14, 1493

by Pam Conrad

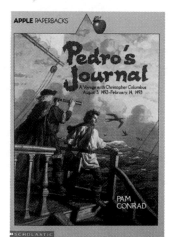

This fiction excerpt presents a boy's version, in diary form, of Columbus's voyage.

How would it have felt to have been aboard the *Santa María* when Christopher Columbus set sail to find the New World? In this excerpt from *Pedro's Journal,* a boy keeps a written account of his adventures on the long voyage.

October 10

This has been the worst day of all for the Captain. I am certain of this. We have doubled all previous records of days and leagues at sea, and we've gone way past the point where he originally said we would find land. There is nothing out here. Surely we are lost. And everyone is certain now as well.

This morning the men <u>responded</u> slowly to orders, scowling and slamming down their tools and lines. They whispered in pairs and small groups on deck and below. The air was thick with <u>mutiny</u> and <u>betrayal</u>, until finally everything came to a dead stop. The wind howled through the <u>shrouds</u>, and the men just stood there on deck and did not move aside when Columbus came.

Reading Instruction

DAY 1	• Teacher Read Aloud • Preparing to Read • Reading the Selection, Segment 1
DAY 2	• Reading the Selection, Segment 2 • Responding
DAY 3	• Revisiting the Text • Comprehension Skill Instruction
DAY 4	• Comprehension Skill Reteaching • Reading the Content Link • Information and Study Skills Instruction
DAY 5	• Comprehension Skill Review • Activity Choices

OBJECTIVES

Students listen to the selection and use story details and personal knowledge to predict what might happen to the characters.

▶ Activate Prior Knowledge

Connecting to the Theme Tell students that you are going to read aloud an excerpt from a story, written in diary form, about what one boy might have experienced during a voyage with Christopher Columbus. Help students connect the selection with what they know, using these suggestions:

■ Discuss with students what they know about Columbus and his voyage from Spain.

■ Ask students what they think life on board Columbus's ship would have been like for a boy. What would his duties have been? What would be exciting about the voyage? What might have been dangerous?

1 "Enough," one of the men said to his face. "This is enough. Now we turn back."

The other men grumbled their <u>assent</u> and nodded, their fists <u>clenched</u>, their chests broad. And they remained motionless and unmoved while Columbus paced the deck, telling them how close he figured we must be, that land could be right over the next horizon. He told them again of the fame and fortune that would be theirs if they could only last a little longer. And they laughed at him, the cruel laughter of <u>impatient</u> and <u>defeated</u> men.

2 "All that aside," he added, "with the fresh easterly wind coming at us and the rising sea, we can't turn a course back to Spain right now. We would stand still in the water."

I looked up at the sails, full and straining, taking us farther and farther from Spain. What if a westerly wind never came? What if we were just blown away forever and ever?

"Let me offer you this," Columbus finally said. "Do me this favor. Stay with me this day and night, and if I don't bring you to land before day, cut off my head, and you shall return."

The men glanced at each other. Some nodded. "One day," they said. "One day, and then we turn around."

"That is all I ask," Columbus said.

Later, when I went down to the cabin with the log, the Captain's door was <u>bolted</u> shut, and when I knocked he didn't answer, so I sat outside the door with the heavy journal in my lap and waited.

1 Why are the men angry? How will Columbus react? (The men have been at sea for months with no sign of land. They are tired and feel that Columbus has lied to them. Columbus will try to convince them to continue westward.)

2 Will Columbus convince the men to continue sailing westward? How? (We know the ship eventually reaches land because Columbus did discover the New World. He gives the men reasons why they can't turn around, but the men are too angry to believe him. Maybe Columbus will offer them higher pay or other rewards to keep going.)

....

Listening Comprehension: ✓ Predicting Outcomes

Remind students that a prediction tells what may happen in the future. It may be about something a character will do or think in the future, a future event, or what will happen following a particular situation in a selection. Explain that a good prediction is based on text clues and on students' own knowledge. Tell students to use details from this selection and their own experiences to make predictions about characters' actions and the events in the selection.

As you read aloud, use the questions in the margin to help determine whether students are making reasonable predictions from the text and their own experiences. Assess students' understanding and decide whether it is necessary to reread any part of the selection for clarification.

Vocabulary *(pages 139S–139T)*
responded: did what was asked; obeyed
mutiny: decision to stop obeying a leader's orders
betrayal: turning against someone; disloyalty
shrouds: ropes that support the mast of a ship
assent: agreement; approval
clenched: closed tightly together
impatient: tired of waiting; unable to stay calm anymore
defeated: frustrated; feeling unable to succeed
bolted: locked

October 11

Through the day, the day that was to have been our last day traveling westward, many things were seen floating in the water, things that stirred everyone's hopes and had the men once again <u>scanning</u> the horizon. We saw birds in flocks, reeds and plants floating in the water, and a small floating board, and even a stick was <u>recovered</u> that had iron workings on it, obviously man-made. Suddenly no one wished to turn around. There was no further word on it.

At sunset, I led the prayers and the men sang the *Salve Regina.* Then the Captain spoke to the seamen from the sterncastle, doubling the night watch and <u>urging</u> everyone to keep a sharp lookout. No one asked about turning back. Then the Captain added a new bonus to his reward of ten thousand maravedis. He added a silk doublet, and some of the men joked with each other. Next the Captain nodded to me, and I sang for the changing of the watch, but my words were lost in the wind that was growing brisker and in the seas that were growing heavier and sounding like breakers all about us. The men <u>dispersed</u> to their watches and their bunks, and the Captain paced the deck. I don't know why, but this night I stayed with him. I stayed still by the gunwale, watching over the side. Once in a while he would stand beside me, silent, looking westward, always westward.

Then, an hour before moonrise, the Captain froze beside me. "Gutierrez!" he called to one of the king's men on board, who came running. He pointed out across the water. "What do you see?"

3 What will happen on this night that Pedro stays on deck with the Captain? Why? (They will probably sight land; there have been many signs of land all day, and Pedro seems excited, as if he expects something to happen.)

3

Teacher's Note

Tip for Read Alouds Before reading aloud, review the story. Look for dialogue and other sections to emphasize. Be sure to read aloud the dates in the title and in the excerpt so that students understand that this selection covers only two days' time, during a voyage that takes many months.

Vocabulary (pages 139U–139V)

scanning: looking at closely

recovered: found

urging: asking strongly; trying to convince

dispersed: went in different directions

tierra (TYEH-ra): Spanish for "land"

plunging: entering suddenly and forcefully

assure: tell someone that something will definitely happen

Gutierrez peered into the west. "I don't see anything," he said. "What? What? What do you see?"

"Can't you see it?" the Captain whispered. "The light? Like a little wax candle rising and falling?"

The man at his side was quiet. I was there beside him, too, straining my own eyes to the dark horizon.

Suddenly another seaman called out across the darkness, "Land! Land!"

"He's already seen it!" I shouted. "My master's already seen it!" And the Captain laughed and tousled my hair.

"*Tierra! Tierra!*" It was heard all across the water from all three ships.

4 I am below now in the Captain's cabin writing, while in the light of the rising moon, with our sails silver in the moonlight, we three exploring ships are rolling and <u>plunging</u> through the swells towards land. Tomorrow our feet will touch soil, and I can <u>assure</u> my dear mother in the hills of Spain that no one will get much sleep on board the *Santa María* tonight!

4 What might happen once the ship reaches land? (Columbus and the crew will go ashore and explore; they may meet other people; the crew might refuse to obey Columbus on land if things become difficult for them again.)

▶ **Discussion**

Summarize After reading, discuss what students found most exciting about Pedro's account of his voyage. Then have them summarize the selection.

Listening Comprehension:
✓ **Predicting Outcomes** Remind students that good predictions are based on selection details, personal knowledge, and their own thinking about characters and events. Then have small groups of students predict how Pedro might react if the men were to threaten mutiny against Columbus again. Would he disagree with the men and remain loyal to Columbus or not? Ask them to support their predictions with details from the story, including how they think Pedro feels about the Captain, and with their own experiences with friends and family. Have each group present their ideas briefly to the other groups.

Personal Response Ask students to describe how they felt as they listened to this selection. Was it exciting or surprising? What pictures did they see in their minds as they listened? Have students describe their favorite part of the selection to a partner or write a paragraph about it.

⭐ **Connecting/Comparing** In both *Across the Wide Dark Sea* and this excerpt from *Pedro's Journal*, the authors have written from the point of view of a young boy. Ask students to evaluate how real each boy and his experiences seem to them. Have them list details that each author uses to make each selection believable.

Anthology

Yunmi and Halmoni's Trip

Sook Nyul Choi *Illustrated by* Karen Dugan

Technology

Get Set for Reading CD-ROM

Yunmi and Halmoni's Trip

Provides background building, vocabulary support, and selection summaries in English and Spanish.

Preparing to Read

▶ Using *Get Set* for Background and Vocabulary

Connecting to the Theme Remind students that this theme is about the adventures travelers have on their journeys. This story, called *Yunmi and Halmoni's Trip*, is a modern-day story about a young girl's visit to Korea. Discuss with students how traveling to another country can be an adventure. Allow volunteers to share their experiences. Then use the Get Set to Read on pages 140–141 to discuss what travelers can learn from a new country and culture.

■ Have someone read aloud "Visiting Another Country." Talk about the photos, and ask a student to read aloud the captions.

■ Point out the passport on page 141, and explain that the story characters must get their passports stamped. Also help students locate Seoul, Korea, on a globe.

■ Ask students to explain the meaning of the Key Vocabulary words in color: *bustling, skyscrapers, sightseeing, customs, foreigner, passport,* and *vendor.*

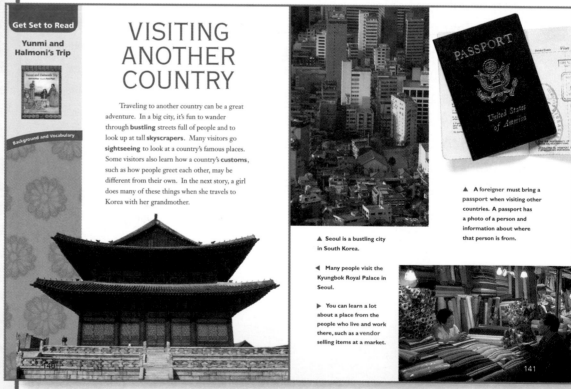

Get Set to Read

Yunmi and Halmoni's Trip

Background and Vocabulary

VISITING ANOTHER COUNTRY

Traveling to another country can be a great adventure. In a big city, it's fun to wander through **bustling** streets full of people and to look up at tall **skyscrapers**. Many visitors go **sightseeing** to look at a country's famous places. Some visitors also learn how a country's **customs**, such as how people greet each other, may be different from their own. In the next story, a girl does many of these things when she travels to Korea with her grandmother.

▲ Seoul is a bustling city in South Korea.

◀ Many people visit the Kyungbok Royal Palace in Seoul.

▶ You can learn a lot about a place from the people who live and work there, such as a **vendor** selling items at a market.

▲ A **foreigner** must bring a passport when visiting other countries. A passport has a photo of a person and information about where that person is from.

English Language Learners

Locate Korea on a map or globe, and ask students who have been to Korea or are from there to share information about the country. Introduce *ushered, allowed, giggled, disappear, overseeing, dipped, pinky, sped, celebrate,* and *selfish.*

▶ Developing Key Vocabulary

Use **Transparency 5–9** to introduce and reinforce Key Vocabulary words that appear in *Yunmi and Halmoni's Trip*.

■ Have a student read the paragraph at the top of the transparency aloud. Then have someone read the first question out loud.

■ Model how to answer the question with an underlined Key Vocabulary word from the paragraph. Also explain how you figured out which word to choose.

■ For each remaining question, ask students to identify the Key Vocabulary word that answers it. Have students explain how they figured out which word to use.

Remind students that it's helpful to use the Phonics/Decoding strategy when they read. For students who need more help with decoding, use the review below.

Practice/Homework Practice Book page 81.

Strategy Review
Phonics/Decoding

Modeling Write the following sentence about *Yunmi and Halmoni's Trip* on the board, and point to the word *embraced*.

> Everyone <u>embraced</u> Halmoni and then hugged Yunmi too.

Think Aloud

First I'll look for word parts I know. I think the first syllable might sound like / ehm /. Then I see a b followed by what looks like the word raced. That syllable should sound like / brayst /. I'll try saying the word, / ehm•BRAYST /. Oh sure, I know that word. It's another word for "hugged."

● Decoding Longer Words, p. 167E–167F

Key Concept
visiting a foreign country

Key Vocabulary

bustling: full of activity; busy

custom: a tradition; a way of doing something that many people follow

foreigners: people who come from a different country or place

passport: a government document that allows a person to travel in foreign countries

sightseeing: visiting interesting places; touring

skyscrapers: very tall buildings

vendor: someone who sells something

See Vocabulary notes on pages 144, 146, 148, 150, 152, 154, and 158 for additional words to preview.

Practice Book page 81

Name _____

Trave

Match e
the lette
the word
the list t

e (1) bu
c (1) cu
a (1) fo
d (1) pa
f (1) si
b (1) ve

1. Durin visit
2. Each in or
3. In N with
4. Man
5. On s vend
6. In A shak

Transparency 5–9

Sightseeing Words

Every <u>foreign</u> visitor has a <u>passport</u> to show the country he or she is from. And every day tour guides must show many of them around the city. Some guides take visitors <u>sightseeing</u> by foot; others show them the city from buses. They take visitors through the <u>bustling</u> city streets full of hurrying people and up to the top of great, tall <u>skyscrapers</u> for a wonderful view. Some guides will stop at an outside cart where a <u>vendor</u> sells food, drinks, or even postcards. A usual <u>custom</u> is to give each tour guide a tip at the end of the tour.

Which word —

• tells about tall city buildings?	1.
• names a government document?	2.
• names a person who sells things?	3.
• describes a busy place?	4.
• names people from other countries?	5.
• is a way of doing something that many people follow?	6.
• tells about touring a new city?	7.

Reading

Strategy/Skill Preview

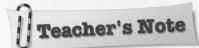

Teacher's Note

Strategy/Skill Connection For a better understanding of *Yunmi and Halmoni's Trip,* students can use the

- Predict/Infer Strategy

- Predicting Outcomes Comprehension Skill

Anticipating how story characters will act and think will help students better understand them, so that students can better predict the characters' reactions to events beyond the story plot.

As students fill in their Character Chart (**Transparency 5–10** and **Practice Book** page 82), they will gain a better understanding of the story characters, which will help them in later skill instruction.

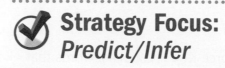

✓ Strategy Focus:
Predict/Infer

> ### Strategy Focus
>
> Use your experiences of meeting new people to **predict** what might happen when a girl visits relatives she has never met before.

Have students turn to page 143. Read aloud the title and author of the selection (*YOON•mee; HAHL•mah•nee*). Then ask someone to read the Strategy Focus. Give students a chance to read the first paragraph on page 145 and to think about the Strategy Focus instructions. Then ask them to predict what will happen in the story; record their responses.

Teacher Modeling Review how to make a good prediction or inference. (Think of a reasonable possibility based on text clues, illustrations, and personal information.) Then model the strategy.

Think Aloud

From the title and illustration, I can predict that the two characters take a trip somewhere. From the first paragraph I learn they go to Korea. Yunmi doesn't live in Korea, so she may not know many Korean words or customs, but she's flying there with her grandmother to visit relatives. I know from personal experience that it's hard to visit with relatives, especially if they speak a different language. I think Yunmi will find her visit to be a challenge.

Ask students to work in pairs or individually to make other predictions and inferences about the characters and to record these in their journals. Remind students to use Predict/Infer and their other reading strategies as they read the story.

✓ Comprehension Skill Focus:
Predicting Outcomes

Character Chart Explain that as students read, they will be listing details about Yunmi, a character in *Yunmi and Halmoni's Trip*. This information will be used for later skill instruction, when students focus on predicting what she might do in new situations. Display **Transparency 5–10**, and demonstrate how to use this graphic organizer.

■ Begin by explaining that readers learn a lot about characters from the way they talk, act, and think. Then ask someone to read page 145 aloud.

■ Ask what students have learned about Yunmi so far. How does she feel about her trip to Korea? (excited, happy, but a bit anxious) Point out those words in the first column in the box labeled *About Her Visit to Korea.*

■ Next, ask what story clues give this information. (The words *Yunmi was very excited;* she held her grandmother's hand.) List those details in the first box of the column labeled *Story Clues.*

■ Have students write the same information in the appropriate places on **Practice Book** page 82.

■ As they read, have students add more information about Yunmi's feelings and the story clues that reveal them. Monitor their work, or have students check one another's charts.

■ Have students wait to answer the last question until later skill instruction.

Graphic Organizer: Character Chart (Accept varied responses.)

Yunmi's Feelings	Story Clues
About Her Visit to Korea excited anxious	*(See page 145.)* from words in the story She held Halmoni's hand.
About Her Korean Cousins fun to be around hard to talk to and understand sometimes jealous	*(See pages 150–153 and 158–160.)* They take her sightseeing. They show her how to make mandoo. Their English is hard to understand and they giggle when she speaks Korean. Halmoni pays so much attension to her cousins.

Transparency 5–10

Character Chart

Yunmi's Feelings	Story Clues
About Her Visit to Korea excited anxious	*(See page 145.)*
About Her Korean Cousins	*(See pages 150–153 and 158–160.)* They take her sightseeing.
jealous	
About Halmoni	*(See pages 152–153 and 157–159.)*
ashamed about being selfish	

What do you think Yunmi will do if her cousins come to visit her in New York? Explain why you think as you do.

VOYAGERS Yunmi and Halmoni's Trip
Graphic Organizer Character Chart

TRANSPARENCY 5–10
TEACHER'S EDITION PAGES 141C AND 1167A

Practice Book page 82

Yunmi and Halmoni's Trip
Graphic Organizer
Character Chart

Name _____

Character Chart

Accept varied responses.

Yunmi's Feelings	Story Clues
About Her Visit to Korea excited anxious	*(See page 145.)* from words in the story **(1)** She held Halmoni's hand. **(1)**
About Her Korean Cousins fun to be around **(1 point)** hard to talk to and understand sometimes **(1)** jealous	*(See pages 150–153 and 158–160.)* They take her sightseeing. They show her how to make mandoo. **(1)** Their English is hard to understand and they giggle when she speaks Korean. **(1)** Halmoni pays so much attention to her cousins. **(1)**
About Halmoni misses her attention **(1)** scared, worried, upset **(1)** ashamed about being selfish	*(See pages 152–153 and 157–159.)* Halmoni is busy visiting and overseeing preparations; she gives all her attention to the cousins. **(1)** She sees how happy Halmoni is with her family in Korea. **(1)** from words in the story; she'd be lonely without Halmoni. **(1)**

What do you think Yunmi will do if her cousins come to visit her in New York? Explain why you think as you do.
Accept responses that students can justify. **(2)**

82 Theme 5: **Voyagers**
Assessment Tip: Total **14** Points

Reading

Options for Reading

▶ **Reading in Segments** Students can read *Yunmi and Halmoni's Trip* in two segments (pages 142–153 and 154–161) or in its entirety.

▶ **Deciding About Support** Clear descriptions and vivid illustrations make this story about a visit to relatives in another country both accessible and enjoyable.

- Because of its easy-to-follow plot structure and realistic characters, most students should be able to follow On Level reading instruction.

- Students who might have difficulty with vocabulary or making inferences may benefit from Extra Support.

- Significantly below-level readers may listen to the Audiotape and read the Selection Summary for *Yunmi and Halmoni's Trip*, and then read "Brothers Are Forever" in the **Reader's Library**.

▶ **Meeting Individual Needs** Use the notes at the bottom of the pages.

Meet the Author Sook Nyul Choi

As a child in Korea, Sook Nyul Choi loved to read about faraway places. When she was older, Choi moved to one of those places — the United States — to go to college. She now lives in Massachusetts with her two daughters. She loves both the United States and Korea, and her books often tell how these two countries are both the same and different.

Other books: *Halmoni and the Picnic, The Best Older Sister*

Meet the Illustrator Karen Dugan

Karen Dugan has been making books since she was in first grade. She would fold paper into a book and then draw pictures. She doesn't fold her own pages anymore, but she still draws great pictures. For this book, she based the main character, Yunmi, on the author's daughters.

Other books: *School Spirit* (by Johanna Hurwitz), *Pascual's Magic Pictures* (by Amy Glaser Gage), *Halmoni and the Picnic* (by Sook Nyul Choi)

Internet

To find out more about Sook Nyul Choi and Karen Dugan, visit Education Place.
www.eduplace.com/kids

Beginning of Segment 1: pages 142–153

142

MEETING INDIVIDUAL NEEDS Classroom Management

On Level
Reading Card 5

While Reading: Character Chart (**Practice Book** page 82); Literature Discussion (p. 152, Reading Card 5); generate questions

After Reading: Literature Discussion (page 160); Wrapping Up Segment 1 (page 153) and Segment 2 (page 161)

Challenge
Reading Cards 4–6

While Reading: Character Chart (**Practice Book** p. 82); Synonyms (p. 149, Reading Card 4); Literature Discussion (p. 152, Reading Card 5); Quiet Games (p. 155, Reading Card 6)

After Reading: Literature Discussion (page 160); Wrapping Up Segment 1 (page 153) and Segment 2 (page 161)

English Language Learners

Intermediate and Advanced Fluency Help students predict what will happen throughout the story. Pause before reading each page and ask: What do you think will happen next?

For English language learners at other proficiency levels, see **Language Development Resources.**

Reading Segment 1: pages 142–153

Selection 2

Yunmi and Halmoni's Trip

Sook Nyul Choi Illustrated by Karen Dugan

Strategy Focus

Use your experiences of meeting new people to **predict** what might happen when a girl visits relatives she has never met before.

143

Reading Segment 1

pages 142–153

Purpose Setting Have students recall the predictions they made for the Strategy Focus on Anthology page 143. Remind them to read to confirm or change their predictions as the story unfolds.

 Journal Writing Students can record their original predictions and inferences about the story in their journals and add new ideas as events unfold.

Reinforcing Comprehension and Strategies

■ Remind students to use Predict/Infer and other strategies as they read and to add to their Character Chart (**Practice Book** page 82).

■ Use the Strategy Focus Notes on pages 152 and 156 to reinforce the Predict/Infer strategy.

■ Use Supporting Comprehension questions beginning on Anthology page 144 to help students develop higher-level understanding of the text.

Extra Support: Previewing the Text

Before each segment, preview the text, using the notes below and on page 154. **While** reading, model strategies (pages 147, 148, and 157). **After** reading, review each segment (pages 152 and 160) before students join the Wrapping Up discussion.

pages 144–147 Halmoni, which means "grandmother" in Korean, takes Yunmi to Korea to visit with Halmoni's family. When they get there, they must have their passports checked. Will Yunmi enjoy her trip?

pages 148–151 A large crowd of Halmoni's family greets them at the airport. For the next few days, Yunmi's cousins take her sightseeing in the city of Seoul. Do you think Yunmi is having fun? Why?

pages 152–153 Halmoni is visiting and preparing for a celebration at Grandfather's tomb. Yunmi worries because Halmoni seems so happy to be back in Korea again. Why might that worry Yunmi?

Reading

....

▶ ## Supporting Comprehension

1 Why do you think Yunmi takes Halmoni's hand in the airplane? (She's excited about the trip but is probably anxious about it too.)

2 Why do you think the author includes details about the family's plans for Grandfather's birthday celebration? (to explain a special Korean custom; to give a reason for the trip)

3 How do you think Halmoni feels about the trip? How do you know? (Thrilled to be seeing her Korean family and to be part of the birthday celebration; she has photos of Yunmi's relatives and talks all during their flight.)

Vocabulary *(page 145)*

passport: a government document that allows a person to travel to foreign countries

Seoul: (SOHL) the capital city of South Korea

Cross-Curricular Connection

Social Studies Korea sits on the east coast of Asia, connecting to China and Russia at its northern end. Although strongly influenced by the Chinese who once ruled the country, Koreans have kept a language and customs truly their own. Respect for elders and family loyalty are very important traditions to many Koreans, who consider extended relatives as family members too.

1 Yunmi settled into the airplane seat and took her grandmother's hand. It was Yunmi's first airplane trip. Her Halmoni, or grandmother, had come from Korea to take care of Yunmi while her parents were at work. Now Halmoni was taking Yunmi for a visit to Korea to meet all her aunts and uncles and cousins. Halmoni also wanted Yunmi to join Grandfather's birthday celebration. Yunmi's grandfather had died many **2** years before, but each year the whole family visited his grave and celebrated his birthday.

3 Yunmi was very excited. She had gotten her very first passport for this trip. And she had promised to send lots of postcards to her best friends Helen and Anna Marie. It was a long flight from New York City across the Pacific Ocean to Seoul. It would take fourteen and a half hours. Halmoni, however, had lots of things to talk about during their flight. She pulled out a thick bundle of photos of Yunmi's many relatives, and began to tell her about each of them. Halmoni said, "I think they will all be at Kimpo Airport. They are so excited to meet you and want to show you all around Seoul."

When the airplane landed, they hurried through the airport to have their passports checked.

145

English Language Learners

Making Predictions Read the first page aloud. Then pause and have students predict what will happen on Yunmi and Halmoni's trip to Korea. Have students flip through the story, using the illustrations in order to help them make predictions.

Reading

▶ ## Supporting Comprehension

4 Why does the author include the scene in which Yunmi and Halmoni stand in different lines to have their passports checked? (to show that Yunmi is an American, but her grandmother is a Korean citizen; to make the story seem realistic)

5 Why do you think Yunmi feels strange as she stands in the foreigners' line? (She has never thought of herself as a foreigner before or experienced being in a different country until now.)

6 After talking to the man checking her passport, why does Yunmi no longer feel as if she's a foreigner? (Meeting someone who knows her grandmother makes her feel less like a stranger.)

Vocabulary *(page 146)*
__foreigners:__ people who come from a different country or place

__nationals:__ citizens from a particular nation or country

4 Halmoni walked Yunmi over to the long line that said "Foreigners." The line moved slowly as the officer checked each passport. Halmoni got to stand in the fast-moving line that said "Nationals." Yunmi looked like all the Koreans in the nationals line, but she had to stand in the foreigners line.
5 It made her feel strange.

But when it was Yunmi's turn, the man checking passports smiled and said, "Welcome to Seoul. Are you here for a visit with your Halmoni?"
"Yes, how did you know?" asked Yunmi.
"I saw you talking with your Halmoni. She was my favorite high school teacher. I heard she went to America to be with her granddaughter. Please tell her Hojun said 'Welcome back.'"
6 Yunmi nodded happily. She wasn't a foreigner after all. People here already knew who she was. She was proud of Halmoni, too.

146

147

Extra Support

Strategy Modeling

Predict/Infer Use this example to model the strategy.

I can infer that Yunmi has never been to Korea before. I note that she feels strange as she stands in the foreigners' line. I can infer that she's never thought of herself as being different from other Koreans, or maybe she's not used to thinking of herself as a "citizen" of the United States. I predict that she'll often feel strange as she meets new relatives and has new experiences in Korea.

Reading Fluency

- **Rereading for Fluency:** Have students choose a favorite part of the story to reread to a partner, or suggest that they read page 146. Encourage students to read with feeling and expression.

- **Assessing Fluency:** See guidelines in the Theme Assessment Wrap-Up, pages 206–207A.

▶ Supporting Comprehension

7 How does Yunmi feel when she first meets her relatives? Why? (She's overwhelmed at the huge crowd of friendly strangers.)

8 Why do you think the author includes the details about Halmoni's Korean house and pets? (to show that Halmoni still has strong ties to Korea and may have reasons to return there one day)

Vocabulary *(pages 148–149)*

embraced: hugged

ushered: led by someone

skyscrapers: very tall buildings

sightseeing: visiting interesting places; touring

Kyong Bok Kung: (kwee•oon bohk juhn)

ministers: people who are in charge of government departments

---

7   Halmoni was waiting for Yunmi, and they walked toward big sliding doors. Suddenly a huge crowd of people rushed toward them, waving and bowing. Yunmi stood still, her eyes wide. Everyone hugged her. Person after person bowed and <u>embraced</u> Halmoni. Halmoni was so happy, she had to wipe tears from her smiling face. Finally they walked past a long line of green and yellow taxis. An uncle <u>ushered</u> Halmoni and Yunmi into his car, and the rest of the relatives piled into cars and cabs.

148

Extra Support

Strategy Modeling

Phonics/Decoding Use this example to model the strategy.

(Point out ushered *on page 148.) I see the word parts* us *and then what could be* here *with a* d *or* her *with an* -ed *ending. /UHS•heerd/, /UHS•hur•ehd/, /UHS•hurd/. None of those sound familiar. Then I remember that the letters* s-h *can stand for the /sh/ sound. I'll try again—/USH•urd/. Oh, I know, that means "being led by someone," like at the movie theater. That makes sense.*

They sped down broad highways, then through streets crowded with skyscrapers. In the middle of the city at the top of a narrow, winding street was a tall brick wall with a pretty iron gate. Inside was Halmoni's house. Halmoni's older sister, who lived there now, rushed out. A cat and a dog with a fluffy tail ran behind her. Halmoni embraced her sister and bent to pet her dog. "Oh, I missed you, too," she said to him. Then she lifted the cat onto her shoulder and carried her inside.

During the next several days, Yunmi's cousins Jinhi and Sunhi took her sightseeing. They went to the royal palace, called Kyong Bok Kung. Yunmi liked running down the center of the wide steps, where only the kings and queens and ministers had once been allowed to walk.

8

149

MEETING INDIVIDUAL NEEDS

Challenge

Reading Card
4

Synonyms

Explain that authors use synonyms to make their writing interesting. Remind students that synonyms are words with the same, or nearly the same, meaning. Provide examples, such as *scared* and *frightened*, or *happy* and *merry*.

- Challenge students to find at least four pairs of synonyms on pages 148 and 149. (sped, rushed; cabs, taxis; embraced, hugged; broad, wide)

- Have students find synonyms for other words in the story.

Reading

▶ Supporting Comprehension

9 Why do you think the author includes factual information about the observatory and book printing? (so readers can experience the sights; to build up interest in and respect for Korea)

10 How does the author make the scene at the East Gate Market come alive? (She appeals to the readers' senses by helping them experience the taste of the cakes and the chants of the vendors.)

11 What difficulties do Yunmi and her cousins have in communicating with each other? (None of them speaks the others' language too well, so it's hard for them to understand one another.)

Vocabulary *(page 150)*

Chomsongdae: (Chuhm•suhn•day) the Star Observatory, believed to be the oldest observatory in Asia

bustling: full of activity; busy

vendor: someone who sells something

parasols: umbrellas that provide shade from the sun

9 They visited the National Museum. There, Yunmi learned that in the seventh century, Koreans built the Chomsongdae Observatory to study the stars. She also learned that in the thirteenth century, Koreans were the first in the world to invent movable metal type to print books.

10 They went to the bustling East Gate Market. A street vendor there was baking little cakes filled with sweet red beans. Jinhi, Sunhi, and Yunmi each bought one and ate the cakes as they roamed the crowded stalls. "Socks for sale," "Silk shirts here," "Parasols on special," the vendors chanted as the girls walked past. Then Yunmi's cousins took her to their favorite stall.

11 There, Yunmi bought two soft lavender and pink silk purses with shiny black tassels for her friends Anna Marie and Helen. Yunmi was having fun with her cousins, but it was a little hard to understand their English. And when Yunmi spoke Korean, her cousins giggled and said she sounded funny.

150

 English Language Learners

Making Inferences Review making inferences with students. Ask students to look at the illustrations as they read. Instruct them to guess what the characters are thinking and feeling. Ask how they can tell. Explain that this activity can help them find the theme of the story.

151

Revisiting the Text ....
Review/Maintain

Comprehension Skill Lesson
Making Generalizations

OBJECTIVES

Students use story details to make generalizations.

Remind students that a generalization

■ is a broad statement that is true most of the time

■ is based on facts or details that can be checked

■ may include clue words such as *most, all, often, always,* and *never*

Display the following sentence and read it aloud: *The East Gate Market is usually crowded and bustling.* Note that it tells what *usually* happens at the East Gate Market. It doesn't always happen but is true most of the time. Ask students to find details in the story that support the generalization. Record their responses in a chart similar to the one below.

Have students work in small groups to make their own generalizations based on story events on pages 152–153 or 157–159. Encourage them to record their statements in a chart like the one below. Allow time for groups to share their work.

Generalization	Supporting Facts
The East Gate Market is usually crowded and bustling.	crowded stalls
	vendors chanted

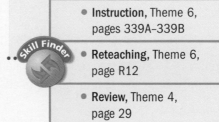

Skill Finder

● **Instruction,** Theme 6, pages 339A–339B

● **Reteaching,** Theme 6, page R12

● **Review,** Theme 4, page 29

▶ Strategy Focus: Predict/Infer

Teacher/Student Modeling Discuss clues on pages 152–153 that can help students predict a future problem for Yunmi. Ask what predictions can be made from the question that Yunmi poses, *"What if Halmoni didn't want to leave?"*

▶ Supporting Comprehension

12 Why does Yunmi wish that everyone would disappear? (She misses her close relationship with Halmoni and isn't used to sharing Halmoni's attention.)

13 What do you think Halmoni has in mind when she puts Sunhi in charge of teaching Yunmi to make mandoo? (She wants the cousins to share a fun experience.)

Vocabulary *(page 152)*

marinated: soaked in sauce or spices to add flavor

dumplings: pieces of dough, often with a filling, that you cook by steaming or boiling

mandoo: a Korean term for dumpling

---

12 Yunmi had hardly seen Halmoni since they arrived. Her grandmother was often out, and when she was home, Yunmi's cousins always sat on her lap and got all her attention. "Halmoni, don't ever leave us again," they kept saying. Halmoni just smiled. Yunmi sometimes wished everyone would disappear so she and Halmoni could talk like they did in New York.

For the next few days, Halmoni did stay home. But all Yunmi's aunts and cousins came over to prepare for the big picnic at Grandfather's tomb. They spent two whole days in the kitchen, making <u>marinated</u> beef, vegetables, <u>dumplings</u>, and sweets. Halmoni rushed about, overseeing <u>everything</u>.

13 "Sunhi," Halmoni said as she gave her a hug, "why don't you be in charge of making the <u>mandoo</u>? You can teach Yunmi. The dumplings are her <u>favorite</u>."

Halmoni rushed back with stacks of thin white dumpling skins, a bowl of water, and a big bowl of meat-and-vegetable filling. Sunhi placed just the right amount of filling on half of a dumpling skin. Then she dipped her pinky in the water and ran it around half the edge of the mandoo skin. She folded it into a half-moon shape and pressed the edge shut. Yunmi tried making them too. Soon they started making funny-shaped mandoo. Some looked like round balls, others like little purses, and some just looked strange. Halmoni smiled as she hurried past.

152

Extra Support

Segment I Review

Before students join the whole class for Wrapping Up on page 153, have them

- check predictions
- take turns modeling Predict/Infer and other strategies they used
- add to **Transparency 5–10**, check and revise their Character Chart on **Practice Book** page 82, and use it to Predict/Infer

---

On Level Challenge

Reading Card 5

Literature Discussion

In mixed-ability groups of five or six, students can discuss their own questions and the discussion prompts on Reading Card 5.

- How do you think Yunmi feels about her visit to Korea? How can you tell?
- Compare and contrast Yunmi's trip to a recent trip you've taken. How were your experiences similar to and different from Yunmi's?

Yunmi saw how happy Halmoni was with all her family, and Yunmi started to worry. What if Halmoni didn't want to leave? In New York, Halmoni had only Yunmi and her parents and Yunmi's friends. She was scared, but tried to think about how much Halmoni loved her.

153

English Language Learners

Pause at the end of page 153 and ask: How has Yunmi changed since the beginning? What is she feeling now? Why does she feel this way? How can you tell? If students do not know the word *jealous*, define it and ask whether they think this is what Yunmi is feeling.

Wrapping Up Segment 1
pages 142–153

First, provide Extra Support for students who need it (page 152). Then bring all students together.

■ **Review Predictions/Purpose** Discuss which predictions were accurate and which needed to be revised. Record any changes and new predictions.

■ **Model Strategies** Refer students to the **Strategies Poster** and have them take turns modeling Predict/Infer and other strategies they used as they read. Provide models if needed (pages 147 and 148).

■ **Share Group Discussions** Have students share their questions and literature discussions.

■ **Summarize** Have students use the transparency and their Character Charts to summarize what they've learned about Yunmi's personality so far.

Comprehension/Critical Thinking

1 How would you describe and explain Yunmi's relationship with her grandmother? (They're quite close, probably because her grandmother takes care of her.) **Making Inferences**

2 Why is Yunmi concerned about the possibility of Halmoni enjoying her stay in Korea too much? (She's worried that her grandmother may want to stay in Korea, which means an end to their close relationship when Yunmi returns home.) **Cause and Effect**

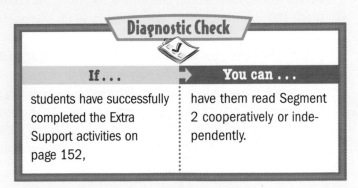

Diagnostic Check	
If...	**You can...**
students have successfully completed the Extra Support activities on page 152,	have them read Segment 2 cooperatively or independently.

Reading

Reading Segment 2
pages 154–161

Purpose Setting Have students summarize the story so far and predict whether Yunmi has good reason to worry about Halmoni's plans. Then have students read pages 154–161 to check their predictions.

 Journal Writing Students can record any revisions they made to their predictions and explain why they changed their minds. Also ask them to write their thoughts on what Yunmi should do to deal with her worries.

Vocabulary *(page 155)*

outskirts: areas away from the center of town

cat's cradle: a traditional game played with string

custom: a tradition; a way of doing something that many people follow

tombstone: a stone that marks where a dead person is buried

154

 Extra Support: Previewing the Text

Before reading Segment 2, preview the text, using the notes below. **While** reading, model strategies (page 157). **After** reading, review the segment (page 160) before students join the Wrapping Up discussion.

pages 154–155 The day of Grandfather's birthday celebration arrives, so the whole family goes to the gravesite to honor him. Where does this scene take place? Why do you think all the family members are bowing?

pages 156–157 Then, as part of the tradition, the family has a picnic. This is very different from Yunmi's other experience at a cemetery. Everyone is busy talking with Halmoni. Why do you think Yunmi is sitting by herself? How do you think she feels? Why?

pages 159–161 Halmoni thinks that Yunmi isn't enjoying her visit. What do you think is really Yunmi's problem? What might Halmoni say to her that will make Yunmi feel better?

The next day was Grandfather's birthday. They loaded all the food and drink into big vans they had rented. Everyone, all the cousins and uncles and aunts, climbed in, and they sped toward the outskirts of Seoul where Grandfather was buried. As they rode through the big city streets and then the winding country roads, Yunmi and her cousins sang Korean songs, played cat's cradle, and folded paper into the shapes of birds and baskets.

They stopped at the bottom of a small mountain. Everyone got out and climbed all the way to the top, to a small field. In the middle was a little hill covered with soft green grass.

There on the hill was a large, flat stone with Grandfather's name on it. Below that were a lot of other names. Yunmi was surprised to see her parents' names and her name. Then she remembered Halmoni telling her it was a Korean custom to list the names of all the children and grandchildren on a tombstone. Yunmi went up and touched the cool stone and felt the warm sunlight on her hand. Meanwhile, Halmoni gathered the whole family. Together they made three deep bows to Grandfather.

Then Halmoni said, "Grandfather will be happy to see us all having a good time visiting him and each other on his birthday. Let's eat and celebrate this beautiful day." They sat down to a picnic with all the food they had prepared.

155

Revisiting the Text

Visual Literacy Lesson
Picturing the Scene

OBJECTIVES

Students compare illustration details with details in the story.

Explain that Karen Dugan, the illustrator, has worked with the author to interpret story details. In this way they can provide ideas that are clearer in pictures than in the text.

Direct students' attention to the illustration on page 154. Ask what the text says the family is doing in this scene. (bowing deeply to Grandfather) Point out the look of respect on the family members' faces, which shows how important the occasion is. The illustrator probably added that detail to show the family's feelings about the special day.

Have students identify other details in the illustration that are also mentioned in the text. (Examples: the flat stone; the little hill covered with green grass) Then have them identify other details not mentioned in the text that the illustrator has added. (Examples: the traditional clothing worn by the women, the faces of the individual family members, the food containers)

Have students work in small groups to discuss other story illustrations. Ask them to list text details and those added by the illustrator. Allow time for groups to share their work.

Strategy Focus: Predict/Infer

Student Modeling Ask students to model their predictions about what will happen as Yunmi's visit comes to an end. If necessary, use the following prompt:

How will Yunmi act as she becomes more and more upset about her grandmother's plans?

▶ Supporting Comprehension

14 What is the author's purpose in contrasting Yunmi's experiences in an American cemetery to her visit to a Korean one? (to show that Koreans have different customs and a different outlook on life)

15 Why do you think Yunmi bursts into tears? (Seeing how much Halmoni is enjoying her visit and attention from relatives, Yunmi fears she'll want to stay in Korea.)

156

 Cross-Curricular Connection

Social Studies Traditional Korean values are greatly influenced by the teachings of Confucius, who emphasized order between generations and family loyalty. The respect shown to older family members extends to ancestors as well, and those still living are charged with caring for the family gravesites. A visit to such places is commonplace on many Korean holidays and special occasions.

 MEETING INDIVIDUAL NEEDS **English Language Learners**

Pause at page 155; consider making paper shapes and playing cat's cradle to help students relate to the story and to reinforce skills like following directions and tangible language use. Most libraries have explanations of how to do origami (Japanese paper folding) and cat's cradle. For materials all you will need is string and paper. Encourage students to work in pairs.

14

Yunmi had only been to a cemetery once before. She had seen people place flowers at a grave, say a prayer, and leave quietly. But in Korea, no one cried or looked sad. The cousins ran through the field collecting flowers and smooth stones for Grandfather's hill.

Yunmi wanted to talk with Halmoni, but everyone was crowded around her. Yunmi went and sat under a big tree all by herself to think. As she watched Halmoni, Yunmi grew more and more afraid that Halmoni would not want to go back to New York.

"Yunmi, help us look for more stones," said Sunhi.

"Why are you all by yourself?" Jinhi asked. "What's wrong?"

"Nothing. Nothing's wrong. Why don't you go sit with Halmoni. She's missed you all year," Yunmi said and burst into **15** tears. She jumped up and ran, tears streaming down her cheeks.

157

Extra Support

Strategy Modeling

Predict/Infer If students need help modeling the strategy, use this example to model it for them.

Yunmi watches everyone crowd around Halmoni and goes off by herself. Then Jinhi finds her and asks what's wrong. When Yunmi replies "Nothing," it's very clear that Yunmi is actually worried and upset. She's afraid Halmoni won't want to return to New York. Then she runs off in tears, which further shows how upset she is.

3 Revisiting the

Tested Skill

Comprehension Skill Lesson
Predicting Outcomes

OBJECTIVES

Students use story clues to predict what characters might do in new situations.

Remind students that good readers look for clues about story characters as they read. That will help them understand why the characters act as they do. It will also help them predict what might happen in a new situation.

Ask what Sunhi and Jinhi do when they see Yunmi sitting by herself. (They show their concern by trying to get Yunmi to join them.) Then explain that those clues would lead you to expect the girls to act the same way if they saw another cousin sitting by herself at a family gathering. That prediction makes sense based on their actions in the story.

Have students work in small groups to answer the following questions. Ask them to write their answers and then list the story clues that helped them make predictions. Have groups share their ideas.

1 If Halmoni were to return to Korea at the same time next year, what plans would she be likely to make?

2 If Halmoni were to ask Sunhi to teach Yunmi how to write Korean words (calligraphy), what would Sunhi be likely to do? What might happen?

Skill Finder

- **Instruction,** pages 167A–167B
- **Reteaching,** page R10
- **Review,** Th. 1, p. 29; Th. 2, p. 173; Th. 4, p. 91

▶ Supporting Comprehension

16 How do Yunmi's actions and thoughts show her mixed feelings? (She runs off to be alone, cries, and thinks how unfair it will be to give up Halmoni; she also thinks she's being selfish because Halmoni is so happy to be back in Korea.)

17 What do you think makes Yunmi say the sentence that begins, *They just want me to stay ...*? Do you think she means it? (She's upset at the idea of Halmoni staying and speaks without thinking. No, she's upset.)

18 Why does Yunmi feel ashamed and selfish? (She realizes she's been putting her happiness first and should be thinking of what's best for her grandmother.)

Vocabulary *(pages 158–159)*

blurted: said suddenly without thinking

ashamed: feeling sorry for doing something wrong

selfish: being mainly interested in yourself rather than others

---

16 When she couldn't run anymore, Yunmi threw herself on the grass and cried and cried. She imagined going back to New York all by herself, and all the lonely afternoons she would spend without Halmoni. She knew Halmoni was happy here, but it all seemed so unfair.

Soon she heard Halmoni's voice. "Yunmi, what's the matter?" She didn't answer.

Halmoni patted her. "Aren't you enjoying your visit? Everyone is so happy you're here. They wish you could stay longer."

17 Yunmi <u>blurted</u>, "They just want me to stay so they can keep you here. I know you want to stay. You're so happy and busy."

158

 English Language Learners

Pause at the end of page 158 and ask: Why is Yunmi so sad? What is she worried about? Then ask students to predict what will happen at the end of the story. Encourage all students to take notes.

Halmoni sighed. "Oh, dear! Have I been that bad? I'm sorry. It's just that I want to take care of everything so I'll be ready to spend another year with you."

Yunmi looked up. "Another year with me?"

"Yes, Yunmi. Another year in New York, just as we planned."

Suddenly Yunmi felt <u>ashamed</u> and <u>selfish</u>. She stared down at the grass. "Halmoni, you have your house, your pets, and all your grandchildren and friends here. In New York, you only have my parents and me. If you want to stay, I understand."

18

159

Revisiting the Text . . . .

Review/Maintain

Comprehension Skill Lesson
Cause and Effect

OBJECTIVES

Students identify the causes and effects of story events.

Remind students that some story events and ideas are related. To figure out these cause and effect relationships, students should ask these questions:

What happens? *(effect)*
Why does it happen? *(cause)*

Point out that when Halmoni sees Yunmi crying, she thinks Yunmi is crying because she's not enjoying her visit to Korea. Readers know, however, that that's not the case. Ask students to identify the real cause of Yunmi's tears. (She fears that Halmoni plans to stay in Korea.) Show the relationship between these two ideas by writing them on a simple chart, similar to the one below.

Have students help you complete the chart by identifying other cause and effect relationships in the story. (Example: Yunmi sees how busy and happy Halmoni is, so she thinks Halmoni will stay in Korea.)

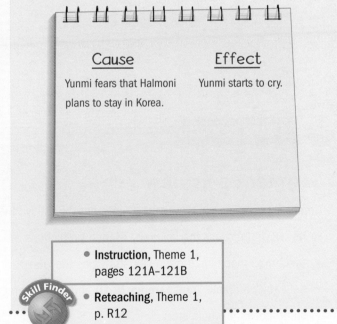

Cause	Effect
Yunmi fears that Halmoni plans to stay in Korea.	Yunmi starts to cry.

Skill Finder

- **Instruction,** Theme 1, pages 121A–121B

- **Reteaching,** Theme 1, p. R12

- **Review,** Theme 3, p. 331

Reading

▶ Supporting Comprehension

19 Why do you think Yunmi suddenly thinks of asking her cousins to visit her in New York? (She realizes how important they are to her; she'd like to share special experiences in the United States with them to return their kindness.)

20 What does the author mean when she says that Yunmi and Halmoni walked over *to join Yunmi's family*? (Instead of thinking of them as just relatives in photos, Yunmi now knows her real-life family members.)

Halmoni smiled. "I do miss everyone here, but I have a family I belong to in New York. And you have a family here too. We're lucky because we both have two families."

Yunmi thought of her cousins Sunhi and Jinhi. "Halmoni, I kept wishing all my cousins would disappear. They were so nice to me, and even helped me buy presents for my friends."

Halmoni stroked Yunmi's hair and said, "They like you so much, you are already one of their favorite cousins."

19 "Halmoni, do you think we can invite Jinhi and Sunhi to New York for a visit? I'd like to show them around," said Yunmi.

Halmoni smiled. "Oh, I know they would love to. Why don't you ask them?"

20 Yunmi heard her cousins calling. She took Halmoni's hand and helped her up. Together they walked over to join Yunmi's family.

160

Extra Support

Segment 2 Review

Before students join in Wrapping Up on page 161, have them:

- review and discuss the accuracy of their predictions
- take turns modeling the reading strategies they used
- help you complete **Transparency 5–10** and their Character Chart
- summarize the whole story

On Level   Challenge

Literature Discussion

Have small groups of students discuss the story, using their own questions or the questions in Think About the Selection on page 162.

161

Wrapping Up Segment 2

pages 154–161

Provide Extra Support for students who need it (page 160). Then bring all students together.

- **Review Predictions/Purpose** Have students compare their predictions with the story itself, suggesting reasons that their predictions varied from the actual outcome.

- **Model Strategies** Have students tell how they used the Predict/Infer strategy, and have them take turns modeling it. Provide models if needed (page 157).

- **Share Group Discussions** Have students compare their understanding of the story by talking about what Yunmi learned on her trip to Korea.

- **Summarize** Have students use their Character Charts to discuss the characters and important clues in the story.

Comprehension/Critical Thinking

1 How is Grandfather's birthday celebration an important event in the story? (It's the main purpose for the trip, minor events build up to it, and it's where Yunmi and Halmoni talk about Halmoni's plans for the future.) **Story Structure**

2 Do you think travel to a foreign country changes a person's views about life? Explain. (Yes; you gain a new understanding of other people's beliefs and customs. No; other people's customs have little effect on daily life at home.) **Making Judgments**

English Language Learners

When all have completed the reading, ask the class to brainstorm on the theme of the story. If they cannot, write a list of possible themes on the board *(learning to share, family love, growing up...)*. For each suggestion, ask students to show examples of the theme in the story. Use a web or outline to record the ideas on the board.

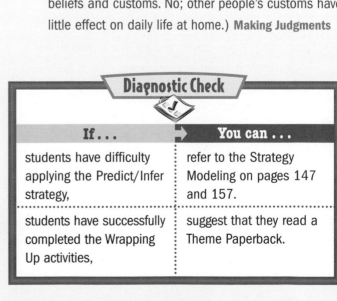

Diagnostic Check

If . . .	You can . . .
students have difficulty applying the Predict/Infer strategy,	refer to the Strategy Modeling on pages 147 and 157.
students have successfully completed the Wrapping Up activities,	suggest that they read a Theme Paperback.

Responding

▶ Think About the Selection

Discuss or Write Have students discuss or write their answers. Sample answers are provided; accept reasonable responses that are supported with evidence from the story.

1 **Making Inferences** They're no longer people in a photo but family members she knows and loves.

2 **Drawing Conclusions** They're possibly following a Korean custom to remember and honor Grandfather.

3 **Cause and Effect** She has a better understanding of Halmoni and the traditions of her Korean family.

4 **Predicting Outcomes** They might be excited to see how their cousin lives; they could be anxious about speaking English.

5 **Making Judgments** Answers will vary.

6 **Connecting/Comparing** Compare and Contrast Both are making a journey to a land unknown to them; they are probably anxious about what is to happen. The boy travels on a leaky ship that takes over two months to reach its destination, a dangerous wilderness where his family plans to start a new life and home. Yunmi travels in a jet that arrives at her destination in about fourteen hours. She is fairly comfortable and plans to visit relatives in a modern city.

Responding

Think About the Selection

1. How does Yunmi feel about her relatives in Korea by the end of the story? Explain your answer.

2. Why do you think that celebrating Grandfather's birthday is so important to Yunmi and Halmoni's family?

3. In what ways does Yunmi change because of her visit to Korea?

4. How do you think Yunmi's cousins would feel about visiting Yunmi in the United States?

5. If someone came to visit you from far away, how would you make them feel welcome?

6. **Connecting/Comparing** Both Yunmi and the boy in *Across the Wide Dark Sea* take long voyages. Compare their experiences.

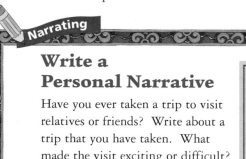

Narrating

Write a Personal Narrative

Have you ever taken a trip to visit relatives or friends? Write about a trip that you have taken. What made the visit exciting or difficult? Tell what was most interesting about your trip.

Tips
- To get started, make a story map of your trip.
- Be sure to keep the events in order.
- Use words that describe sights, sounds, and feelings.

162

 English Language Learners

Beginning/Preproduction Help students make a list of all of the words in the story for Yunmi's relatives. Then ask students to add other words for family members.

Early Production/Speech Emergence Ask: What did Yunmi worry about? What did she learn from her trip?

Intermediate and Advanced Fluency Ask students to describe a visit to relatives or friends they did not know well, especially in another country. Ask what they felt and what they worried about.

Social Studies

Find Out Names for Grandparents

In a small group, list all the names you know for *grandmother* and *grandfather*. Include names from other languages if possible. Compare your group's results with the rest of the class.

Grandmother
Halmoni
Nonna

Grandfather
Abuelo

Listening and Speaking

Be a Tour Guide

Yunmi's cousins give her a tour of their town. Plan a tour of your classroom or school. In a small group, decide what places to show and what to tell about each one. Then ask permission to invite visitors to take the tour.

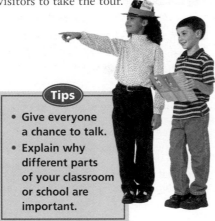

Tips

- Give everyone a chance to talk.
- Explain why different parts of your classroom or school are important.

Internet

Solve a Web Crossword Puzzle

What new words did you learn from *Yunmi and Halmoni's Trip*? Go to Education Place and print out a crossword puzzle about the selection. **www.eduplace.com/kids**

163

Personal Response

Invite volunteers to share their personal responses to *Yunmi and Halmoni's Trip*. As an alternative, ask students to write in their journals about a trip they have made.

▶ Comprehension Check

Assign **Practice Book** page 83 to assess students' understanding of the selection.

Practice Book page 83

Name _____

Yunmi and Halmoni's Trip
Comprehension Check

Finish the Letter

Write story details to finish Yunmi's letter.

Dear Anna Marie,

We've had a wonderful time in Korea! When Halmoni **(2 points)** _____ and I first arrived at the airport, I had to stand in the line for foreigners **(2)** _____. That made me feel strange. However, my Korean family made me feel welcome. I loved sightseeing and shopping, and my cousins Jinhi and Sunhi helped me buy a silk purse for you **(2)** _____. For a time I became sad, because I thought that my grandmother wanted to stay in Korea **(2)** _____. Then we went to my grandfather's gravesite to celebrate his birthday **(2)**. That's where Halmoni told me that she would be coming back to New York **(2)** _____.

Next year I hope that my cousins will come to New York for a visit. You can help me take them sightseeing! I'll be home soon, and I can't wait to see you.

Your friend,
Yunmi

Theme 5: **Voyagers** 83
Assessment Tip: Total **12** Points

English Language Learners

Remind students that their stories need a strong beginning, middle, and end. Encourage less proficient students to write their stories in comic strip form with pictures and words/phrases. You may want to recommend that all students begin with the comic strip exercise in order to map out the order of events. Then instruct students to make a word dictionary sheet for the names of *grandmother* and *grandfather*. Ask: What do you call your grandparents? Have you heard of other names from your friends, in stories, or on television?

End-of-Selection Assessment

Selection Test Use the test in the **Teacher's Resource Blackline Masters** to assess selection comprehension and vocabulary.

Student Self-Assessment Have students assess their reading with additional questions such as

- What parts of this selection were difficult for me? Why?

- What strategies helped me understand the story?

- Would I recommend this story to my friends? Why?

Art Link

pages 164–167

▶ **Skill: How to Look at Fine Art**

Read aloud the title of the link. Explain that in "Journeys Through Art," students will be examining four paintings and one sculpture, each by a different artist. Explain that while everyone views works of art in their own unique, personal way, it can be helpful to follow some general guidelines, especially when experiencing a new kind of art form. Direct students to the left column of page 164 and review these tips.

■ Explain to students that they will learn how to "read" each picture by **looking** at the entire image and considering how it makes them feel.

■ After this initial overview, instruct students to view the art in greater depth, **focusing** on smaller details. Prompt them to **notice** colors, shapes, textures, mood, lighting, and other sensory qualities.

■ Have students make an evaluative **response**. Do they like it? Why or why not? Have students complete the sentence "I like it *because ...*" or "I don't like it *because ...*"

Point out that critical art viewers observe a work carefully, as well as reflect on how the work affects the viewer—that is, how it makes the viewer think or feel. Urge students to ask themselves what the work is about or what the artist is trying to express. To encourage students to approach the link with the necessary critical eye, have them use the Evaluate strategy while they examine the artwork.

Art Link

Journeys Through Art

Skill: How to Look at Fine Art

❶ **Look** at the whole painting or sculpture. **Think** about how it makes you feel.

❷ Then look more carefully. **Focus** on small details or parts. **Notice** colors and shapes.

❸ **Respond** to the art. Tell a friend how the art makes you feel or what it makes you think about.

Geese in Flight, 1850 or later
Leila T. Bauman

The Seven Ri Ferry Boat Approaching Kuwana, 1855
Ando Hiroshige

164

 Classroom Management

All Students

Viewing the Art Involve all students in How to Look at Fine Art, Art Chart, Visual Literacy, and Comprehension Check activities. Instead of conducting the Art Chart activity with the entire class, you may prefer to have students work in small groups.

▶ **Art Chart**

Explain that keeping track of the details they observe in the artwork—and of their own impressions of the art—can help students reflect on their understanding of it. Draw a three-column chart on the board. Have students help you fill in the chart for *Geese in Flight*. Then have them fill in new charts independently for the remaining artwork featured in the link.

Geese in Flight

Look at the Entire Art Work	Focus on Details	Respond
small town by the sea	geese flying away	I like it because it makes me think of traveling someplace far away.
boats coming and going	train going by	

Purpose Setting Have students examine the examples of fine art and determine what each one conveys. Suggest that they use the Question strategy as well as other appropriate strategies.

Noting Details

If students have difficulty focusing their thoughts on what the artwork conveys, guide them in noting details. Ask them to list the objects they see that suggest motion. (birds, boats, trains, airplanes, cars) Then have them look for other details that give the feeling of motion. (ocean waves, full sails, smoke from the train) Students can then refer to these details as they reflect on what the art expresses.

Art Link *continued*
pages 164–167

Revisiting the Text

Visual Literacy
Cubism

OBJECTIVES

Students identify characteristics of cubist art.

Explain that *Airplane Over Train* is an example of a modern art form called cubism, a style of art that began in the early 1900s. Draw a three-dimensional cube on the board, and then draw a one-dimensional square. Explain that a cubist artist would be more interested in painting an item using shapes with cubic qualities. Tell students that, unlike other painting approaches, cubism

- often breaks up a figure

- tries to show hidden, or invisible, qualities

- does not always look like the thing it is representing

- can be a challenging art form, requiring a different kind of focus from viewers

Ask students to identify the characteristics of cubism in *Airplane Over Train*. Then have students experiment with cubism by choosing an object to sketch, color, or paint in the cubist style.

Airplane Over Train, 1913
Natalia Goncharova

166

English Language Learners

Some students may be quite accustomed to viewing and analyzing art. Others may not. To help all students learn how to respond to art, look together at the first painting and ask: What do you see? List all the details mentioned in the chart. Prompt interpretation by asking, Who is on a journey? Does this painting make you feel happy, sad, afraid? Finally, assign one painting to each pair of students and instruct them to repeat the analysis, using a chart.

View of the Pont de Sèvres and the Slopes of Clamart,
St. Cloud, and Bellevue, 1908
Henri Rousseau

Car, 1943
Alexander Calder

167

▶ **Comprehension Check**

Art Chart Have selected students share their completed Art Chart entries with the class.

Comprehension/Critical Thinking Have students refer to the chart and the selection as they answer these questions.

1 Why do you think these pieces of art were chosen to be shown in a theme entitled *Voyagers*? (They all feature some form of transportation.) **Making Generalizations**

2 In what ways are the three paintings *Geese in Flight, View of the Pont de Sèvres,* and *Airplane Over Train* different, and how are they similar? (They all show objects in motion; they show methods of transportation; *Geese in Flight* features birds rather than airplanes; *Geese in Flight* and *View of the Pont de Sèvres* are landscapes and are more realistic.) **Compare and Contrast**

3 How can you tell that all of the works of art on pages 166–167 were created in the 1900s? (Airplanes and cars were not invented before 1900.) **Drawing Conclusions**

4 **Connecting/Comparing** What idea or theme do these works of art express that relates to *Yunmi and Halmoni's Trip,* and what clues does page 164 give you? (the idea of going somewhere; the clue is the word *journeys*) **Making Inferences**

MEETING INDIVIDUAL NEEDS **Challenge**

Art

Using encyclopedias, art books, or the Internet, have selected students research further examples of fine art by their favorite of the artists featured in the link. If this is not practical, have them research the artistic genre that most intrigues them, such as *cubism*. Have students share their findings with the class.

Comprehension Skills

 Predicting Outcomes

▶ Teach

Remind students that they can use story clues from *Yunmi and Halmoni's Trip* to predict outcomes—or what might happen to the story characters in new situations. Use **Transparency 5–10** to review the details they noted about Yunmi. Then discuss

■ what the story details tell about her feelings

■ how those details can be used to predict her feelings and actions if her cousins come to visit her in New York.

During discussion allow students to refer to the selection and to **Practice Book** page 82. Then have them write their own responses to the question below the chart. Discuss their ideas.

Graphic Organizer: Character Chart (Accept varied responses.)

Yunmi's Feelings	Story Clues
About Her Visit to Korea excited anxious	*(See page 145.)* from words in the story She held Halmoni's hand.
About Her Korean Cousins fun to be around hard to talk to and understand sometimes jealous	*(See pages 150–153 and 158–160.)* They take her sightseeing. They show her how to make mandoo. Their English is hard to understand and they giggle when she speaks Korean. Halmoni pays so much attention to her cousins.

Modeling Remind students that the way story characters talk, act, feel, and even the choices they make give clues as to how they may act in a new situation. Have students take turns rereading pages 158–159 aloud. Discuss what story clues reveal more about Yunmi's and Halmoni's relationship. Help students realize that Yunmi is able to share her thoughts and feelings with her grandmother. Then ask students to consider how Yunmi might react if she learned that Halmoni had to return to Korea for two months to care for her sick sister. As students keep their ideas in mind, model by using this think aloud.

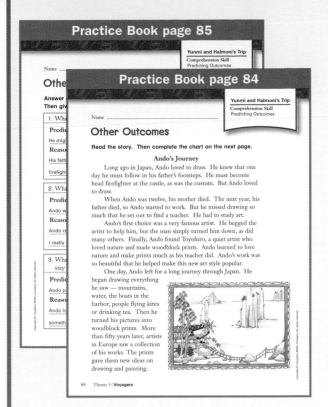

Practice Book page 85

Practice Book page 84

Yunmi and Halmoni's Trip
Comprehension Skill
Predicting Outcomes

Name _____

Other Outcomes

Read the story. Then complete the chart on the next page.

Ando's Journey

Long ago in Japan, Ando loved to draw. He knew that one day he must follow in his father's footsteps. He must become head firefighter at the castle, as was the custom. But Ando loved to draw.

When Ando was twelve, his mother died. The next year, his father died, so Ando started to work. But he missed drawing so much that he set out to find a teacher. He had to study art.

Ando's first choice was a very famous artist. He begged the artist to help him, but the man simply turned him down, as did many others. Finally, Ando found Toyohiro, a quiet artist who loved nature and made woodblock prints. Ando learned to love nature and make prints much as his teacher did. Ando's work was so beautiful that he helped make this new art style popular.

One day, Ando left for a long journey through Japan. He began drawing everything he saw — mountains, water, the boats in the harbor, people flying kites or drinking tea. Then he turned his pictures into woodblock prints. More than fifty years later, artists in Europe saw a collection of his works. The prints gave them new ideas on drawing and painting.

84   Theme 5: **Voyagers**

Think Aloud

When Yunmi fears that Halmoni will stay in Korea, she thinks how lonely the afternoons will be without her. So I can predict that if Halmoni had to go back to Korea, Yunmi would probably miss her and be lonely. But it also says that Yunmi realizes how much Halmoni cares about her Korean family. I predict that Yunmi would try not to be selfish. She'd want what's best for Halmoni.

Discuss students' predictions. Then ask what story clues reveal about Halmoni. Have students predict her reaction to news about a sick relative in Korea.

▶ Practice

Provide possible scenarios similar to the ones below. Have small groups of students predict what the characters might do in each instance. Ask them to write their predictions and list the story clues that helped them.

- Yunmi's younger cousin is coming to New York to go to school for the year.

- Halmoni decides to go back to school so she can get a job to help the family.

- Halmoni returns for a visit to Korea at the same time next year.

MEETING INDIVIDUAL NEEDS

Extra Support

- Reteaching, page R10

- **Reader's Library:** *Voyagers* Selection 2, "Brothers Are Forever"

▶ Apply

Use **Practice Book** pages 84–85 to diagnose whether students need Reteaching. Students who do not need Reteaching may work on Challenge/Extension Activities, page R11. Students who need Extra Support may apply the skill to an easier text using "Brothers Are Forever," Selection 2 of the **Reader's Library**, and its Responding activity.

 Skill Finder

• Revisiting, p. 157	• Review, Th. 1, p. 29; Th. 2, p. 173; Th. 4, p. 91	• Reteaching, p. R10

Diagnostic Check

If...	You can...
students need extra help with predicting outcomes,	use the Reteaching Lesson on page R10.
students have successfully met the lesson objectives,	have them do the Challenge/Extension Activities on page R11.

Reading

Students

- identify the steps in SQRR
- use graphic organizers to record information gathered with SQRR

Information & Study Skills
Using Graphic Organizers

▶ **Teach**

Explain to students that if they were traveling to Korea, they might first read a book or an article about the country. Display a book or magazine article about Korea (or another country). Point out that graphic organizers can help them identify and organize the information they learn while reading. Write SQRR on the board and explain that this is a method for reading articles. The abbreviation stands for the different steps of this reading method. List the steps individually, explaining each one before writing the next:

S survey
Q question
R read
R review

Explain that survey means to quickly look over the book or article to get a general idea of what it is about. Look at the title, pictures, headings, and the first and last paragraphs. Students should then come up with questions about each part of the book or article. Show them how to create a simple, two-column chart to record their questions.

Questions   Answers

Explain that as they read, they should look for answers to their questions. Finally, students should review their questions and answers when they're finished reading.

Modeling Have students look at "Young Voyagers" on pages 134–137. Then model how to use SQRR and a graphic organizer.

Think Aloud

The first thing I do is look at the title, the bold type below it, the diagram, and then the title and heading on the next page. All this tells me that the article is about the lives of children in Pilgrim times. I have a few questions right away: Where did the children travel on the ship? How was life different for them than it is today? I write these in my chart and then read to find the answers. I learn that the 'tween decks was where the passengers lived, although the children could play on deck in good weather. I also learn that children worked more and bathed less than they do today. I note these answers in my chart. Later, I will review what I wrote.

▶ Practice

Ask students to read or reread an article in their Anthology, such as "I Work in the Ocean" on pages 66–69. Have them work in pairs as they read to practice the SQRR technique. Have both students in each pair read the article and then share the questions they each come up with. Have pairs create a simple question/answer chart to record their questions and answers.

▶ Apply

Invite students to research a country that interests them. It might be a country they have read about or one they would like to visit. Using SQRR, have students find three to five interesting details about the place they have selected. Have them share this information either orally or by means of fact cards.

Teacher's Note

Students may need additional help in learning how to generate questions. You may suggest that if they can't think of any questions, they should begin by asking *who, what, when, where, why,* and *how* questions.

Decoding Longer Words

 Structural Analysis: Possessives

Word Work Instruction	
DAY 1	• Spelling Pretest • Spelling Instruction
DAY 2	• Structural Analysis Instruction • Spelling Practice
DAY 3	• Phonics Instruction • Spelling Practice
DAY 4	• Structural Analysis Reteaching • Vocabulary Skill Instruction • Spelling Game
DAY 5	• Expanding Your Vocabulary • Spelling Test

OBJECTIVES

Students

- read singular and plural possessives
- read words and syllables with the vowel sound in *bought*
- use the Phonics/Decoding strategy to decode longer words

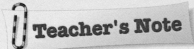 **Teacher's Note**

Point out the difference between words in which an apostrophe and *s* form a contraction, and those in which an apostrophe and *s* form a possessive noun. Use these sentences as examples.

Yunmi's going on her first airplane trip. (Yunmi's = Yunmi is)

Yumni's cousins took her sightseeing. (Yunmi's cousins = the cousins belonging to Yunmi)

▶ **Teach**

Write these sentences on the board: *Yunmi took <u>grandmother's hand</u>. Yunmi was surprised to see her <u>parents' names</u> on the stone.* Underline the words *grandmother's hand* and circle the apostrophe and *s*. Explain that *grandmother's* is a possessive noun. It shows ownership. *Grandmother's hand* is a way of saying "the hand that belongs to grandmother."

Explain that you can also show that something belongs to more than one person or animal. Underline *parents' names* and circle the *s* followed by an apostrophe. Explain that *parents' names* is a short way of saying "the names that belong to her parents." Point out that when forming a possessive noun only an apostrophe is added to a plural noun that already ends in *s*. Have students review the Phonics/Decoding strategy. Explain that this strategy will help them decode other possessive nouns.

Modeling Display the following sentence and model how to decode the word *Grandfather's: The next day was <u>Grandfather's</u> birthday.*

Think Aloud

When I read this word from left to right I see the shorter words grand *and* father. *It's a compound word—grandfather. I see that it ends in* s, *so maybe it means more than one grandfather. I notice the apostrophe before the* s; *the word is a possessive. It means "the birthday that belongs to Grandfather."*

▶ **Practice**

Write these phrases on the board and have students copy them: *Yunmi's relatives; the foreigners' line; Halmoni's house; her cousins' favorite stall; Grandfather's hill; Halmoni's voice.* Have students work in pairs. Tell students to underline the possessive noun in each phrase and decide its meaning, including whether it refers to one or more than one person.

▶ **Apply**

Have students complete **Practice Book** page 86.

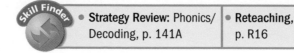

Skill Finder

• Strategy Review: Phonics/ Decoding, p. 141A	• Reteaching, p. R16

Phonics: Vowel Sound in bought

▶ Teach

Tell students that understanding the vowel sound in *bought* can help them use the Phonics/Decoding strategy to decode unfamiliar words. Explain that

■ the spelling patterns *ough* and *augh* can have the / ô / sound as in *bought*

Modeling Write this sentence and model how to decode *granddaughter*:

> *She went to America to be with her* <u>*granddaughter*</u>.

 Think Aloud

When I look at this word, I recognize the shorter word grand. *Next I see the letter* d *followed by the* augh *spelling pattern. I know this pattern can have the / aw / sound as in* bought, *so I think this part of the word might sound like / daw /. The last part probably sounds like / ter / as in the word* water. *When I try putting it all together, I say / GRAND•daw•tur /. I know that word—it's* granddaughter, *which makes sense in the sentence.*

▶ Practice

Write these phrases on the board and have students copy the underlined words: *Sunmi* <u>*taught*</u> *Yunmi how to make dumplings. Yunmi* <u>*thought*</u> *her grandmother wanted to stay in Korea.* Tell students to circle the *ough* or *augh* spelling in each word, pronounce the word, and see if it makes sense. Call on individuals to model the Phonics/Decoding strategy at the board.

▶ Apply

Tell students to decode the following phrases and discuss their meanings: *bought cakes; brought home gifts; ought to say thank you; should not act naughty.*

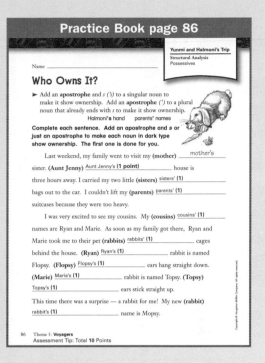

Practice Book page 86

Yunmi and Halmoni's Trip
Structural Analysis
Possessives

Name _____

Who Owns It?

▶ Add an **apostrophe** and *s* (*'s*) to a singular noun to make it show ownership. Add an **apostrophe** (*'*) to a plural noun that already ends with *s* to make it show ownership.
    Halmoni's hand   parents' names

Complete each sentence. Add an apostrophe and *s* or just an apostrophe to make each noun in dark type show ownership. The first one is done for you.

Last weekend, my family went to visit my (**mother**) mother's

sister. (**Aunt Jenny**) Aunt Jenny's (**1 point**) _____ house is

three hours away. I carried my two little (**sisters**) sisters' (**1**) _____

bags out to the car. I couldn't lift my (**parents**) parents' (**1**) _____

suitcases because they were too heavy.

I was very excited to see my cousins. My (**cousins**) cousins' (**1**) _____

names are Ryan and Marie. As soon as my family got there, Ryan and

Marie took me to their pet (**rabbits**) rabbits' (**1**) _____ cages

behind the house. (**Ryan**) Ryan's (**1**) _____ rabbit is named

Flopsy. (**Flopsy**) Flopsy's (**1**) _____ ears hang straight down.

(**Marie**) Marie's (**1**) _____ rabbit is named Topsy. (**Topsy**)

Topsy's (**1**) _____ ears stick straight up.

This time there was a surprise — a rabbit for me! My new (**rabbit**)

rabbit's (**1**) _____ name is Mopsy.

86   Theme 5: **Voyagers**
Assessment Tip: Total **10** Points

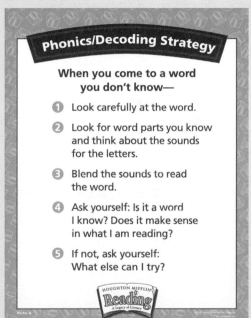

Phonics/Decoding Strategy

When you come to a word you don't know—

1. Look carefully at the word.

2. Look for word parts you know and think about the sounds for the letters.

3. Blend the sounds to read the word.

4. Ask yourself: Is it a word I know? Does it make sense in what I am reading?

5. If not, ask yourself: What else can I try?

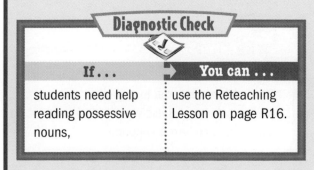

Diagnostic Check

If . . .	You can . . .
students need help reading possessive nouns,	use the Reteaching Lesson on page R16.

Word Work

OBJECTIVES

Students write spelling words that have the vowel sound in *bought*.

Spelling Words

Basic Words

caught	**fought**
thought*	**daughter***
bought*	**taught**
laugh	**brought**
through*	**ought**
enough	**cough**

Review Words†

teeth

was*

Challenge Words

sought

granddaughter*

---

*Forms of these words appear in the literature.

†Because this lesson presents these spelling patterns for the first time, the Review Words do not contain the lesson's patterns.

Extra Support

Basic Word List You may want to use only the left column of Basic Words with students who need extra support.

Spelling

✓ The Vowel Sound in bought

Day 1   Teaching the Principle

Pretest Use the Day 5 Test sentences. Say each underlined word, read the sentence, and then repeat the word. Have students write only the underlined word.

Teach Write *bought* and *caught* on the board. Read the words aloud and have students repeat after you. Ask students to name each word's vowel sound. (/ ô /) Then underline the *ough* and *augh* patterns and explain that these are two spellings for the / ô / sound.

Add *laugh, through, enough,* and *cough* to the board. Say each word and have students repeat it. Explain that these words are special because their *augh* or *ough* patterns do not spell the / ô / sound. (In *laugh, augh* spells the / ăf / sounds; in *through, enough,* and *cough, ough* spells the / o͞o / sound, the / ŭf / sounds, and the / ôf / sounds respectively.)

List the remaining Basic Words on the board, say each word, and have students repeat it. Underline the / ô / spelling patterns in the words.

Practice/Homework Assign **Practice Book** page 185. Tell students to use this Take-Home Word List to study the words they missed on the Pretest.

Day 2   Reviewing the Principle

Practice/Homework Review the spelling principle and assign **Practice Book** page 87.

Day 3   Vocabulary

Word Family for *laugh* Write *laugh* and *laughter* on the board and ask students to say each word after you. Tell students that these words are in the same word family because they are related in spelling and in meaning. Ask students to suggest other words in the same family. (Some possible answers include *laughs, laughed, laughing, laughingly, laughable.*)

Next, list the Basic Words on the board. Have students use each word orally in a sentence. (Sentences will vary.)

Practice/Homework For spelling practice, assign **Practice Book** page 88.

(167G)   THEME 5: **Voyagers**

Day 4 Question Relay

Ask students to form groups of three to five, and ask each group to make a set of word cards for the Basic Words. Tell students to mix up the cards and place them facedown. Then explain these rules:

- Player 1 picks a card. The other players take turns asking questions that can be answered with yes or no, such as "Is it the opposite of *cry*?"

- A player can ask a question and make a guess in the same turn. The player must then spell the word correctly to score a point. If the player misspells the word, the next player may try to score a point by spelling it correctly.

- The first player to spell the word correctly draws the next card. The player with the highest score at the end of the game wins.

Practice/Homework For proofreading and writing practice, assign **Practice Book** page 89.

Day 5 Spelling Assessment

Test Say each underlined word, read the sentence, and then repeat the word. Have students write only the underlined word.

Basic Words

1. How many fish were <u>caught</u>?
2. I <u>thought</u> you were home.
3. Is that the cat you <u>bought</u>?
4. The clowns make me <u>laugh</u>.
5. We walked <u>through</u> the park.
6. Did you eat <u>enough</u> fish?
7. We <u>fought</u> to change the rules.
8. Is that girl your <u>daughter</u>?
9. My dad <u>taught</u> me to swim.
10. We <u>brought</u> chairs to sit on.
11. You <u>ought</u> to go before dark.
12. The nurse heard him <u>cough</u>.

Challenge Words

13. I <u>sought</u> out Fred to be my friend.
14. She made a doll for her <u>granddaughter.</u>

Technology

Spelling Spree! ™

Students may use the **Spelling Spree!™** for extra practice with the spelling principles taught in this lesson.

Practice Book page 185

Take-Home Word List   Take-Home Word List   Take-Home Word List

Practice Book page 89

Yunmi and Halmoni's Trip

Practice Book page 88

Yunmi and Halmoni's Trip

Practice Book page 87

Yunmi and Halmoni's Trip
Spelling The Vowel Sound in *bought*

Name _____

The Vowel Sound in *bought*

When you hear the /ô/ sound, remember that it can be spelled with the pattern *ough* or *augh*.
/ô/   **bought, caught**

▶ In the starred words *laugh, through, enough,* and *cough,* the *ough* and *augh* patterns spell other sounds.

Write each Spelling Word under its *ough* or *augh* spelling pattern. Order of answers for each category may vary.

Spelling Words

1. caught
2. thought
3. bought
4. laugh*
5. through*
6. enough*
7. fought
8. daughter
9. taught
10. brought
11. ought
12. cough*

ough

thought (1 point)   fought (1)
bought (1)   brought (1)
through (1)   ought (1)
enough (1)   cough (1)

augh

caught (1)   daughter (1)
laugh (1)   taught (1)

Theme 5: **Voyagers**   87
Assessment Tip: Total **12** Points

···· **Houghton Mifflin Spelling and Vocabulary** ····
Correlated instruction and practice

MEETING INDIVIDUAL NEEDS
Challenge

Challenge Word Practice Have students use the Challenge Words to write some quotes that Halmoni might say upon her return to New York.

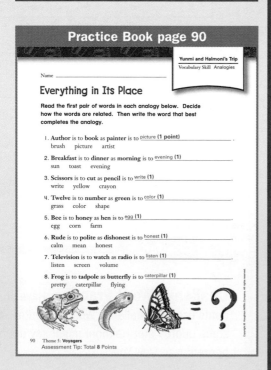

Transparency 5–11

Analogies

Six Steps to Solve an Analogy

Frog is to **jump** as **worm** is to

1. Take the analogy apart. See it as two pairs of words (one pair will have a blank instead of a word).

first pair of words   second pair of words

Frog is to **jump** as **worm** is to

2. Read the first pair of words. In this analogy, they are *frog* and *jump*.

3. Decide how the first pair of words are related to each other.

4. Using the first pair of words, make up a sentence that shows how they are related. For example:
A **frog** will **jump** to move from place to place.

5. Using the same sentence, replace the first pair of words with the second pair:
A **worm** will _____ to move from place to place.

6. Now fill in the blank with a word that makes sense in the sentence. Then go back to the analogy and use the same word.
A **worm** will _____ to move from place to place.

Frog is to **jump** as **worm** is to _____

Practice Book page 90

Everything in Its Place

Read the first pair of words in each analogy below. Decide how the words are related. Then write the word that best completes the analogy.

1. **Author** is to **book** as **painter** is to picture (1 point)
brush picture artist

2. **Breakfast** is to **dinner** as **morning** is to evening (1)
sun toast evening

3. **Scissors** is to **cut** as **pencil** is to write (1)
write yellow crayon

4. **Twelve** is to **number** as **green** is to color (1)
grass color shape

5. **Bee** is to **honey** as **hen** is to egg (1)
egg corn farm

6. **Rude** is to **polite** as **dishonest** is to honest (1)
calm mean honest

7. **Television** is to **watch** as **radio** is to listen (1)
listen screen volume

8. **Frog** is to **tadpole** as **butterfly** is to caterpillar (1)
pretty caterpillar flying

90   Theme 5: **Voyagers**
Assessment Tip: Total **8 Points**

Vocabulary Skills

Vocabulary: Analogies

▶ Teach

Display **Transparency 5–11**, explaining that an analogy is a kind of comparison. One pair of words is compared to a second pair. Words in the second pair should be related to each other in the same way as the words in the first pair. For example, if the first pair of words are synonyms, then the second pair of words should be synonyms. If the first pair of words describe an object and its color, then the second pair of words should describe an object and its color.

Read steps 1–6, *Six Steps to Solve an Analogy*. Point out that some analogies offer answer choices, while others do not. Tell students that they should always begin by focusing on the word pairs. If answer choices are given, students should try not to look at them until they have completed step 5.

Modeling Write this analogy on the board and model how to solve it:
Airplane is to *sky* as *ship* is to _____.

Think Aloud

First, I find the first pair of words. They are airplane *and* sky. *Then I ask myself how these words are related. I know that an airplane is a form of travel, and that it goes in the sky. Now I need to make a sentence:* An airplane travels in the sky. *Next I replace* airplane *and* sky *with the second set of words,* ship *and a blank. I get this sentence:* A ship travels in the _____. Sea, water, *and* ocean *all make sense in the blank. I'll pick the word I like best,* ocean. *So* airplane *is to* sky *as* ship *is to* ocean.

▶ Practice

Write the following analogies on the board and have students work in pairs to solve them:

Lemon is to *sour* as *honey* is to _____ (sweet).

Hair is to *scissors* as *lawn* is to _____ (lawnmower).

Have students share the sentences they made showing how the word pairs are related.

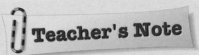

Teacher's Note

The /m/ sound is one of the earliest sounds that a baby makes, so it is probably no coincidence that many different languages feature this sound in words and nicknames for *mother*. Here are just a few examples:

mother, mommy, mama (English)

madre, mamá (Spanish)

mère, maman (French)

Mutter, Mutti (German)

Have students suggest more words or nicknames from other languages they might know.

···· **Houghton Mifflin Spelling and Vocabulary** ····
Correlated instruction and practice

▶ **Apply**

Have students complete **Practice Book** page 90.

Expanding Your Vocabulary
Family Words

The selection contains a number of terms that describe different family members. Have students identify as many of these terms as possible and begin a word web, similar to the following:

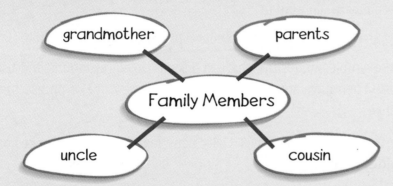

Have students work with partners to find additional words that either describe family relationships or are special family titles, such as *Nana, Gramps,* or *Sis.*

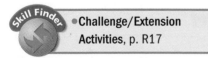
•Challenge/Extension
Activities, p. R17

Writing and Language Instruction

DAY 1	• Daily Language Practice • Grammar Instruction • Journal Writing
DAY 2	• Daily Language Practice • Write a Message • Journal Writing • Grammar Practice
DAY 3	• Daily Language Practice • Grammar Instruction • Write a Personal Narrative
DAY 4	• Daily Language Practice • Listening/Speaking/Viewing • Writing: Improving Your Writing • Grammar Practice
DAY 5	• Daily Language Practice • Grammar: Improving Your Writing

OBJECTIVES

Students

- identify object pronouns
- use object pronouns in sentences
- proofread and correct sentences with grammar and spelling errors
- use correct pronouns to improve writing

Wacky Web Tales

Students may use the **Wacky Web Tales** floppy disk to create humorous stories and review parts of speech.

Grammar Skills

Object Pronouns

Day 1

Display the two sentence pairs at the top of **Transparency 5–12**.

Remind students that a pronoun takes the place of one or more words. Have students tell what words are replaced in each sentence. Then go over the following rules and definitions with students:

■ The pronouns *me, you, him, it, us,* and *them* are object **pronouns**.

■ *It* and *you* are both subject and object pronouns.

■ Use *I* as the subject of a sentence. Use *me* as an object pronoun.

■ Always capitalize the word *I*.

■ Name yourself last when you talk about another person and yourself.

Display the examples under the chart to discuss object pronouns and using *I* and *me* correctly. Then have students choose the correct word or phrase to complete each sentence.

Then have them correct the Day 1 Daily Language Practice sentences on **Transparency 5–14**.

Day 2

Practice/Homework Have students correct the Day 2 Daily Language Practice sentences. Then assign **Practice Book** page 91.

Day 3   The Object Comes After

Have students create note cards for each object pronoun: *me, you, him, it, us, them.*

Then have students create a second set of note cards that show these words: *gives, shows, helps, teaches, thanks, to, for, with, of, at.*

Students shuffle the cards and take turns drawing one card from each stack and using them in a sentence. Students might write sentences about Yunmi and her grandmother. Help students place the verb or preposition *before* the object pronoun. For example, if students select *us* and *thanks*, they first arrange the cards to show the phrase *thanks us*. They might then write the sentence *Yunmi thanks us for the gift*. Then have students correct the Day 3 Daily Language Practice sentences.

Day 4

Practice/Homework Have students correct the Day 4 Daily Language Practice sentences. Then assign **Practice Book** page 92.

Day 5 — Improving Your Writing

Using the Correct Verb Form: Tell students that good writers take care to use the correct pronouns. After writing a sentence, it is always a good idea to check all pronouns. Have students read the sentences on **Transparency 5–13** and correct any mistaken pronouns.

Then have students review a piece of their own writing to see whether they can improve their use of subject and object pronouns.

Practice/Homework Have students correct the Day 5 Daily Language Practice sentences. Then assign **Practice Book** page 93.

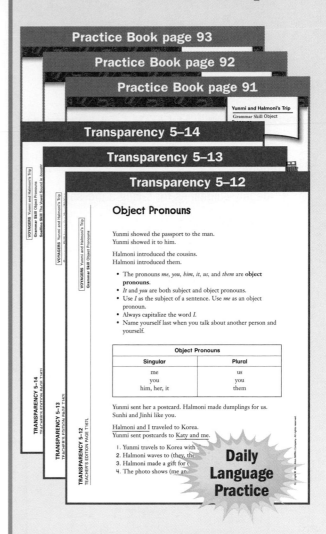

Object Pronouns

Yunmi showed the passport to the man.
Yunmi showed it to him.

Halmoni introduced the cousins.
Halmoni introduced them.

- The pronouns *me, you, him, it, us,* and *them* are **object pronouns.**
- *It* and *you* are both subject and object pronouns.
- Use *I* as the subject of a sentence. Use *me* as an object pronoun.
- Always capitalize the word *I*.
- Name yourself last when you talk about another person and yourself.

Object Pronouns	
Singular	**Plural**
me	us
you	you
him, her, it	them

Yunmi sent her a postcard. Halmoni made dumplings for us.
Sunhi and Jinhi like you.

Halmoni and I traveled to Korea.
Yunmi sent postcards to Katy and me.

1. Yunmi travels to Korea with
2. Halmoni waves to (they, th
3. Halmoni made a gift for
4. The photo shows (me an

Daily Language Practice

·········· **Houghton Mifflin English** ··········
Correlated instruction and practice

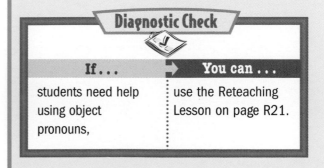

Diagnostic Check

If . . .	You can . . .
students need help using object pronouns,	use the Reteaching Lesson on page R21.

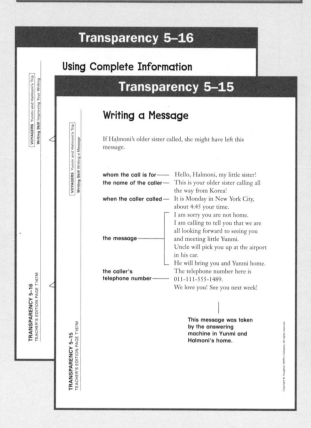

Students

- identify guidelines for taking a message
- write a message
- record complete information when taking a message

Writing Skills
Writing a Message

▶ Teach

In *Yunmi and Halmoni's Trip*, Yunmi and her grandmother visit their relatives in Korea. Before they left New York, Halmoni's sister in Korea might have called and left a message for Halmoni, reminding her of something that needs to be done or something that needs to be purchased for the trip. Taking a message is a big responsibility. Every message should include who called, whom the call was for, the time and date of the call, the message itself, the name of the person who took the message, and the phone number of the person who called.

▶ Practice

Display **Transparency 5–15**. Have students read the message and check that all the important information is in it.

Ask:

■ Whom is the phone call for? (Halmoni)

■ Who called? (Halmoni's older sister)

■ When did she call? (Monday, 4:45)

■ What is the message? (Uncle will pick you up at the airport in his car and will drive you and Yunmi home.)

■ What is the caller's telephone number? (011-111-555-1489)

■ Who took the message?

Help students visualize the structure of a message with a graphic organizer.

Graphic Organizer: Phone Message Form	
Date:_____	Time:_____
For:_____	Message taken: _____
From:_____	Telephone number:_____
Message:_____	
_____	
_____	

Discuss with students the guidelines for writing a message.

Guidelines for
Writing a Message

All messages should include the following information:
- the name of the person the message is for
- the name of the caller (the person who called)
- the time and date of the call
- the message
- the caller's phone number
- the name of the person who took the message

▶ **Apply**

Students can use **Practice Book** page 94 to help them plan and organize their writing. Have pairs of students role-play making telephone calls and taking messages.

Improving Your Writing
Writing Complete Information

Teach Remind students that a message must be exact and complete. Explain that *exact* means that the written message is correct and matches the message heard. *Complete* means that important information is there.

Practice To model how to write messages that are complete and exact, display **Transparency 5–16**. Have students read the voice balloon and the message taken. Then have them correct misinformation and add any missing information. Remind students that when they listen to answering machine messages, they can replay them to check the messages they write down.

Encourage students to use abbreviations to speed message taking.

Apply Assign **Practice Book** page 95. Then have students review their messages to check that they contain all the necessary information and that all the information is correct.

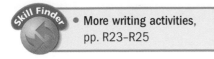

Skill Finder
- More writing activities, pp. R23–R25

Technology

Type to Learn™

Students may use **Type to Learn™** to learn proper keyboarding technique.
©Sunburst Technology Corporation, a Houghton Mifflin Company. All Rights Reserved.

·········· **Houghton Mifflin English** ··········
Correlated instruction and practice

Portfolio Opportunity

Save students' messages as samples of their writing development.

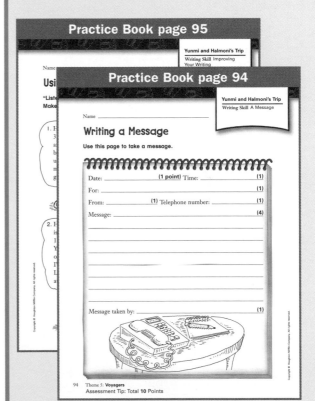

Practice Book page 95

Practice Book page 94

Yunmi and Halmoni's Trip
Writing Skill A Message

Name _____

Writing a Message

Use this page to take a message.

Date: _____ **(1 point)** Time: _____ (1)
For: _____ (1)
From: _____ **(1)** Telephone number: _____ (1)
Message: _____ (4)

Message taken by: _____ (1)

94   Theme 5: **Voyagers**
Assessment Tip: Total **10 Points**

Listening/Speaking/Viewing

Develop Nonverbal Communication Skills

▶ Teach

Tell students that many people go to Korea and to other countries without knowing the language. Yet they can still communicate in other ways. Point out that there are many ways to communicate without words. As an example, mention school crossing guards, who signal for traffic to stop by holding up a hand, with the palm facing traffic. Demonstrate this, and then show how the guard might signal the traffic to move forward again.

Explain that nonverbal communication takes many forms. Have students brainstorm some of these, guiding them to include the following:

▶ Practice

Divide students into pairs. Then, on small slips of paper, write words or phrases such as the following: *"Come here!"; "Go away!"; sadness; anger; fear.* Have each pair of students pick a slip and decide how they would nonverbally communicate that word or phrase. Afterward, students may enjoy demonstrating for the rest of the class.

• facial expression
• gesture
• posture
• movement
• pantomime

▶ Apply

In small groups or pairs, have students select a scene or detail from the story to act out without words. Encourage them to select one that shows strong emotion, such as the scene at the airport where Yunmi and Halmoni are greeted by family members. After the scene has been selected, have each student decide what emotion or message she or he wants to communicate nonverbally and decide upon the best way to do so.

Teacher's Note

Explain to students that the popular and fun game of charades simply involves practicing nonverbal communication. You may wish to have a brief game in class, or encourage students to play during recess or in their free time.

Improving Presentation Skills

Explain to students that they can use what they know about nonverbal communication to improve their presentation skills. Explain that they can follow the same steps that many speakers and professionals do when they make public presentations. Suggest the following:

- They stand up straight.

- They move with confidence and control.

- They keep their eyes on the audience.

- They wear a pleasant expression.

- They wait for silence before beginning to speak.

- They often use gestures and facial expressions to enhance their words to the audience.

Students may enjoy demonstrating these steps and contrasting them with their opposites.

Selection 3

Trapped by the Ice!
Different texts for different purposes

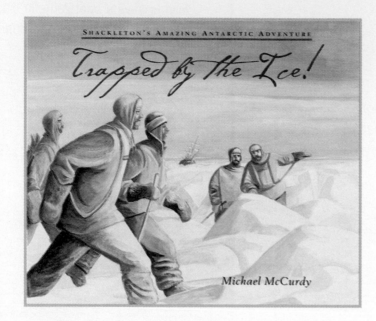

Michael McCurdy

Anthology: Main Selection
Purposes

- strategy focus: monitor/clarify
- comprehension skill: text organization
- vocabulary development
- critical thinking, discussion

Genre: Narrative Nonfiction
A series of actual events comes to life in this telling of a true story.

Award
★ American Bookseller "Pick of the Lists"

Selection Summary
During Sir Ernest Shackleton's 1914–1916 Antarctic expedition, his ship was trapped and crushed in the frozen Weddell Sea. Shackleton and his men made a long and perilous journey across ice and stormy seas to reach inhabited land. Not one man was lost.

Teacher's Edition: Read Aloud

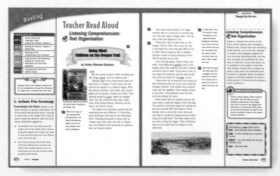

Purposes
- listening comprehension: text organization
- vocabulary development
- critical thinking, discussion

Anthology: Get Set to Read

Purposes
- background building: Antarctica
- developing key vocabulary

Anthology: Content Link

Purposes
- content reading: media
- skill: how to read a photo essay
- critical thinking, discussion

Leveled Books and Resources

See Cumulative Listing of Leveled Books.

Reader's Library

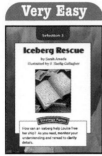

Very Easy

Iceberg Rescue
by Sarah Amada

(Also available on blackline masters)

Purposes
- fluency practice in below-level text
- alternate reading for students reading significantly below grade level
- strategy application: monitor/clarify
- comprehension skill application: text organization
- below-level independent reading

Lesson Support
- Guided Reading lesson, page R6
- Alternate application for Comprehension Skill lesson on text organization, page 205A
- Reteaching for Comprehension Skill: text organization, page R12

Selection Summary Masters

Trapped by the Ice!
Teacher's Resource Blackline Masters

Audiotape

Trapped by the Ice!
Audiotape for *Voyagers*

 Inclusion Strategy

Significantly Below-level Readers

Students reading so far below level that they cannot read *Trapped by the Ice!* even with the suggested Extra Support should still participate with the class whenever possible.

- Include them in the Teacher Read Aloud (p. 167U) and Preparing to Read (pp. 168A–169C).
- Have them listen to *Trapped by the Ice!* on the audiotape for *Voyagers* and read the Selection Summary while others read Segment 1 of the selection.
- Have them read "Iceberg Rescue" in the Reader's Library collection for *Voyagers* while others read Segment 2 of *Trapped by the Ice!*.
- Have all students participate in Wrapping Up Segment 2 (p. 199) and Responding (p. 200).

Theme Paperbacks

Easy

The Josefina Story Quilt
by Eleanor Coerr

Lesson, TE page 139I

On Level

A Child's Glacier Bay
by Kimberly Corral

Lesson, TE page 139K

Challenge

Balto and the Great Race
by Elizabeth Cody Kimmel

Lesson, TE page 139M

 **Technology**

Get Set for Reading CD-ROM
Trapped by the Ice!

Provides background building, vocabulary support, and selection summaries in English and Spanish.

Education Place
www.eduplace.com
Log on to Education Place for more activities relating to *Trapped by the Ice!*.

Book Adventure
www.bookadventure.org
This Internet reading incentive program provides thousands of titles for students to read.

Suggested Daily Routines

Instructional Goals	Day 1	Day 2

Reading
 	
Strategy Focus: Monitor/Clarify
 	
 Comprehension Skill: Text Organization
 	
Comprehension Skill Review: Sequence of Events; Topic, Main Idea, Supporting Details
 	
 Information and Study Skills: Using a Time Line
	Teacher Read Aloud
	Going West: Children on the Oregon Trail, 167U
	Preparing to Read *Trapped by the Ice!*
	• Get Set: Background and Vocabulary, *168A*
	• Key Vocabulary, *169A*
	  Selection Vocabulary, **Practice Book**, *96*
	• Strategy/Skill Preview, *169B*
	  Text Organization Chart, **Practice Book**, *97*
	
	Reading Segment 1
	Trapped by the Ice!, 170–183
	• Supporting Comprehension
	• Strategy Focus, *176*
	
	Wrapping Up Segment 1, *183*
		Reading Segment 2
		Trapped by the Ice!, 184–199
		• Supporting Comprehension
		• Strategy Focus, *186*
		
		Wrapping Up Segment 2, *199*
		Responding
		• Comprehension Questions: Think About the Selection, *200*
		• Comprehension Check, **Practice Book**, *98*
		
		Revisiting the Text
		• Comprehension: Text Organization, *187*

Word Work *Spelling:* The VCCV Pattern *Decoding Longer Words:* *Structural Analysis:* VCCV Pattern *Phonics:* Double Consonants *Vocabulary:* Homophones	**Spelling** • Pretest, *205G* • Instruction: The VCCV Pattern, *205G* • Take-Home Word List, **Practice Book:** *Handbook*	**Decoding Longer Words Instruction** • Structural Analysis: VCCV Pattern, *205E* • *Practice Book, 101* **Spelling** • *Practice Book, 102*
Writing & Language *Grammar:* Possessive Pronouns *Writing:* Write a Learning Log Entry; Writing Dates and Times *Listening/Speaking/Viewing:* Practice Group Problem Solving	Daily Language Practice, *205L* **Grammar Instruction** • Possessive Pronouns, *205K* **Writing** • Journal Writing, *171*	Daily Language Practice, *205L* **Grammar Instruction** • Possessive Pronouns, **Practice Book**, *106* **Writing Instruction** • Write a Learning Log Entry, *205M* • Journal Writing, *184*

 = tested skills

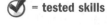 **Leveled Books** See Cumulative Listing of Leveled Books.

Reader's Library
• **Very Easy** *Iceberg Rescue*, Lesson, *R6*
Book Links: Anthology, *106*
Bibliography: Teacher's Edition, *102C*

Theme Paperbacks, Lessons, *139H–139N*
• **Easy** *The Josefina Story Quilt*
• **On Level** *A Child's Glacier Bay*
• **Challenge** *Balto and the Great Race*

Houghton Mifflin Classroom Bookshelf, Level 3

Allow time every day for students to read independently from self-selected books.

Technology

Lesson Planner CD-ROM:
Customize your planning for *Trapped by the Ice!* with the Lesson Planner.

Day 3

Revisiting the Text
- Writer's Craft: Setting, *193*
- Genre: Narrative Nonfiction, *197*

Comprehension Skill Instruction
- Text Organization, *205A*
- *Practice Book,* 99

Phonics Instruction
- Double Consonants, *205F*

Spelling
- *Practice Book,* 103

Daily Language Practice, *205L*

Grammar Instruction
- Our Perilous Journey, *205K*

Writing
- Responding: Write a Speech, *200*

Day 4

Comprehension Skill Instruction
- Reteaching Text Organization with Reader's Library, *R12*
- Independent Application, *Practice Book,* 100

Reading the Media Link
- "Shakelton's Real-Life Voyage," *202–205*
- Visual Literacy: Photography, *204*

Information and Study Skills Instruction
- Using a Time Line, *205C*

Decoding Longer Words
- Reteaching Structural Analysis: VCCV Pattern, *R18*
- Challenge/Extension Activities, *R19*

Spelling
- *Practice Book,* 104

Vocabulary Skill Instruction
- Homophones, *205I*
- *Practice Book,* 105

Daily Language Practice, *205L*

Grammar
- Reteaching, *R22*
- Our Perilous Journey, *Practice Book,* 107

Writing
- Writing Dates and Times, *205N*

Listening/Speaking/Viewing
- Practice Group Problem Solving, *205O*

Day 5

Revisiting the Text: Comprehension Review Skill Instruction
- Sequence of Events, *175*
- Topic, Main Idea, Supporting Details, *177*

Rereading for Fluency
Trapped by the Ice!, 170–199

Activity Choices
- Responding Activities, *201*
- Challenge/Extension Activities, *R13*
- Cross-Curricular Activities, *R26*

Vocabulary Expansion
- Words Used on Ships, *205J*

Spelling
- Posttest, *205H*

Daily Language Practice, *205L*

Grammar
- Proofreading for *its* and *it's,* *205L*
- *Practice Book,* 108

Writing
- Proofreading for *its* and *it's,* *205L*
- Writing Activities, *R23*
- Sharing Students' Writing: Author's Chair

Reading-Writing Workshop: Description

Based on the **Student Writing Model** in the Anthology, this workshop guides students through the writing process and includes skill lessons on—

- Ordering Information
- Using Sensory Language
- Writing Complete Sentences

See Teacher's Edition, *pages 138–139G.*

Allow time every day for students to write independently on self-selected topics.

Reading Instruction

DAY 1	• Teacher Read Aloud • Preparing to Read • Reading the Selection, Segment 1
DAY 2	• Reading the Selection, Segment 2 • Responding
DAY 3	• Revisiting the Text • Comprehension Skill Instruction
DAY 4	• Comprehension Skill Reteaching • Reading the Content Link • Information and Study Skills Instruction
DAY 5	• Comprehension Skill Review • Activity Choices

OBJECTIVES

Students listen to the selection, identify how the text is organized, and use this information to recognize and understand the main ideas.

▶ Activate Prior Knowledge

Connecting to the Theme Explain to students that you are going to read aloud a nonfiction article that describes what it was like to travel west on the Oregon Trail. Help students connect the selection with what they know, using these suggestions:

■ Ask students what they know about the western part of the United States. Discuss geographic features, the people, the weather. How would the west have been different about 200 years ago?

■ How would traveling west in the 1800s have been different from traveling west today? Have students discuss ways we travel today and how the pioneers would probably have traveled.

Teacher Read Aloud

Listening Comprehension: ☑ Text Organization

1

Going West Children on the Oregon Trail

by Helen Wieman Bledsoe

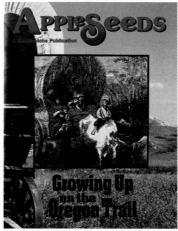

Appleseeds *magazine published this article about traveling on the Oregon Trail.*

1 What is the topic of this selection? (children going west on the Oregon Trail) What text features tell you this? (title, quotation, introductory paragraphs)

"*In the month of April 1844, my father got the Oregon fever and we started west.*"

Matilda Sager wrote these words from her new home in Oregon. To get there, she traveled for six months in a covered wagon. With her parents, brothers, and sisters, she crossed plains and mountains, deserts and rivers. They traveled along the route called the Oregon Trail. The trail stretched more than 2,000 miles, from Independence, Missouri, all the way to the Pacific Ocean.

The Sagers were pioneers, people who do something new and different. In those days, most Americans lived east of the Mississippi River. Traveling thousands of miles west to Oregon was a new idea. And life in Oregon was very different from anything the pioneers had ever known before!

2 Like many other pioneers, the Sagers traveled west in a long line of covered wagons. This was called a wagon train. The trip was a hard and dangerous one.

3 What was it like to travel west on the Oregon Trail in 1844? First of all, you had to get ready for a very long and difficult trip. It might take as long as a year to prepare. Families needed to bring everything necessary for months on the trail.

Once you got going, it was a long, long walk. Only babies and <u>toddlers</u> rode in the wagons with their mothers. All other children and adults had to walk. There wasn't room in the wagon for everyone, and the load would have been too heavy for the <u>oxen</u> to pull.

There was a lot to keep you busy along the trail. Everyone had a job to do. Girls cared for younger children. They helped their mothers cook over the campfire. They washed clothes in the rivers. They gathered wood for fires. And they milked the cows.

Boys looked after the animals and got the oxen ready to pull the wagons every morning. They added to the food supply by hunting rabbits and squirrels with their fathers. When families had to cross wide rivers, boys and men had to unload the wagons and put everything into small boats. The oxen swam across the river, pulling the wagon. Then everything had to be put back into the wagons on the other side.

Crossing a River

2 In what ways is this first section a good introduction to the article? (It includes background information: time it took to travel the route; what the land was like; how long the trail was; where it started and ended; what a pioneer is; what a wagon train was.)

3 What does the question that opens this paragraph tell you? (what kind of information to expect next; for example, you'll find out details about life on the trail)

Listening Comprehension:
 Text Organization

Explain to students that authors of non-fiction articles organize their materials in different ways. Remind them that identifying certain features, such as the title, headings or subtitles, and paragraphs organized by main ideas and supporting details, can help them recognize and understand the main ideas of a selection. As you read aloud, use the questions in the margin to help determine whether students both recognize the author's main points and understand how the article is organized. Based on students' responses, determine whether you need to clarify any part of the selection by pausing to reread or discuss it.

MEETING INDIVIDUAL NEEDS

English Language Learners

Discuss covered wagons. Define *hardship* and *settler*. Then ask: What are some hardships people faced on the Oregon Trail? What are some of the dangers and difficulties of a trip like this? What duties do you think the children will have? As you read ask students to listen for the answers to these questions.

Vocabulary *(pages 167U–167V)*

fever: great excitement about something

route: a path for getting from one place to another

toddlers: very small children who have just learned to walk

oxen: adult male cattle

4 What details support the main idea "There was a lot to keep you busy along the trail"? (information about girls' and boys' chores, such as cooking, cleaning, gathering wood and food, tending animals, loading the wagons; details about what travelers did for fun)

The trip wasn't all work, though. Late every afternoon, the wagon train stopped for the night. Usually, all the wagons pulled together into a circle. The animals were **4** <u>penned</u> inside. Now it was time for games, stories, songs, and lessons. Sometimes adults would read aloud around the campfire, often from the Bible.

There were many dangers along the trail. In the Great Plains, the grass was so tall that small children sometimes got lost in it. Playing near the rolling wagons was dangerous too. Pioneer Amelia Stewart wrote about one day: "Chet had a very <u>narrow</u> escape from being run over.... He escaped with only a bad scare." Catherine Sager wasn't so lucky, though. Her leg was badly broken under a wagon wheel.

Illness was always a threat. Diseases like measles, mumps, cholera, malaria, and mountain fever took many lives. When <u>fever</u> struck the Sagers's wagon train, both Mr. and Mrs. Sager died.

Teacher's Note

Tip for Read Alouds If students are confused by the two different meanings for the word *fever* in the selection, pause and clarify the word for them.

Vocabulary *(page 167W)*

penned: kept inside; closed in

narrow: uncomfortably close; almost unsuccessful

fever: very high body temperature

5   Friendly families offered to divide the seven Sager children among the wagons. But the Sagers wanted to stay together. The youngest was only five months old. John, the oldest, was fourteen. With other families to help them, the brave Sager children made it all the way to Oregon.

5 How is the end of the article like the beginning? (It talks about the Sager family again; both parts give specific details about one family, which helps to make the general information in the article more meaningful.)

▶ **Discussion**

Summarize After reading, ask students what fact they found most interesting about life on the Oregon Trail. Then have them summarize the main ideas of the selection.

Listening Comprehension:
☑ **Text Organization** Remind students that they can use the organization of a text to recognize and understand the main ideas in a selection. Then ask them to describe the organization of this selection: title, introduction (including the quotation), main ideas with supporting details, and an ending. Write students' ideas on the board or on a chart. Discuss the main ideas of the selection and the details that support those ideas. List the details beneath the main ideas. As you write, create an outline for the selection that students can use as a group to summarize the article.

Personal Response Ask students what qualities they admire in the Sager family and in the pioneers who traveled west. Talk about how they might have felt if they had traveled the Oregon Trail.

⭐ **Connecting/Comparing** Have students compare Yunmi's trip to Korea with the Sager children's trip west. Discuss how long the trips took, what was fun or difficult about them, and how they think Yunmi and the Sager children each felt about their trips.

Anthology

SHACKLETON'S AMAZING ANTARCTIC ADVENTURE

Trapped by the Ice!

Michael McCurdy

Technology

Get Set for Reading CD-ROM

Trapped by the Ice!

Provides background building, vocabulary support, and selection summaries in English and Spanish.

Preparing to Read

▶ Using *Get Set* for Background and Vocabulary

Connecting to the Theme Remind students that the stories in this theme all deal with voyages. Now they will read *Trapped by the Ice!*, a true story about a perilous voyage to Antarctica. Discuss with students what challenges a voyage to Antarctica, the continent located at the South Pole, might bring. Then use the Get Set to Read on pages 168–169 to explain some hazards of Antarctic travel.

- Have students read aloud "Exploring Antarctica." Point out the map and the photo showing the location of Antarctica and its topographical features.

- Ask students to explain the meaning of the boldfaced Key Vocabulary words: *barren, crevasse, deserted, floes, grueling, impassable, perilous,* and *terrain.* Have them use those words as they predict what challenges Shackleton and his crew will encounter.

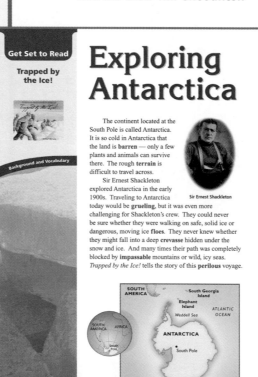

Get Set to Read

Trapped by the Ice!

Exploring Antarctica

The continent located at the South Pole is called Antarctica. It is so cold in Antarctica that the land is **barren** — only a few plants and animals can survive there. The rough **terrain** is difficult to travel across.

Sir Ernest Shackleton explored Antarctica in the early 1900s. Traveling to Antarctica today would be **grueling**, but it was even more challenging for Shackleton's crew. They could never be sure whether they were walking on safe, solid ice or dangerous, moving ice **floes**. They never knew whether they might fall into a deep **crevasse** hidden under the snow and ice. And many times their path was completely blocked by **impassable** mountains or wild, icy seas. *Trapped by the Ice!* tells the story of this **perilous** voyage.

Sir Ernest Shackleton

SOUTH AMERICA · **South Georgia Island** · **Elephant Island** · **ATLANTIC OCEAN** · **Weddell Sea** · **ANTARCTICA** · **South Pole**

168

169

MEETING INDIVIDUAL NEEDS

English Language Learners

Help students define sea adventure words: *horizon, ice cap, slip, skipper, mounted, stalking, rifle, sores, slammed, swelled, permanent, canvas,* and *bailed.* Use magazine photographs or the illustrations and pantomime to explain the words. Encourage students to act out the words with you.

▶ Developing Key Vocabulary

Use **Transparency 5–17** to introduce Key Vocabulary from *Trapped by the Ice!*

■ Model how to use context clues to figure out the meaning of the word *barren* from clues in the first item.

■ For each remaining sentence with a blank to fill in, ask students to find clues to the meaning of the Key Vocabulary word. Have them explain how they figured out each word.

Remind students that it's helpful to use the Phonics/Decoding strategy when they read. For students who need more help with decoding, use the review below.

Practice/Homework **Practice Book** page 96.

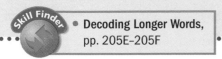

Strategy Review
Phonics/Decoding

Modeling Write this sentence from *Trapped by the Ice!* on the board, and point to *exhausting*.

> After an <u>exhausting</u> week battling the sea, the men nearly lost all hope.

Think Aloud

I think I can figure out this long word if I break it into parts. The beginning probably sounds like /ehks/ as in the word extra. Next I recognize the a-u spelling pattern from the word August. It probably makes the /aw/ sound, and when I blend it with the letters around it I say /hawst/. I also see the -ing ending. When I put it all together I say /ehks•haust•ihng/. That's close to a word I know, /ihg•ZAWST•ihng/. It means "really tiring." It makes sense that the men would be really tired after a week at sea.

Skill Finder
• Decoding Longer Words, pp. 205E–205F

Key Concept
Sir Ernest Shackleton's historic Antarctic journey

Key Vocabulary

barren: having little plant or animal life

crevasse: deep hole or crack

deserted: empty; not lived in, or having few or no people

floes: large sheets of floating ice

grueling: very tiring

impassable: not able to be crossed or traveled through

perilous: very dangerous

terrain: land, ground, or earth

See Vocabulary notes on pages 172, 174, 176, 178, 182, 184, 186, 188, 190, 192, 194, and 196 for additional words to preview.

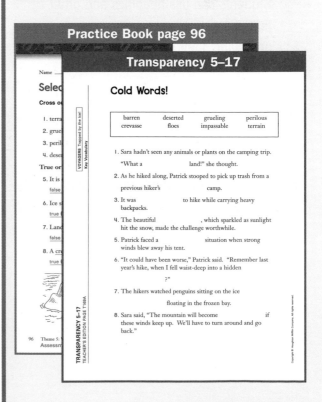

Practice Book page 96

Transparency 5–17

Cold Words!

| barren | deserted | grueling | perilous |
| crevasse | floes | impassable | terrain |

1. Sara hadn't seen any animals or plants on the camping trip. "What a _____ land!" she thought.

2. As he hiked along, Patrick stooped to pick up trash from a previous hiker's _____ camp.

3. It was _____ to hike while carrying heavy backpacks.

4. The beautiful _____, which sparkled as sunlight hit the snow, made the challenge worthwhile.

5. Patrick faced a _____ situation when strong winds blew away his tent.

6. "It could have been worse," Patrick said. "Remember last year's hike, when I fell waist-deep into a hidden _____?"

7. The hikers watched penguins sitting on the ice _____ floating in the frozen bay.

8. Sara said, "The mountain will become _____ if these winds keep up. We'll have to turn around and go back."

Reading

Strategy/Skill Preview

▶ **Strategy Focus:**
Monitor/Clarify

Strategy Focus

Can Shackleton and his crew escape from the ice? **Monitor** your reading to make sure you understand what happens. Reread to **clarify**.

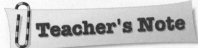

Teacher's Note

Strategy/Skill Connection For a better understanding of *Trapped by the Ice!*, students can use the:

• Monitor/Clarify Strategy

• Text Organization Comprehension Skill

Students can use headings and other features of text organization to monitor and clarify their understanding as they read.

Students can use their answers on the *Trapped by the Ice!* Text Organization Chart (**Practice Book** page 97 and **Transparency 5–18**) to review different sections of the selection and to check their understanding.

Have students turn to page 171 and follow along as you read aloud the title and author of the story. Ask someone to read the Strategy Focus. Remind students that to *monitor* means to check your understanding as you read. Remind them that to *clarify* means to reread, think about what you know, and read ahead to make clear confusing parts or unknown word meanings. Then have students read the first paragraph of the story on page 172 and apply the strategy by asking themselves if what they just read makes sense and by trying to clarify any unclear details.

Teacher Modeling Review how students can monitor their reading by asking themselves if they understand what they've read. Remind them that rereading, thinking about what they already know, or reading ahead can help them clarify difficult information or words. Model the strategy.

Think Aloud

The first two sentences tell me that the Endurance is trapped in the ice. From the title, I know that this selection is about some voyagers who get trapped by the ice on a journey to Antarctica. I guess the Endurance is the name of their ship. Yes, the next sentence gives me another clue. It says that Shackleton is standing on the deck. I know that a deck is a part of a ship.

Encourage students to record in their journals parts of the story that they find hard to understand and also how they tried to clarify these parts. Remind them to use their other reading strategies to help them understand the selection.

Comprehension Skill Focus:
Text Organization

Text Organization Chart Explain that as students read the selection, they will focus on text organization. To develop the skill, students will identify pages in the selection that show specific features of text organization. Display **Transparency 5–18**, and demonstrate how to use this graphic organizer.

■ Have a student read aloud the first text feature (headings) listed on the Text Organization Chart.

■ Have another student read aloud the first example in the selection of this text feature. (October 27, 1915)

■ Model how to identify and record on the chart the page number (172) where the heading *October 27, 1915* is found.

■ Ask students to fill in the same answer in the second column of the chart on **Practice Book** page 97.

■ Tell students to complete the Text Organization Chart as they read the selection. Monitor their work, or have students check each other's charts.

Graphic Organizer: Text Organization Chart

Text Feature	Where It Is	Purpose
heading (date)	pp. 172, 174, 176, 180, 182, 184, 186, 190, 192, 196, 198	helps readers follow the order of events
photograph, caption, illustration	pp. 172–199	helps readers understand the text; gives more details
definition	p. 190: "Graybeards are monstrous waves that come quietly and quickly, threatening everything in their path."	helps readers understand the meaning of a special term
chronological sequence	p. 172: The first event takes place on October	helps readers understand the order

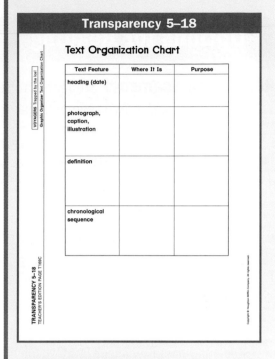

Transparency 5–18

Text Organization Chart

Text Feature	Where It Is	Purpose
heading (date)		
photograph, caption, illustration		
definition		
chronological sequence		

Practice Book page 97

Name _____

Trapped by the Ice!
Graphic Organizer Text Organization Chart

Text Organization Chart

Text Feature	Where It Is	Purpose
heading (date)	pp. 172, 174, 176, 180, 182, 184, 186, 190, 192, 196, 198 **(1 point)**	helps readers follow the order of events **(1)**
photograph, caption, illustration	pp. 172–179 **(1)**	helps readers understand the text; gives more details **(1)**
definition	p. 190 "Graybeards are monstrous waves that come quietly and quickly, threatening everything in their path." **(1)**	helps readers understand the meaning of a special term **(1)**
chronological sequence	Page 172: The first event takes place on October 27, 1915. Page 198: The last event takes place on May 20, 1916. **(1)**	helps readers understand the order of events **(1)**

Theme 5: **Voyagers** 97
Assessment Tip: Total 8 Points

Reading

Options for Reading

▶ **Reading in Segments** Students can read *Trapped by the Ice!* in two segments (pages 170–183 and 184–199) or its entirety.

▶ **Deciding About Support** Real-life action, danger, suspense, and heroism make *Trapped by the Ice!* exciting for students to read.

- Because of the familiar genre (narrative nonfiction) and the division of the story into sections (indicated by dates), most students should be able to follow On Level reading instruction.

- Students who have difficulty with vocabulary will benefit from Extra Support.

- Significantly below-level readers can listen to the Audiotape and read the Selection Summary for *Trapped by the Ice!* and then read "Iceberg Rescue" in the **Reader's Library.**

▶ **Meeting Individual Needs** Use the notes at the bottom of the pages.

MEET THE AUTHOR AND ILLUSTRATOR

Michael McCurdy

Fact File

- Michael McCurdy has illustrated nearly 200 books, including classic stories such as *The Wonderful Wizard of Oz*. He has also written many books himself.

- In art school, McCurdy was a roommate of David McPhail, another children's author and illustrator.

- To create an illustration, McCurdy usually carves a picture on a wood block, covers the carving with ink, and stamps it on paper. But it's never too late to try something new — this story is the first book McCurdy has ever illustrated with paintings.

- McCurdy lives with his family in Massachusetts, where he works on his books in a big red barn. He enjoys playing the piano and hiking.

If you'd like to learn more about Michael McCurdy, stop by Education Place.
www.eduplace.com/kids

170

 Classroom Management

On Level
Reading Card 8

While Reading: Text Organization Chart (**Practice Book** page 97); Literature Discussion (p. 182, Reading Card 8); generate questions

After Reading: Literature Discussion (p. 198); Wrapping Up Segment 1 (page 183) and Segment 2 (page 199)

Challenge
Reading Cards 7–9

While Reading: Text Organization Chart (**Practice Book** p. 97); Point of View (p. 178; Card 7); Literature Discussion (p. 182, Card 8); Heroism and Courage (p. 187; Card 9)

After Reading: Literature Discussion (p. 198); Wrapping Up Segment 1 (page 183) and Segment 2 (page 199)

English Language Learners

Intermediate and Advanced Fluency
For this long selection, encourage both individual and group reading.

For English language learners at other proficiency levels, see **Language Development Resources.**

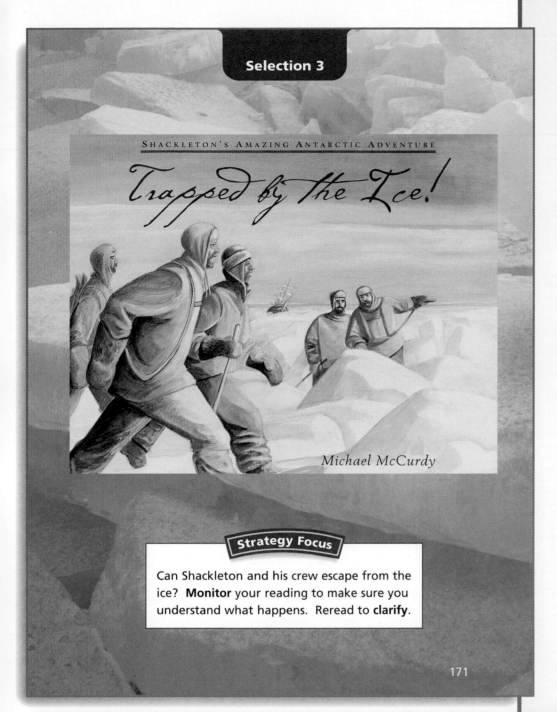

Selection 3

SHACKLETON'S AMAZING ANTARCTIC ADVENTURE

Trapped by the Ice!

Michael McCurdy

Strategy Focus

Can Shackleton and his crew escape from the ice? **Monitor** your reading to make sure you understand what happens. Reread to **clarify**.

171

Reading Segment 1
pages 171–183

Purpose Setting Have students preview the story and think about the title. Then ask them to predict what will happen in the story. Remind them to revise and add to their predictions as they read.

 Journal Writing Students can use their journal to record their original predictions and to add new ones.

Reinforcing Comprehension and Strategies

■ Remind students to use Monitor/Clarify and other strategies as they read and to add to their Text Organization Charts (**Practice Book** page 97).

■ Use the Focus Strategy notes on pages 176 and 186 to reinforce Monitor/Clarify strategies.

■ Use Supporting Comprehension questions beginning on page 172 to help students develop higher-level understanding of the text.

Extra Support: Previewing the Text

Before each segment, preview the text, using the notes below and on page 184. **While** reading, model strategies (pp. 175, 188, and 197). **After** reading, review each segment (pp. 182 and 198) before students join the Wrapping Up discussion.

Pages 172–175 Trapped and crushed by the ice, the *Endurance* cannot take Shackleton and his crew any farther. How do you think the voyagers will survive, in Antarctica with nobody around to help them?

Pages 176–179 The men face many challenges, like moving supplies to their camp, and even fighting off an attacking sea leopard! What would be difficult about these tasks? How do you think the men feel?

Pages 180–183 The men camp on ice floes until they can reach open water and steer their lifeboats to Elephant Island, the nearest land. How important is teamwork in keeping safe and surviving?

▶ Supporting Comprehension

1 What can you infer about the fact that even though Shackleton's main goal was to become the first person to cross the South Pole's ice cap, now *his only concern was for his men?* (He's a good leader who feels responsible for his crew and thinks that keeping them safe is more important than the fact that he won't achieve his goal.)

2 Why does the author describe the *Endurance* as *a sad sight*? (The ship has been the crew's home and provided warmth, travel, and safety for many months; now, it is a crushed wreck. It is a sad sight to see it transformed from what it used to be to the miserable, useless state it's now in; the men may also feel sad when looking at the ship.)

3 How do you think the crew members feel at this point? (scared, sad, worried)

Vocabulary *(page 172)*

horizon: the line where the earth and the sky meet

delay: wait until later to do something

rations: supplies, usually food, that are limited

hulk: the body of an old or wrecked ship; something large and clumsy

stranded: trapped or stuck in a difficult situation

October 27, 1915

The *Endurance* was trapped. Giant blocks of ice were slowly crushing her sides. From the deck, Sir Ernest Shackleton looked at the snow and ice that spread to the horizon. Ten months before, all he had wanted was to be the first person to cross the South Pole's ice cap.

1 Now his only concern was for his men. What would happen to them — and how much longer did the ship have before it broke apart? The *Endurance* was leaking badly. Shack could not delay.

Shack ordered his crew off the *Endurance* and camp was set up on the frozen Weddell Sea. Tools, tents, scrap lumber for firewood, sleeping bags, and what little food rations and clothing the men had left were saved from their ship, along with three lifeboats in case they ever reached open water.

2 The *Endurance* was a sad sight now, a useless hulk lying on its side. For months she had been the crew's home. Now they would have to get used to life on the ice — stranded hundreds of miles

3 from the nearest land.

172

English Language Learners

Pause after reading page 172. Ask students to say where the men are and to describe what has happened to the ship. Call on a student to read the date aloud. Discuss what communications and travel were like in 1915. Ask: Do you think anyone can rescue the sailors? Why or why not?

173

▶ Supporting Comprehension

4 Why do you think the sound of crushing wood startles the men? (Even though they probably knew that the ship might be crushed, it is still shocking to them because they didn't know when it would happen; it is loud.)

5 Why do you think the author says that the *Endurance* is *swallowed* by the Weddell Sea? (to add to the suspense by making the sea seem like something alive; to emphasize that the ship has disappeared forever)

6 What kinds of things might Shackleton, Worsley, and Wild have to think about when making a plan for what to do next? (how to travel and carry their supplies; food; water; staying warm; finding shelter; getting off the ice and on land; getting rescued or making it back home)

Vocabulary *(pages 174–175)*

startled: surprised, alarmed, or shocked

stern: the rear part of a ship or boat

tremble: to shake or shiver

skipper: captain

November 21, 1915

4 Almost one month later, the sound of crushing wood <u>startled</u> the men. It was what they had feared. Turning toward the ship's wreckage, they saw her <u>stern</u> rise slowly in the air, <u>tremble</u>, and slip quickly beneath the ice.

174

 Cross-Curricular Connection

Social Studies Keeping warm and dry on the ice was a constant challenge for the voyagers, whose gear was vastly inferior to that of adventurers today. As he evacuated the *Endurance*, Shackleton issued each man a sleeping bag and warm clothing. The sailors received the warmer reindeer skin bags, while the officers took the less protective woolen ones. All the men had windproof—but not waterproof—tunics. The voyagers camped in five linen tents, which were so thin that the light of the moon showed through.

Minutes later, the hole had frozen up over the ship. She was gone forever, swallowed by the Weddell Sea. Shack talked with the ship's skipper, Frank Worsley, and his next-in-command, Frankie Wild. Among them, they would have to decide what to do next.

5

6

175

Extra Support

Strategy Modeling

Monitor/Clarify Use this example to model the strategy.

I'm a little confused about how the Endurance sinks on page 175. I know that it's been trapped in the ice for about one month. Is there water beneath the ice? On page 174, it says that the men hear a crushing sound before the ship sinks. Maybe the ice froze around the ship so tightly that it cracked a hole in it and the ship filled up with water. That must be right.

Comprehension Skill Lesson
Sequence of Events

OBJECTIVES

Students relate story events in sequential order.

Remind students that the sequence of events is the order in which things happen in a story. In *Trapped by the Ice!* events are presented in chronological order (from first to last in time). Point out that thinking about the order of events helps readers

- understand what is happening and why
- tell how the events in a story fit together
- summarize a selection

Draw on the board a chart like the one below. Use the chart to show students how to put events in sequential order. Point out that the events do not make sense in the wrong order.

And Then What Happened?

1. The Endurance is trapped in the ice.
2.
3.

Have students copy the chart from the chalkboard and add to it as they continue listing the sequence of events. Consulting with a partner can help students decide which events are important enough to add to the list.

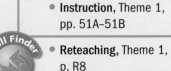

- **Instruction**, Theme 1, pp. 51A–51B
- **Reteaching**, Theme 1, p. R8
- **Review**, Theme 1, p. 83; Theme 4, p. 57

Reading

▶ **Strategy Focus: Monitor/Clarify**

Teacher/Student Modeling Discuss details on pages 176–177 that can help students clarify the original plan for reaching land. (The lifeboats, loaded with supplies, are mounted on sleds; the men are harnessed to the sleds to pull the 2,000-pound loads.) Then ask students to reread page 177 to clarify why and how the original plan is changed. (The loaded boats are too heavy to move, so the men must wait for the floating ice to carry them to open water.)

▶ **Supporting Comprehension**

7 How do you think Shackleton feels when making decisions and giving orders ? (He probably feels pressure and enormous responsibility.)

8 Why do you think Shackleton decides to try the first plan—pulling the loads instead of floating on the ice floes—even though it seems (and turns out to be) impossible? (He couldn't know for sure if they would succeed unless they tried, they didn't have many other options, and it would have been faster than floating on the ice.)

Vocabulary *(pages 176–177)*

executing: carrying out or doing

barren: having little plant or animal life

sledge: a sled, usually pulled by animals, used to carry loads across snow and ice

harnessed: wearing straps attached to a vehicle or tool such as a sled or plow

current: the path or flow of moving water, such as a river or sea

---

December 23, 1915

Executing their plan would be difficult. By pulling the lifeboats, loaded with supplies, they would try to cross the barren ice to open water. If they made it, they would use the three boats to reach the nearest land. Shack studied the unending snow and ice ahead of him. Was it possible?

7

176

 English Language Learners

MEETING INDIVIDUAL NEEDS

Taking Summary Notes Encourage students to take summary notes each time they stop reading and to reread their notes before they begin again. Pause at page 176 to model with a Think Aloud:

I know now that the boat was crushed by moving ice, so the explorers have to leave. They put everything they need on three boats that they hope will take them out of Antarctica. I will write down these notes.

Each boat was mounted on a <u>sledge</u>. <u>Harnessed</u> like horses, the men pulled, one boat at a time. Pulling 2,000-pound loads was hard work. Soon everybody was so tired and sore that no one could pull anymore. The crew would have to wait for the ice, moved by the sea's <u>current</u>, to carry them north to open water.

8

177

Revisiting the Text

Review/Maintain

Comprehension Skill Lesson
Topic, Main Idea, Supporting Detail

OBJECTIVES

Students

- identify the topic of a selection
- identify main ideas about the topic
- identify details that support the main ideas

Explain to students that

■ the topic of a selection is what it is about

■ the main idea of a paragraph or paragraphs explains the topic

■ supporting details are facts, examples, or other small pieces of information that explain (support) each main idea

Identify the topic of *Trapped by the Ice!* by asking, What is this selection mainly about? Have a student read aloud the paragraph on page 176. Model the skill for students by identifying the main idea (executing the plan would be hard) and supporting details. (The men would have to haul the lifeboats, loaded with supplies, all the way to open water.) Then have students read page 177. Have students complete the chart below.

Main Idea	Supporting Detail
Pulling the lifeboats was hard work.	All the men got so tired that they couldn't pull anymore.

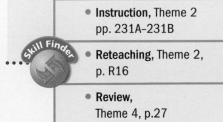

- **Instruction,** Theme 2 pp. 231A–231B

- **Reteaching,** Theme 2, p. R16

- **Review,** Theme 4, p.27

Skill Finder

▶ Supporting Comprehension

9 How does the author tell you that the men eat penguins and seals? (by writing that the men who provide food for everyone have to search farther because penguins and seals were becoming scarce)

10 How is Tom like a penguin to the sea leopard? (Like a penguin, Tom is prey to the sea leopard.)

11 What reversal (a situation that suddenly turns into the opposite) does the author tell about on page 178? (The sea leopard tries to eat humans and is eaten by humans instead.)

Vocabulary *(page 178)*

scarce: not enough

lunged: moved forward suddenly

stalking: moving secretly while tracking prey

---

9 Over the next few months, food was always a concern, and it was Tom Orde-Lees's job to find it. Penguins and seals were growing scarce. To find meat to eat, hunters had to go farther away.

10 This was dangerous. Once, when Tom was skiing back to camp, a monstrous head burst from the ice. A giant sea leopard lunged at Tom, only to slip quickly back into the dark water, stalking Tom from below, as sea leopards do when they hunt penguins.

Tom tripped and fell. The huge animal lunged again, this time springing out of the water and right onto the ice. Back on his feet, Tom tried to get away. He cried for help, and Frankie Wild rushed over from camp carrying a rifle.

11 The sea leopard now charged Frankie, who dropped calmly to one knee, took careful aim, and fired three shots. The sea leopard fell dead. There was plenty to eat for days afterward!

178

MEETING INDIVIDUAL NEEDS · **Challenge**

Reading Cards 7

Point of View

The selection is told from the third-person point of view. A narrator outside the action describes the voyage. Have students discuss how the story might be different if it were told from the first-person point of view.

- Would the reader feel closer or farther away from the perils of the voyage?

- What details would the reader miss out on?

- Would the reader trust the narrator more or less—and be more or less likely to believe the information?

179

► ## Supporting Comprehension

12 In the first paragraph, why do you think the author describes the men in such detail? (to help the reader understand what they look like, how they feel, and how hard their voyage has been)

13 How does the author remind you that Shackleton continues to observe the men and revise his plan as needed? (by describing how Shackleton revises his plan after seeing that all his men would not survive a 700-mile journey in an open boat)

14 Based on Shackleton's decision, what can you predict about the open boat journey to Elephant Island? (It will be very difficult and possibly deadly, but not as potentially dangerous or hard as sailing to South Georgia Island.)

Vocabulary *(page 180)*

sapped: weakened

floes: large sheets of floating ice

grueling: very tiring

April 8, 1916

The men smelled terrible. During their five and a half months on the ice they hadn't had a bath. Clothes were greasy and worn thin, and **12** they rubbed against the men's skin, causing painful sores. Hands were cracked from the cold and wind, and hunger <u>sapped</u> everyone's strength.

By now, the ice <u>floes</u> were breaking up into smaller and smaller pieces all around the men as they drifted closer to the edge of the polar sea. Shack thought it was a good time to launch the lifeboats, rigged with small canvas sails. He **13** knew his men could not all survive the <u>grueling</u> 800-mile open-boat journey to the whaling station **14** on South Georgia Island. So he decided to try to reach Elephant Island first.

180

English Language Learners

Role-Playing Dialogue Pause at page 180 to ask students to imagine how the men are feeling. Challenge partners to create short dialogues, imagining they are the explorers on the trip. Instruct them to include "I feel" and "I hope" statements. Have volunteers role-play for the class.

181

▶ ## Supporting Comprehension

15 Do you think it is just the noise that the killer whales make that keeps the men from sleeping well? (No, it is also the strange, unfamiliar situation and the possibility that the whales might attack or injure them or damage their boats or their ice floe.)

16 How was the crevasse that Ernie Holness falls in formed? (A powerful wave hit an ice floe with such force that it made a crack in the ice floe. The crack traveled quickly across the ice floe, splitting it in two and forming a crevasse.)

17 How does the author create suspense by choosing the words *wriggling shape* to describe what Shackleton first observes in the crevasse? (The words *wriggling shape* make you think that either a man has fallen into the crevasse and that he is weak, helpless, and possibly injured, or that an animal is lurking there.)

Vocabulary *(page 182)*

crevasse: deep hole or crack

---

11 p.m. April 8, 1916

Steering around the blocks of ice was hard. The boats bumped into ice floes — or crashed into icebergs. As night fell, the boats were pulled up onto a big floe and the tents were raised. But sleeping was difficult with damp bags and blankets, and with noisy killer whales circling around.

15

One night, Shack suddenly felt something was wrong. He shook Frankie, and they crawled out of their tent for a look. A huge wave smacked headlong into the floe with a great thud, and the floe began to split into two pieces. The crack was headed straight toward Tent Number 4!

16

Then Shack heard a splash. Looking into the crevasse, he saw a wriggling shape below in the dark water. It was a sleeping bag — with Ernie Holness inside! Shack acted quickly. Reaching down, he pulled the soggy bag out of the water with one mighty jerk. And just in time, too — within seconds the two great blocks of ice crashed back together.

17

182

Extra Support

Segment 1: Review

Before students join the whole class for Wrapping Up on page 183, have them

- check their predictions

- take turns modeling Monitor/Clarify and any other strategies they used

- help you add to **Transparency 5–18**, check their Text Organization Chart on **Practice Book** page 97, and use it to Summarize

---

On Level   Challenge

Reading Card 8

Literature Discussion

In mixed-ability groups of five or six, students can discuss their own questions and the discussion prompts on Reading Card 8.

- What challenges do Shackleton and his men face before and after the *Endurance* is trapped by the ice?

- How do you think Shackleton felt after the *Endurance* was trapped? How do you think the crew felt?

End of Segment 1: pages 170–183

Wrapping Up Segment 1
pages 170–183

First, provide Extra Support for students who need it (page 182). Then bring all students together.

- **Review Predictions/Purpose** Have students compare what they thought would happen with the selection itself. Have them discuss which predictions needed to be revised.

- **Model Strategies** Refer students to the **Strategies Poster** and have them take turns modeling Monitor/Clarify and other strategies they used as they read. Provide models if needed (page 175).

- **Share Group Discussions** Have students share their questions and literature discussions.

- **Summarize** Have students use their text organization charts to summarize what has happened in the story so far.

Comprehension/Critical Thinking

1 Why do all the voyagers camp out for five and a half months on the ice? Why do they sail in the boats after this time has passed? (Their ship has sunk and they are unable to pull the loaded lifeboats, so they must wait for the sea's current to move the ice floes—with them on top—to open water; they've reached open water and are now trying to reach the closest, safer land, Elephant Island.) **Cause and Effect**

2 Do you think Shackleton is a good leader? Explain your answer. (Yes, because he consults with others, adjusts his plans to changing conditions, and shows concern for his men.) **Making Judgements**

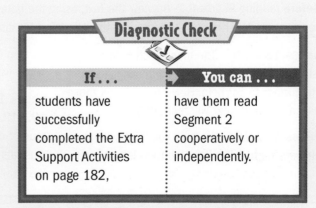

Diagnostic Check

If . . .	You can . . .
students have successfully completed the Extra Support Activities on page 182,	have them read Segment 2 cooperatively or independently.

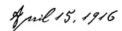

Beginning of Segment 2:
pages 184–199

Reading Segment 2

pages 184–199

Purpose Setting Have students summarize the story so far and predict what will happen as Shackleton and his men push on toward the whaling station. Then ask students to read pages 184–199 to check their predictions.

Journal Writing Students can record any revisions they make to their predictions and explain what made them change their minds.

Vocabulary *(page 184)*

savage: wild

furiously: violently

dehydration: sickness caused by not having enough water

quench: to satisfy

exhausting: very tiring

jagged: ragged, full of parts sticking up and out

April 13, 1916

Finally, the men reached open water. The savage sea slammed furiously into the three little boats — called the *James Caird*, the *Dudley Docker*, and the *Stancomb Wills*. Tall waves lifted them up and down like a roller coaster. Blinding sea spray blew into the men's faces. Most of them became seasick.

Worst of all, they were very thirsty, because seawater had spoiled the fresh water. The men's tongues had swelled so much from dehydration they could hardly swallow. Shack had his men suck on frozen seal meat to quench their thirst. They *had* to make land. They had to get to Elephant Island!

April 15, 1916

After an exhausting week battling the sea, the men nearly lost all hope. Big Tom Crean tried to cheer the men with a song, but nothing worked. Finally, something appeared in the distance. Shack called across to Frank Worsley in the *Dudley Docker*, "There she is, Skipper!" It was land. It was Elephant Island at last. It looked terribly barren, with jagged 3,500-foot peaks rising right up out of the sea, yet it was the only choice the men had.

184

MEETING INDIVIDUAL NEEDS **Extra Support: Previewing the Text**

Before reading Segment 2, preview the text, using the notes below. **While** reading, model strategies (pp. 188 and 197). **After** reading, review the segment (p. 198) before students join the Wrapping Up discussion.

pages 184–187 The men reach Elephant Island, but some must travel with Shackleton still further to get help. How do you think those asked to sail farther will feel? Why?

pages 188–191 What do you think will be challenging or difficult for the men left to camp on Elephant Island, waiting for Shackleton to return with help?

pages 192–195 The illustration on pages 192–193 shows that Shackleton and his men reach South Georgia Island. What does the illustration on pages 194–195 suggest about the challenge that they face there?

pages 196–199 Shackleton tries to reach a whaling station on the opposite side of the island, where he may find people who can help. What equipment do you think the men will need to make this journey? Will they be able to return and rescue the remaining men on Elephant Island?

185

▶ Strategy Focus: Monitor/Clarify

Student Modeling Ask students to clarify Shackleton's decision to take five men on to South Georgia Island, leaving twenty-two men behind on Elephant Island. If necessary, use the following prompt:

What things must Shackleton consider when deciding the best way to reach safety?

▶ Supporting Comprehension

18 Reread the first sentence on page 186. Why do you think the author uses a dash instead of a comma between the last two items in the series? (to draw special attention to the wind on Elephant Island, which was so strong that it blew the tents away)

19 Most or all of the men probably have frozen fingers. Why do you think the author describes only Chippy's condition? (Because, as the carpenter, Chippy has to have use of his fingers to do his job.)

Vocabulary *(pages 186–187)*

<u>pitched:</u> put up (tents)

<u>deserted:</u> empty; not lived in, or having few or no people

---

April 24, 1916

18 Elephant Island was nothing but rock, ice, snow — and wind. Tents were <u>pitched</u> but quickly blew away. Without resting, Shack planned his departure for South Georgia Island. There he would try to get help. Twenty-two men would stay behind while Shack and a crew braved the 800-mile journey in the worst winter seas on earth.

186

 English Language Learners

Making Predictions Pause after reading page 187 to help students make predictions. Ask: What do you think will happen? Do you think all the men on Elephant Island will survive? Why or why not? Do you think that Shackleton's brave crew will make it to the whaling station? What makes you think that?

The five ablest men were picked: Frank Worsley; Big Tom Crean; the carpenter, Chippy McNeish; and two seamen, Tim McCarthy and John Vincent. With frozen fingers and a few tools, Chippy prepared the *Caird* for the rough journey ahead. Only nine days after the men had first sighted the <u>deserted</u> island, Shack and his crew of five were on open water once again.

19

187

MEETING INDIVIDUAL NEEDS

Challenge

Reading Card
9

Heroism and Courage

Most students would probably agree that Shackleton and the crew members are courageous, and even heroic. Have students discuss what they believe bravery and heroism are. Is bravery fighting a sea leopard, putting aside your own self for the sake of others, or both? Can a person be a hero in his or her everyday life? Students can write or tell about examples of courage and heroism they've heard about or witnessed in their own lives. Then have students look through the selection to list examples of ways Shackleton and his men are brave and heroic.

Revisiting the Text

Tested Skill

Comprehension Skill Lesson
Text Organization

OBJECTIVES

Students identify the section to which a given heading and a topic apply.

Explain to students that readers can use text organization to recognize the main ideas in a selection. Features of text organization include

- titles

- headings

- illustrations

Write on the board the heading *April 24, 1916.* Ask students to locate the section in their books to which the heading applies. (pages 186–189) Then give students the main idea *Preparing for the Trip to South Georgia Island.* Ask students to raise their hands when they can identify the page of their books to which the main idea applies. When all students have raised their hands, call on someone to give the answer. (page 187)

Write more main ideas and headings on the board. Have students work in pairs or in groups to identify the pages on which the headings or main ideas appear. Alternatively, you may wish to pass out cards or strips of paper with main ideas, headings, and page numbers on them, then have students try to find other students with the appropriate corresponding page numbers, main ideas, or headings as necessary.

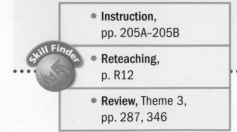

Skill Finder

- **Instruction,** pp. 205A–205B

- **Reteaching,** p. R12

- **Review,** Theme 3, pp. 287, 346

▶ Supporting Comprehension

20 What might have happened if the men on Elephant Island hadn't had materials to build a permanent shelter? (They might have frozen to death.)

21 What do you think are the challenges of living in the dark and cramped hut without knowing when or if Shack will return? (not fighting in such close quarters; not giving up hope; the cold, wet darkness and the smell)

22 How, in only a few words, does the author show you what life is like for the men left behind on Elephant Island? (by choosing vivid details, such as the bird droppings that smelled terrible as they melted in the heat of the hut)

Vocabulary *(page 188)*

permanent: meant to last for a long time

hut: small, simple house or shelter

cramped: crowded

wick: the cord that burns on a candle or a lamp

frigate birds: a type of sea bird

---

20 For the men who stayed behind, permanent shelter was now needed or they would freeze to death. Frankie Wild had the men turn the two remaining boats upside down, side by side. Then the boats were covered with canvas and a cookstove was put inside.

21 The hut was dark and cramped, lit only by a burning wick. And something happened that the **22** men had not expected: heat from their bodies and the stove melted the ice under them as well as piles of frozen bird droppings left for years by the frigate birds and penguins. The smell was terrible!

Day after day the men looked toward the sea, wondering if Shack would make it back to rescue them. How long would they be left here? Was Shack all right?

188

Extra Support

Strategy Modeling

Monitor/Clarify Use this example to model the strategy.

How do the boats keep the men on Elephant Island warm? I'll go back and reread. The boats are turned upside down and covered with canvas, and a stove is put inside. The stove keeps the air under the boats warm. Yes, I see. It says that the hut—that's the upside-down boat—was cramped. That's because all the men are under there.

189

▶ Supporting Comprehension

23 How and why does the author shift the setting on page 190? (To continue the story of what happens on Shackleton's voyage, the author shifts the scene from the men left behind on Elephant Island to Shackleton's small group sailing on to South Georgia Island.)

24 How does the author build suspense in his description of the graybeard? (First the author explains what a graybeard is, which makes the reader afraid that the men will face one. Next the author shows Shackleton screaming from the tiller, which makes the reader aware—before all the men know—that a graybeard is ahead.)

25 How do you think the jagged rocks in the hull of the *Caird "saved the day"*? (by holding the boat down, so that it stayed upright as it spun around in the giant wave)

Vocabulary *(page 190)*

rancid: having a nasty smell or taste

tiller: part used to steer a boat

impact: crash

bailed: got water out of a boat by filling containers and emptying them, over and over

hull: the body or frame of a ship or boat

capsizing: turning bottom side up

May 5, 1916

23 The *Caird* made her way through the storm-tossed seas, while Shack and his men drank <u>rancid</u> seal oil to prevent seasickness. The ocean swelled and hissed and broke over the small boat as the men worried about the terrible graybeards found in these waters. Graybeards are monstrous waves that come quietly and quickly, threatening everything in their path.

24 The men had to battle to keep the boat free of ice, because any added weight might sink the *Caird*. Suddenly, Shack screamed from the <u>tiller</u>. The men turned around to face the biggest wave they had ever seen. It was a graybeard!

25 The boat shuddered on <u>impact</u> as the mountain of water spun it around like a top. Water filled the *Caird* while the men <u>bailed</u> furiously. Jagged rocks in her <u>hull</u>, which Chippy had used to keep the boat from <u>capsizing</u>, saved the day.

190

English Language Learners

Ask students to choose a scene that they liked from the story so far. Ask them to write a diary entry as if they were a character from the story experiencing that scene. Model diary entries for students by choosing your own favorite scene and writing an entry on the board or on an overhead projector.

191

▶ **Supporting Comprehension**

26 What new problems do the men have as they finally approach South Georgia Island? (Their supply of freshwater has run out; they are terribly weakened; they have to land on the opposite side of the island from the whaling station; for nine hours, they fight the worst hurricane they've had.)

27 How do you think the author chose which parts of the men's seventeen days at sea to include in the selection? (The author probably thought about which parts of the seventeen days are the most dramatic or the most important to the larger story of Shackleton's voyage.)

28 Based on the facts in this part of the selection, would you rather have been part of the crew that stayed behind on Elephant Island or part of the crew that traveled with Shackleton to South Georgia Island? Explain your answer. (Answers will vary.)

Vocabulary *(pages 192–193)*

dimly: not seen easily or clearly

miraculously: amazingly; seemingly impossibly

May 10, 1916

26
27 Finally, after seventeen grueling days at sea, young McCarthy shouted, "Land ho!" South Georgia Island lay dimly ahead. The whaling station was on the other side of the island, but the men had to land *now* or die. Their fresh water was gone, and they were too weak to battle the sea to the other side of the island.

192

While the men planned their landing attempt, they were hit by the worst hurricane they had ever encountered. For nine terrible hours they fought to keep afloat. <u>Miraculously</u>, just as things looked hopeless, the sea calmed enough to allow the *Caird* to land safely on the rocky beach of King Haakon Bay. 28

193

 English Language Learners

Adjectives The author uses well chosen adjectives throughout the story. On pages 192–193 are some examples of these strong adjectives. Pair students with English-speaking partners or work as a group to list the adjectives on these pages. These include: *grueling, weak, worst, terrible,* and *hopeless.* Discuss how these words contribute to the overall feeling of the story.

Revisiting the Text

Writer's Craft Lesson
Setting

 OBJECTIVES

Students identify elements of setting in a nonfiction narrative.

Explain that setting is the time and place of the action or events in a story or nonfiction selection. It is the background in which the fictional or real-life characters live and act. Ask students what the general, overall setting of this selection is. (Antarctica) Then read aloud the following from page 192:

> *May 10, 1916. Finally, after seventeen grueling days at sea, young McCarthy shouted, "Land ho!" South Georgia Island lay dimly ahead. The whaling station lay on the other side of the island, but the men had to land now or die.*

Point out that, in this passage, the author makes more clear and specific the general Antarctic setting of the story. He gives a date and details that show the men's location in relation to their goal. For example, the phrase *"Land ho!"* shows that the men are in the sea near the coast of South Georgia Island.

Have students identify other words or phrases on pages 192–193 that show the setting of the scene. Then ask students to find a phrase on page 193 that shows a change, from sea to land, in the setting. (the sea calmed enough to allow the *Caird* to land safely on the rocky beach of King Haakon Bay)

▶ Supporting Comprehension

29 On page 194, the author shifts the focus of the story from the whole group that pushed on to South Georgia Island to what each individual man in the group is doing. Why do you think the author shifts the focus as he does? (to help readers relate more deeply to the story by making a personal connection with the individuals involved; to emphasize that the group of healthy, strong men gets smaller and smaller as the voyage continues)

30 If you were in the party on South Georgia Island, would you rather be in the weaker group left behind to rest in the cave or in the stronger group that attempts the dangerous mountain hike to the whaling station? Explain your answer. (Answers will vary.)

31 How do you think Shackleton, Big Tom, and Skipper Worsley feel when they set out on their hike to the whaling station? (nervous or scared, because it's the most dangerous hike they've ever faced; excited or happy, because they've already traveled far and survived much, and because they are close to reaching people who might be able to help them rescue the others and return home)

29
30
The men landed near a small cave with a freshwater spring nearby. The cave would become a temporary home for John Vincent and Chippy McNeish. Both had suffered too much on the voyage and could not survive the long hike across the island to the whaling station. Tim McCarthy stayed behind to take care of the two sick men. Fortunately, water for drinking, wood from old shipwrecks for fire, and albatross eggs and seals to eat meant those who stayed behind would be all right while waiting for their rescue.

194

Vocabulary (page 194)

temporary: lasting for only a short time

albatross: a large sea bird

But Shack, Big Tom, and Skipper Worsley would have to climb over a series of jagged ridges that cut the island in half like a saw blade. All they could carry was a little Primus stove, fuel for six meals, fifty feet of rope, and an ice ax. Their only food consisted of biscuits and light rations that hung in socks around their necks. On their eighth day ashore, May 18, it was time to set off on the most dangerous climb they had ever attempted. **31**

195

Reading Fluency

- **Rereading for Fluency:** Have students choose a favorite part of the story to reread to a partner, or suggest that they read pages 194–195. Encourage students to read with feeling and expression.

- **Assessing Fluency** See guidelines in the Theme Assessment Wrap-Up, pages 206–207A.

Reading

▶ Supporting Comprehension

32 What are the many challenges of the men's hike across the mountains? (They are weakened, exhausted, and poorly equipped when they start; they have hardly any food or sleep while hiking; they climb up mountains three times only to find them impassable and have to go back down; they have to slide 1,500 feet down the mountain; they have to lower themselves by rope through an icy, thirty-foot waterfall.)

33 What are the risks of sliding down the mountain on Shackleton's makeshift toboggan? Why do the men laugh when they hit the snowbank? (They could have crashed into a something or been thrown off the toboggan and fallen 1,500 feet down the mountain, risking serious injury or death; they laugh because they are happy and relieved to have defeated yet another risk, against great odds, and survived unhurt.)

34 How does the author hold your interest in the last stages of the hike to the whaling station? (by presenting interesting details, such as the men at the whaling station looking like insects from a distance, and stressing, through Shackleton's caution on the descent, that the voyage is perilous up to the very end)

May 19, 1916

32 Three times the men struggled up mountains, only to find that the <u>terrain</u> was <u>impassable</u> on the other side. The men stopped only to eat a soup called "hoosh," to nibble on stale biscuits, or to nap five minutes, with each man taking a turn awake so that there would be someone to wake the others.

On and on the exhausted men hiked. From one mountain <u>summit</u> they saw that night was coming fast. Being caught on a peak at night meant certain death. They had to make a dangerous <u>gamble</u>. **33** Shack assembled a <u>makeshift</u> toboggan from the coiled-up rope and the men slid 1,500 feet down the mountain in one big slide. Despite the <u>perilous</u> landing, they couldn't help but laugh with relief after they had crashed, unhurt, into a large snowbank.

The men had survived the long slide, but danger still lay ahead. They had been hiking for more than thirty hours now without sleep. Finally, all three heard the sound of a far-off whistle. Was it the whaling station?

They climbed a ridge and looked down. Yes, there it was! Two whale-catchers were docked at the pier. From this distance, the men at the station were the size of insects.

34 Shack fought against being too <u>reckless</u>. The three still had to lower themselves down a thirty-foot waterfall by hanging on to their rope and swinging through the icy <u>torrents</u>. At last, the ragged explorers stumbled toward the station. They had done it!

196

Vocabulary *(page 196)*

terrain: land, ground, or earth

impassable: not able to be crossed or traveled through

summit: the highest point

gamble: a risky action

makeshift: something used as a temporary substitute for something else

perilous: very dangerous

reckless: not careful or cautious

torrents: violent, fast-moving streams of liquid

197

Revisiting the Text

Genre Lesson
Narrative Nonfiction

OBJECTIVES

Students identify elements of narrative nonfiction in the selection.

Explain to students that narrative nonfiction text

- tells about real people, animals, places, or events

- is told in story form

- gives facts about the subject

- usually describes events in chronological order

- may include photographs, captions, illustrations, and graphic aids to convey information

Point out that the text on page 196 tells about real people (Shack, Big Tom, and Skipper Worsley), in a real place (South Georgia Island), doing a real thing (crossing mountains to reach the whaling station at the other end of the island). Then ask students to identify other details from the scene that make *Trapped by the Ice!* a piece of narrative nonfiction.

Have small groups list examples of narrative nonfiction traits in the selection. Allow time for groups to compare their work.

Have students point out characteristics of narrative nonfiction as they continue to read the selection.

 Extra Support

Strategy Modeling

Phonics/Decoding Use this example to model the strategy.

When I look at the word t-o-b-o-g-g-a-n, *I notice the shorter word* to. *I think* b-o-g *probably has the short vowel sound because there's a single vowel followed by a consonant.* /bahg/ *The last part probably has the short vowel sound like in the word* man, /gan/. *When I put it all together, I say* /too•bahg•gan/. *I've got it. The word is* /tuh•BAHG•uhn/. *That's a kind of sled.*

▶ Supporting Comprehension

35 From the facts in the selection, what can you infer about Thoralf Sørlle? (By Sørlle's concern for the men in their terrible condition and the tears that well up in his eyes when he recognizes Shackleton, it can be inferred that he is a kind, caring person.)

36 How can you figure out the meaning of the words *pack ice* on page 198? (From the sentence context. The phrase *to break through* and the adjective *winter* are context clues that show the meaning, "a thick mass of ice.")

37 What kind of summary does the author provide at the end of the story? (The author summarizes the rescue efforts that end with all of Shackleton's men finally reaching safety.)

4 p.m. May 20, 1916

Thoralf Sørlle, the manager of the whaling station, heard a knock outside his office and opened the door. He looked hard at the ragged clothes and blackened faces of the men who stood before him. "Do I know you?" he asked.

35

"I'm Shackleton," came the reply. Tears welled up in Sørlle's eyes as he recognized his old friend's voice.

The three explorers received a hero's welcome from the whaling crew. The whalers knew that no one had ever done what Shack had accomplished. The next day, Skipper Worsley took a boat and picked up McCarthy, Vincent, and McNeish while Shack began preparations for the Elephant Island rescue.

36

37

It would take more than three months — and four attempts — to break through the winter pack ice and save the stranded men. But Shack finally did it — and without any loss of life. The men were glad to have a ship's deck once again under their feet. Finally, they were going home!

198

Extra Support

Segment 2 Review

Before students join in Wrapping Up on page 199, have them:

- review and discuss the accuracy of their predictions
- take turns modeling the reading strategies they used
- complete their Text Organization Charts
- summarize the entire selection

On Level / Challenge

Literature Discussion

Have small groups of students discuss the story, using their own questions or the questions in Think About the Selection on page 200.

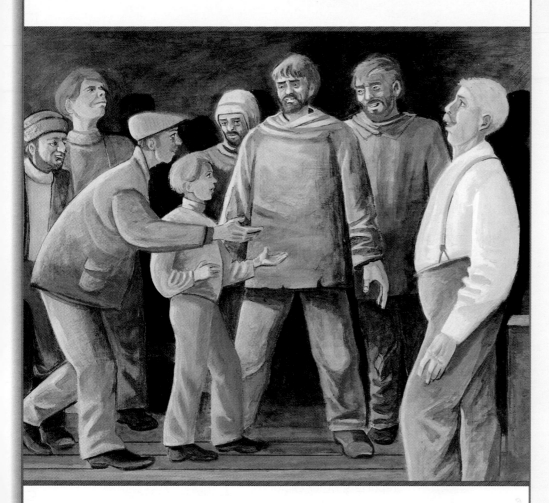

Wrapping Up Segment 2
pages 184–199

Provide Extra Support for students who need it (page 198). Then bring all students together.

■ **Review Predictions/Purpose** Have students discuss whether their predictions were or were not accurate.

■ **Model Strategies** Have students tell how they used the Monitor/Clarify strategy, and then have them take turns modeling it. Ask what other strategies they found helpful while reading.

■ **Share Group Discussions** Have students share their questions and literature discussions. Invite them to share their opinions of whether Shackleton is a hero.

■ **Summarize** Have students use their Text Organization Charts to recall and summarize the main events of the story.

Comprehension/Critical Thinking

1 Why do you think the author uses headings, in the form of dates, to introduce each section of the story? (to help readers follow the order of events in a story that takes place over many months) **Text Organization**

2 Throughout the selection, why do you think the author chooses to refer to Shackleton as *"Shack"*? Do you think this is a good idea? Use facts from the story to support your answer. (Answers will vary.) **Making Judgments**

End of Segment 2:
pages 184–199

English Language Learners

As a class or in two groups, rewrite the story as a short skit. Assign tasks to students, including characters, authors, set designers (those who arrange the tables and chairs), and costumers (those who gather hats, coats, and mittens). Check the script for accuracy before students begin practicing. If the skit is brief enough, encourage students to memorize their lines. Perform for each other with classroom lights off, to set the mood.

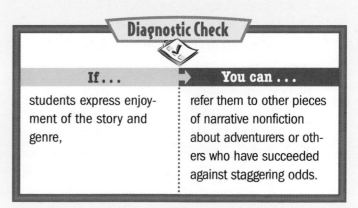

Diagnostic Check

If . . .	You can . . .
students express enjoyment of the story and genre,	refer them to other pieces of narrative nonfiction about adventurers or others who have succeeded against staggering odds.

Responding

> ## Think About the Selection

Discuss or Write Have students discuss or write their answers. Sample answers are provided; accept reasonable responses that are supported with evidence from the story.

1 **Making Judgments** Answers will vary.

2 **Making Inferences** The crew members left behind were probably mostly grateful that their lives were spared. They were left in an area with shelter, food, and water. However, they were probably also scared or worried that Shackleton wouldn't be able to find help and make it back to rescue them.

3 **Making Judgments** Answers will vary. Possible answers: a person would need to be able to withstand hardships, to be physically fit, to work well in a team, to be creative and able to think of ideas and make plans, quickly and under pressure, to be able to adapt to change and new situations or circumstances, and to remain hopeful.

4 **Making Judgments** Answers will vary.

5 **Drawing Conclusions** Shackleton was a hero because of his leadership in surviving incredible hardships without losing any members of his crew.

6 **Connecting/Comparing** Compare and Contrast Shackleton's voyage and the voyage of the *Mayflower* were alike in that the people aboard the ships were traveling into the unknown. Both voyages were attempting to be the first to achieve a goal, both experienced hardships at sea. The people aboard the *Mayflower* were in search of religious freedom while Shackleton and his crew were attempting to be the first to cross the South Pole's ice cap. The *Mayflower* journey took place nearly 300 years earlier and included families while the *Endurance* included explorers and crew.

Think About the Selection

1. What do you think would have been the most difficult part of Shackleton's Antarctic voyage?

2. When Shackleton went to find help, how do you think the crew members who were left behind felt?

3. Name some qualities a person would need to survive a voyage like Shackleton's.

4. Would you have gone back with Shackleton to rescue the men on Elephant Island? Explain your answer.

5. Why do people call Shackleton a hero even though he didn't succeed in crossing the South Pole's ice cap?

6. **Connecting/Comparing** How is Shackleton's sea voyage like the *Mayflower* voyage? How is it different?

Informing

Write a Speech

Shackleton gave speeches telling people about his adventures. Choose a group Shackleton might have spoken to, such as reporters, other explorers, or students. Write a short speech Shackleton might have given to this group.

Tips

- Say *hello* and *good-bye* to the group. At the end, thank them for listening.
- Choose only a few parts of the voyage. Describe them in detail.
- Read your speech aloud to hear how it sounds.

200

MEETING INDIVIDUAL NEEDS
English Language Learners

Beginning/Preproduction Ask students to draw a scene from the story. Then help them write a caption for the drawing.

Early Production/Speech Emergence Ask students to retell the story based on the illustrations. Have each student take a turn.

Intermediate and Advanced Fluency Ask: What qualities do you think an explorer needs to have? How has exploration changed?

Science

Investigate Ice

In a small group, talk about the way water freezes into ice and melts back into water. Then discuss the following questions.

- Why doesn't the stove melt the ice at the men's first camp? (pages 174–175)

- How can the ice carry Shackleton's crew north? (page 177)

- Why do the ice floes break up at the edge of the polar sea? (page 180)

Social Studies

Make a Time Line

Record Shackleton's journey on a time line. On paper, draw a straight line. For each date, draw and label a dot on the line. Below each dot, write what happened on that date. Keep the events in order from left to right.

Bonus Figure out when Shackleton began his journey and when he rescued the men on Elephant Island. Add these events to your time line.

Internet

Take a Web Field Trip

You've read about three exciting voyages — now do some exploring of your own! Visit Education Place and link to Web sites for young travelers. **www.eduplace.com/kids**

201

Personal Response

Invite volunteers to share their personal responses to *Trapped by the Ice!* As an alternative, ask students to write reviews in their journals, to draw pictures of scenes in the selection, or to respond in their own way.

▶ Comprehension Check

Assign **Practice Book** page 98 to assess students' understanding of the selection.

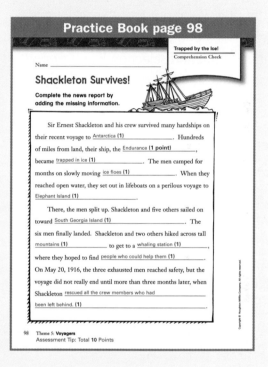

English Language Learners

Have English language learners work with English speakers to prepare Shackleton's speech. As an alternative, have English language learners prepare the questions that reporters and other listeners may have asked. For the Social Studies activity, list the important events of the story randomly on the board. Challenge pairs of students to reorder the events correctly. Show an example of a time line before asking the students to make their own. Then they can make a final time line with sketches and sentence labels.

End-of-Selection Assessment

Selection Test Use the test in the **Teacher's Resource Blackline Masters** to assess selection comprehension and vocabulary.

Student Self-Assessment Have students assess their reading with additional questions such as

- What parts of this selection were difficult for me? Why?

- What strategies helped me understand the story?

- Would I recommend this story to my friends? Why?

Media Link

pages 202–205

▶ ## Skill: How to Read a Photo Essay

Read aloud the title. Point out that "Shackleton's Real-Life Voyage" is a photo essay. Since it differs from a narrative nonfiction selection like *Trapped by the Ice!*, students should read it differently. Instead of focusing mainly on the words, they should focus equally on the photos to understand the topic. Remind students to maintain a dual focus on the words and photos.

Impress upon the class that, while many of the images in *Trapped by the Ice!* are reconstructed by an artist, these photos are actual moments of drama that are frozen in time. Emphasize that in a photo essay each photograph, sentence, and caption gives important information that places the photo in context. Have students read each step in the box in the left column on page 202.

■ Students should begin by **reading** the title and introductory text. Have them get an overview of the link by **scanning** the photos.

■ Next, students should **view** each photo in order, **reading** the corresponding captions as they go along.

■ Remind students to focus on the **details** of individual photos. How does each image add to their **understanding** of the topic?

Media Link

Skill: How to Read a Photo Essay

❶ **Read** the title and introduction. **Scan** the photos.

❷ **View** the photos one at a time.

❸ **Read** the caption that describes each photo.

❹ **Note details** in the photos. Ask yourself what each photo shows you and how it helps you understand the topic.

Shackleton's Real-Life Voyage

Frank Hurley

The story of Shackleton's Antarctic journey is so amazing, it's hard to believe it really happened. But it did, and everyone survived. One crew member, Frank Hurley, even took photos during the voyage.

Hurley didn't know if he would return home. He wasn't sure if anyone would ever see his photos. However, he never gave up hope. He worked hard to protect the photos from ice, snow, water, wind, and freezing cold. Today, his photos still help people understand what this incredible adventure was like.

Hurley photographed the entire crew soon after the ship was caught in the ice.

202

MEETING INDIVIDUAL NEEDS
Classroom Management

All Students

Reading the Photo Essay Involve all students in the activities under How to Read a Photo Essay, Noting Visual Details Chart, Visual Literacy Lesson, and Comprehension Check. Pair visual learners and students who learn by speaking or listening to study the link together. One student can read and clarify the text while the other student points out important elements in the photos. Have students periodically refer back to the selection *Trapped by the Ice!* to help them to contextualize the images.

The *Endurance* was slowly crushed by the powerful ice.

203

▶ Noting Visual Details Chart

Have students copy the following chart. Walk them through the examples shown below, then ask them to fill out charts for each of the remaining photos in the link. Prompt students to fill in their charts based on inferences drawn from the photographic details combined with their reading of the captions and *Trapped by the Ice!*

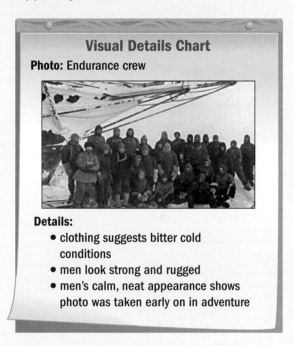

Visual Details Chart

Photo: Endurance crew

Details:
- clothing suggests bitter cold conditions
- men look strong and rugged
- men's calm, neat appearance shows photo was taken early on in adventure

Purpose Setting Have students read "Shackleton's Real-Life Voyage" to supplement their understanding of the crew's dire situation and how the voyagers overcame it. Encourage students to use the Evaluate strategy as they read to decide how effectively the photo essay shows what it was like to be a member of the Antarctic journey.

MEETING INDIVIDUAL NEEDS

Extra Support

Primary Sources

Some students may have difficulty understanding the significance of Hurley's photographs, which will likely not appear as spectacular to students as photographs in geography magazines today. Emphasize that Hurley's photographs are an eyewitness report that supports the stories the voyagers told after their ordeal and extends their experience to viewers today. This fact makes the photos especially valuable. Explain that such eyewitness accounts are called primary sources, and help historians and writers greatly in their work to tell readers what *really* happened.

The crew tried to chop a path out of the ice. But the ice was too solid and thick, and there was too much of it.

Media Link *continued*
pages 202–205

pages 202–205

Revisiting the Text

Visual Literacy
Photography

OBJECTIVES

Student discussion promotes appreciation of primary source photos.

Explain that a photographer can strongly influence what people learn about an event by his or her choice of subject, lighting, and camera angle. Following are some possible points of discussion to lead students to develop a deeper appreciation of the photos featured in the essay:

■ Have students discuss what, specifically, makes these photos so dramatic and exciting.

■ Ask students to identify their favorite photo from the essay. Have them explain their choice. Ask them to list as many descriptive adjectives as they can.

■ Impress upon students that during the period these photos were taken, photography was a much more difficult, cumbersome process than it is today, requiring far more effort and preparation.

As the ice destroyed their ship, the crew had to camp in the freezing cold.

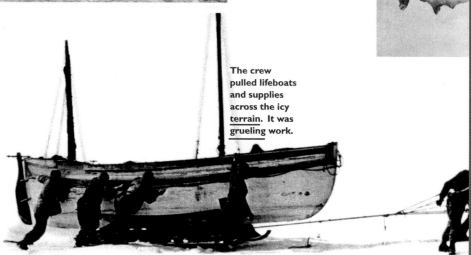

The crew pulled lifeboats and supplies across the icy terrain. It was grueling work.

204

Vocabulary *(page 204)*
terrain: land
grueling: tiring and difficult

English Language Learners

As a group, look at the photographs. Ask students to note small details. Assign groups of students one photograph each, which they will describe in detail and then write an alternate caption for. Remind them of the possible use of quotes, dates, and narrative descriptions. Have a class sharing in which one member of each group reads the photo description and another reads the caption.

The smashed wreck sank slowly into the ice. One sad day, it disappeared forever.

Rescued! Shackleton used a rowboat to carry the twenty-two men from Elephant Island to the *Yelcho*, the ship in the background. Finally, after nearly two years on the ice, the crew traveled home.

205

Art

Have selected students use family photographs to create a photo essay of a voyage (trip) that they may have taken. Alternatively, if resources permit, have volunteers create a photo essay to document a class field trip or other class activity.

▶ **Comprehension Check**

Noting Visual Details Chart Mark on the board the results of students' chart entries and discuss.

Comprehension/Critical Thinking Ask students to read aloud the parts of the photo essay, or point to the elements of the photographs, that support their answers.

1 Why are Frank Hurley's photographs more valuable to us than the drawings of an artist who was not present on the voyage? (The photographs help people understand what Shackleton's voyage was really like. They are eyewitness accounts.) **Making Judgments**

2 How do the photograph and caption on page 203 work together to give information? (The photo shows how the *Endurance* was crushed by ice; the text tells that it happened slowly.) **Text Organization**

3 How does the photograph of the crew pulling the lifeboat especially sum up the men's situation? (It shows how arduous their daily struggle for survival really was.) **Drawing Conclusions**

4 **Connecting/Comparing** How does the photo essay add to what you learned about the voyage in the selection? (It deepens appreciation of the voyagers' plight.) **Compare and Contrast**

Transparency 5-10

Character Chart

Yunmi's Feelings	Story Clues
About Her Visit to Korea excited anxious	*(See page 145.)*
About Her Korean Cousins	*(See pages 150–153 and 158–160.)* They take her sightseeing.
jealous	
About Halmoni	*(See pages 152–153 and 157–159.)*
ashamed about being selfish	

What do you think Yunmi will do if her cousins come to visit her in New York? Explain why you think as you do.

Practice Book page 82

Name _____

Yunmi and Halmoni's Trip
Graphic Organizer
Character Chart

Character Chart

Accept varied responses.

Yunmi's Feelings	Story Clues
About Her Visit to Korea excited anxious	*(See page 145.)* from words in the story **(1)** She held Halmoni's hand. **(1)**
About Her Korean Cousins fun to be around **(1 point)** hard to talk to and understand sometimes **(1)** jealous	*(See pages 150–153 and 158–160.)* They take her sightseeing. They show her how to make mandoo. **(1)** Their English is hard to understand and they giggle when she speaks Korean. **(1)** Halmoni pays so much attention to her cousins. **(1)**
About Halmoni misses her attention **(1)** scared, worried, upset **(1)** ashamed about being selfish	*(See pages 152–153 and 157–159.)* Halmoni is busy visiting and overseeing preparations; she gives all her attention to the cousins. **(1)** She sees how happy Halmoni is with her family in Korea. **(1)** from words in the story; she'd be lonely without Halmoni. **(1)**

What do you think Yunmi will do if her cousins come to visit her in New York? Explain why you think as you do.

Accept responses that students can justify. **(2)**

82   Theme 5: **Voyagers**
Assessment Tip: Total **14** Points

Comprehension Skills

✓ Text Organization

▶ Teach

Review the text organization of *Trapped by the Ice!* Use **Transparency 5–18** to discuss how authors use text organization to

- help readers learn new information
- present this information clearly, so that it is easier to understand

Students can refer to the selection and to **Practice Book** page 97.

Graphic Organizer: Text Organization Chart

Text Feature	Where It Is	Purpose
heading (date)	pp. 172, 174, 176, 180, 182, 184, 186, 190, 192, 196, 198	helps readers follow the order of events
photograph, caption, illustration	pp. 172–199	helps readers understand the text; gives more details
definition	p. 190: "Graybeards are monstrous waves that come quietly and quickly, threatening everything in their path."	helps readers understand the meaning of a special term
chronological sequence	p. 172: The first event takes place on October 27, 1915. p. 198: The last event takes place on May 20, 1916	helps readers understand the order of events

Modeling Have students examine the selection to identify the type of headings (dates) that the author primarily uses to organize information. Ask students to look at page 190 as you think aloud.

Think Aloud

I read the heading May 5, 1916, on page 190. The heading helps me locate story events in time. On May 5, a graybeard hit the Caird, spinning the lifeboat around and around and almost causing it to capsize.

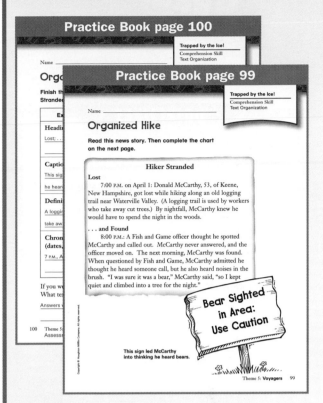

Explain to students that they can use headings and other text features—such as photographs, illustrations, captions, definitions, and chronological (time) sequence—to follow the events and the author's ideas better. By breaking down the text into smaller parts, organized by a certain theme (in this case, the date), these features also help readers find the main ideas and supporting details in the selection. Explain that, although every page does not have a date, the approximate date of a story event can be inferred by looking at the surrounding dates.

▶ Practice

Ask students to identify other information the author might have included in the headings and how it might help readers. Have students record their answers on a chart similar to the one below.

Additional Information That Could Appear in Headings	How This Information Could Help
(Location)	Knowing where the events take place might help a reader follow and understand the selection.

▶ Apply

Use **Practice Book** pages 99–100 to diagnose whether students need reteaching. Students who do not need Reteaching may work on Challenge/Extension Activities, page 13. Students who need Extra Support may apply the skill to an easier text using **Reader's Library**, Selection 3, "Iceberg Rescue," and its Responding activity.

Skill Finder	• Revisiting, p. 187	• Review, Theme 3, pp. 287, 346	• Reteaching, p . R12

Extra Support

- Reteaching, page R12
- **Reader's Library,** Selection 3, "Iceberg Rescue"

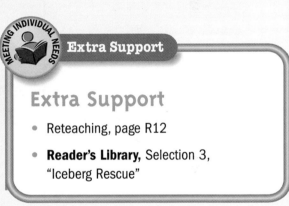

Diagnostic Check

If...	▶ You can...
students need extra help identifying features of text organization,	use the Reteaching Lesson on page R12.
students have successfully met the lesson objectives,	have them do the Challenge/Extension Activities on page R13.

Comprehension Skills (205B)

Information & Study Skills

Using a Time Line

▶ Teach

Time Lines Explain that a time line is a quick, efficient way to picture the order in which important, related events took place. It also shows at a glance whether a short time or a long time passed from one event to the next. It is an easy way to view the chronology of potentially complicated historical events.

Display **Transparency 5–19**. Point out the time line shown at the top. Have students read aloud the time line title and the historical events shown on the time line. Point out that this time line, like many others, uses the present tense, even though the events took place in the past.

Time Line Time Spans Also explain to students that most time lines are drawn to span the period from the earliest event listed to the latest event listed. Time periods before the earliest event and after the latest event need not necessarily be shown. Most time lines have dated events spaced out proportionally. For example, there will be far less space separating events having taken place in 1945 and 1946 than there will be for events marked down for 1945 and 1970.

Modeling Using the time line on **Transparency 5–19**, demonstrate for students how to find information on a time line. Point to labels and information on the time line as you explain how it is organized.

Think Aloud

The first event in the selection about Shackleton's Antarctic adventure was dated October 27, 1915. This time line starts with October and shows what happened in the months that followed. It organizes the information from the selection so that I can clearly see what was happening during each month. Without the time line, figuring out the sequence of events could get pretty confusing. I can see that the Endurance sank in November. This shows that the men set out to cross the ice in December. The bracket on the time line shows that for these three months, they were on the ice traveling north. The selection does not include any dates for those months, so this helps me understand how long it took.

OBJECTIVES

Students

- use a time line to locate information
- summarize information from a nonfiction selection by creating a time line

Transparency 5–19

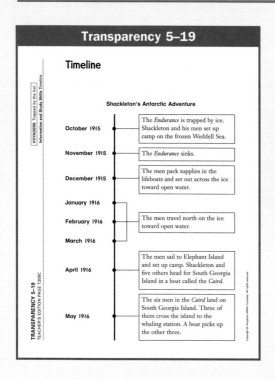

▶ Practice

Ask students to use the time line to answer questions such as the following:

■ Which took longer, traveling on the ice toward open water, or sailing to Elephant Island? (traveling on the ice toward open water)

■ In what month did the men reach Elephant Island? (April)

■ In what month did Shackleton reach the whaling station? (May)

■ About how long did it take Shackleton to reach the whaling station after the *Endurance* sank? (about six months)

■ How much time, in total, elapsed from the beginning of the time line, to the end? (eight months)

▶ Apply

Point out to students that some months were much more eventful for Shackleton and his men than others. Most of the entries in the selection tell about what happened in just two of the eight months: April and May. In large scale on the board, draw a time line like the one on the transparency. Label eight points as follows: April 8, April 13, April 15, April 24, May 5, May 10, May 19, May 20. Assign pairs of students to summarize what happened on each of these dates. Have them write summaries neatly on paper and attach them to the appropriate points along the time line.

Word Work Instruction

DAY 1	• Spelling Pretest • Spelling Instruction
DAY 2	• Structural Analysis Instruction • Spelling Practice
DAY 3	• Phonics Instruction • Spelling Practice
DAY 4	• Structural Analysis Reteaching • Vocabulary Skill Instruction • Spelling Game
DAY 5	• Expanding Your Vocabulary • Spelling Test

OBJECTIVES

Students

• read words with the VCCV pattern

• read words that have double consonants

• use the Phonics/Decoding strategy to decode longer words

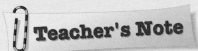
Teacher's Note

Explain that:

• Many words with the VCCV pattern have only one syllable, to which the ending -ed has been added. For example, *trapped, rigged,* and *lunged.* Students should try one-syllable and two-syllable pronunciations and decide which is correct.

• When two consonants spell one sound such as *th* in *gather* or *ck* in *rocket,* the word is divided before or after the two consonants.

Decoding Longer Words

✓ Structural Analysis: VCCV Pattern    Spelling·Connection

▶ Teach

Write this sentence on the board:

Remind students that when they encounter unfamiliar words in their reading, one good strategy for decoding is to look for spelling patterns. Point to the word *concern* in the sentence. Underline the letters *o-n-c-e.* Explain that when there are two consonants in the middle of

Now his only concern was for his men.

a word with a vowel before and after, this is called the VCCV pattern. Write the letters VCCV on the board over the letters as you say the words *vowel, consonant, consonant, vowel.* Tell students that this pattern often indicates two syllables, with a division between the two consonants. Draw a line between the *n* and the *c* in the word *concern* and pronounce each syllable distinctly.

Modeling Display the following sentence and model how to decode *canvas*: *The lifeboats were rigged with small <u>canvas</u> sails.*

Think Aloud

When I look at the underlined word, I see the VCCV pattern a-n-v-a. When I break the word between the consonants n and v, I can easily say each syllable /CAN•vuhs/. I know canvas *is a kind of thick material. That makes sense in this sentence.*

▶ Practice

Write these phrases on the board and have students copy the underlined words: *wanted to be the first <u>person</u>, scrap <u>lumber</u> for firewood, in the <u>distance</u>, a hero's <u>welcome</u>.* Have pairs of students underline the VCCV pattern in each word, draw a line between the syllables, and pronounce the word. Call on individuals to model the Phonics/Decoding strategy at the board.

▶ Apply

Have students complete **Practice Book** page 101.

Phonics: Double Consonants

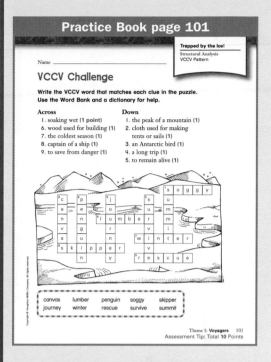

Practice Book page 101

Name _____

VCCV Challenge

Write the VCCV word that matches each clue in the puzzle.
Use the Word Bank and a dictionary for help.

Across
1. soaking wet (1 point)
6. wood used for building (1)
7. the coldest season (1)
8. captain of a ship (1)
9. to save from danger (1)

Down
1. the peak of a mountain (1)
2. cloth used for making tents or sails (1)
3. an Antarctic bird (1)
4. a long trip (1)
5. to remain alive (1)

| canvas | lumber | penguin | soggy | skipper |
| journey | winter | rescue | survive | summit |

Theme 5: **Voyagers** 101
Assessment Tip: Total **10** Points

▶ Teach

Tell students that understanding double consonants can help them use the
Phonics/Decoding strategy to decode unfamiliar words. Explain that

■ A VCCV word may have a double consonant. Divide between the consonants to
find the syllables.

Modeling Display this sentence and model how to decode *skipper*:

> The ship's <u>skipper</u> was Frank Worsley.

 Think Aloud

*When I look at this word, I see the double consonants in the middle. Since the
word contains the VCCV pattern, I'll try splitting it into syllables between the two
p's. / skihp•pur / Oh, it's / SKIHP•ur /. I know that word. A skipper is a person who
is in charge of a ship. That makes sense.*

▶ Practice

Write these sentences on the board and have students copy the underlined
words: *The ice was moved by the sea's <u>current</u>. He pulled the <u>soggy</u> bag out of
the water. The boat <u>shuddered</u> on impact.* Have students circle the double consonant spellings and decode each word. Call on individuals to model the
Phonics/Decoding strategy at the board.

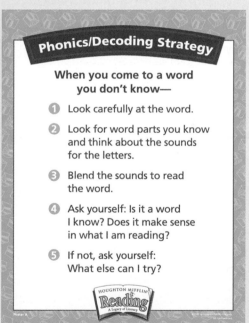

Phonics/Decoding Strategy

**When you come to a word
you don't know—**

1 Look carefully at the word.

2 Look for word parts you know
and think about the sounds
for the letters.

3 Blend the sounds to read
the word.

4 Ask yourself: Is it a word
I know? Does it make sense
in what I am reading?

5 If not, ask yourself:
What else can I try?

HOUGHTON MIFFLIN
Reading
A Legacy of Literacy

▶ Apply

Tell students to decode the following words from *Trapped by the Ice!* and discuss their meanings: *terrible*, page 180; *killer whales*, page 182; *swallow*, page
184; *jagged*, page 184; *suffered*, page 194; *nibble*, page 196.

 Skill Finder

• Strategy Review: Phonics/ Decoding, p. 169A	• Reteaching, p. R18

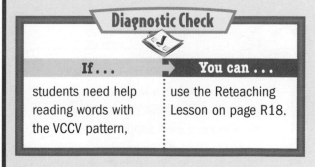

Diagnostic Check

If . . .	You can . . .
students need help reading words with the VCCV pattern,	use the Reteaching Lesson on page R18.

Spelling Words
Basic Words

Monday	dollar
sudden*	window
until	hello
forget	market
happen*	pretty
follow	order*

Review Words	Challenge Words
after*	stubborn
funny	expect*

*Forms of these words appear in the literature.

 Extra Support

Basic Word List You may want to use only the left column of Basic Words with students who need extra support.

Spelling

✓ The VCCV Pattern

Day 1   Teaching the Principle

Pretest Use the Day 5 Test sentences. Say each underlined word, read the sentence, and then repeat the word. Have students write only the underlined word.

Teach Write *Monday* and *sudden* on the board, say the words, and have students repeat them. Tell students that each word has two syllables, and then point out each word's vowel-consonant-consonant-vowel pattern.

Next, explain that finding the syllables of VCCV words will help students to spell the words. Draw lines to syllabicate the examples. *(Mon | day, sud | den)* Tell students that words with the VCCV pattern are divided between the two consonants, whether the consonants are different or the same.

Add the remaining Basic Words to the board, say each word, and have students repeat it. Call on students to identify each word's VCCV pattern and tell you where to divide the word into syllables.

Practice/Homework Assign **Practice Book** page 185. Tell students to use this Take-Home Word List to study the words they missed on the Pretest.

Day 2   Reviewing the Principle

Practice/Homework Review the spelling principle and assign **Practice Book** page 102.

Day 3   Vocabulary

Classifying Write the Basic Words on the board. Then dictate the following word groups and ask students to write the Basic Word that fits in each group.

nickel, quarter,	(dollar)
store, shop,	(market)
door, porch,	(window)
Sunday, Thursday,	(Monday)

Next, have students use each Basic Word from the board orally in a sentence. (Sentences will vary.)

Practice/Homework For spelling practice, assign **Practice Book** page 103.

Day 4 | Match Game

Ask pairs of students to make a set of 24 syllable cards, one for each syllable of the twelve Basic Words. Then ask the pairs to shuffle the cards and arrange them facedown in four rows of six cards each.

To play, players take turns turning over two cards at a time, hoping to make a match of the two syllables in a Basic Word. If the cards match, the player may keep the cards after using the word correctly in a sentence. If the cards do not match, they are turned facedown again. The player with more cards at the end wins.

Practice/Homework For proofreading and writing practice, assign **Practice Book** page 104.

Day 5 | Spelling Assessment

Test Say each underlined word, read the sentence, and then repeat the word. Have students write only the underlined word.

Basic Words

1. School starts on <u>Monday</u>.
2. The car came to a <u>sudden</u> stop.
3. We can play outside <u>until</u> dark.
4. Did you <u>forget</u> your lunch?
5. What will <u>happen</u> next?
6. We will <u>follow</u> the trail.
7. What can I buy with a <u>dollar</u>?
8. Did you shut the <u>window</u>?
9. The friendly clown said <u>hello</u>.
10. We can buy jam at the <u>market</u>.
11. This pond looks so <u>pretty</u>!
12. Write the numbers in <u>order</u>.

Challenge Words

13. Your brother is very <u>stubborn</u>.
14. I do not know what to <u>expect</u> next.

Spelling Spree!™

Students may use the **Spelling Spree!™** for extra practice with the spelling principles taught in this lesson.

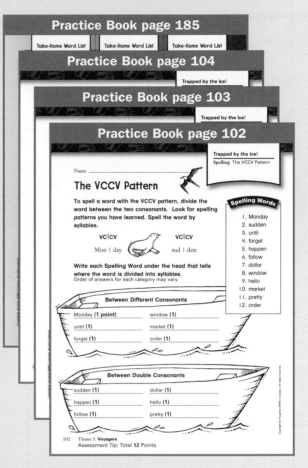

Practice Book page 185

Take-Home Word List   Take-Home Word List   Take-Home Word List

Practice Book page 104

Trapped by the Ice!

Practice Book page 103

Trapped by the Ice!

Practice Book page 102

Trapped by the Ice!
Spelling The VCCV Pattern

Name _____

The VCCV Pattern

To spell a word with the VCCV pattern, divide the word between the two consonants. Look for spelling patterns you have learned. Spell the word by syllables.

vcIcv   vcIcv
Mon I day   sud I den

Write each Spelling Word under the head that tells where the word is divided into syllables.
Order of answers for each category may vary.

Spelling Words
1. Monday
2. sudden
3. until
4. forget
5. happen
6. follow
7. dollar
8. window
9. hello
10. market
11. pretty
12. order

Between Different Consonants

Monday (1 point) ____   window (1) ____
until (1) ____   market (1) ____
forget (1) ____   order (1) ____

Between Double Consonants

sudden (1) ____   dollar (1) ____
happen (1) ____   hello (1) ____
follow (1) ____   pretty (1) ____

102   Theme 5: Voyagers
      Assessment Tip: Total 12 Points

•• **Houghton Mifflin Spelling and Vocabulary** ••
Correlated instruction and practice

Challenge

Challenge Word Practice Students can use the Challenge Words to write sentences from a speech given to honor the crew of the *Endurance*.

Students

- read and understand words that are homophones
- use sentence context to identify the appropriate homophone

Practice Book page 105

Transparency 5–20

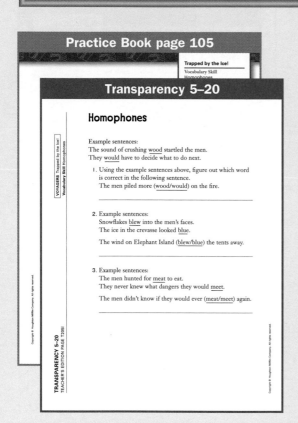

Vocabulary Skills

✓ Homophones

Teach

Display **Transparency 5–20**, blocking out all but the first two sentences. Read the two sentences aloud. Point out the underlined words, *wood* and *would*. Remind students that words that sound alike but have different meanings and spellings are called *homophones*.

Modeling On the transparency, uncover practice sentence 1 and read it aloud. Explain how students can use the example sentences to help them determine which of the two homophones, *would* or *wood*, correctly completes the sentence.

Think Aloud

In the first example sentence, I can see that the word wood *is a noun. It names something that makes a sound when it is crushed. In the second sentence, the word* would *is a verb. To fill the blank in sentence 1, I need a word that names something the men piled on a fire, so it must be a noun. Wood is used to build ships and can be used to start a fire. The word* wood *in the first example sentence makes sense in sentence 1.*

▶ Practice

Uncover the second set of example sentences and practice sentence 2 on the transparency. Read the examples and the practice sentence aloud. Then ask students which homophone correctly completes the sentence. (blew) Ask students to explain why *blew* is correct in this sentence rather than *blue*. Then uncover the remainder of the transparency and proceed in the same manner, reading the sentences, and asking a volunteer to complete practice sentence 3. (meet)

Point out that several other words in the sentences on the transparency are homophones: *to, sea, for, knew,* and *know*. Write the following word groups on the board: *to/two/too; sea/see; for/four/fore; knew/new; know/no*. Discuss the meanings of the words. In pairs or small groups, have students create sentences that use each of these words correctly.

▶ **Apply**

Have students complete **Practice Book** page 105.

Expanding Your Vocabulary
Words Used on Ships

Point out that *Trapped by the Ice!* includes many terms that are used on board a ship. Begin a word web that includes words relating to ships from the selection, as in the following example:

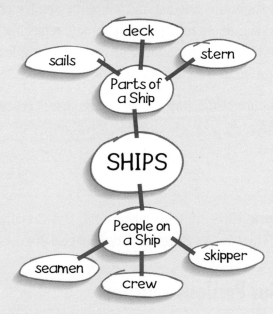

Have students work with partners to define each of the words in the web and to find additional words that tell about ships and people who work on ships. Add the additional words to the word web.

• **Challenge/Extension**
  Activities, p. R19

Writing and Language Instruction

DAY 1	• Daily Language Practice • Grammar Instruction • Journal Writing
DAY 2	• Daily Language Practice • Write a Log Entry • Journal Writing • Grammar Practice
DAY 3	• Daily Language Practice • Grammar Instruction • Write a Speech
DAY 4	• Daily Language Practice • Listening/Speaking/Viewing • Writing: Improving Your Writing • Grammar Practice
DAY 5	• Daily Language Practice • Grammar: Improving Your Writing

OBJECTIVES

Students

- identify possessive pronouns

- use possessive pronouns in sentences

- proofread and correct sentences with grammar and spelling errors

- proofread for *its* and *it's* to improve writing

Technology

Wacky Web Tales

Students may use the **Wacky Web Tales** floppy disk to create humorous stories and review parts of speech.

Grammar Skills

 Possessive Pronouns

Day 1

Remind students that pronouns replace one or more words. Display the two sets of sentences at the top of **Transparency 5–21**.

Have students identify the words replaced by pronouns. Help students recognize that in these sentences, the pronouns *his* and *its* replace possessive nouns. Then go over the following definitions:

■ A possessive pronoun shows ownership.

■ The pronouns *my, your, her, his, its, our,* and *their* are possessive pronouns.

Display the chart to show the singular and plural possessive pronouns. Have students study the next sentences on the transparency, replacing the underlined word or words with possessive pronouns. In the last examples, have students choose the correct pronoun from the choices at the end of the sentence.

Then have students correct the Day 1 Daily Language Practice sentences on **Transparency 5–23**.

Day 2

Practice/Homework Have students correct the Day 2 Daily Language Practice sentences. Then assign **Practice Book** page 106.

Day 3 **Our Perilous Journey**

Have students imagine that they were members of Shackleton's crew. Ask them to write sentences from their diaries. Each sentence should include one possessive pronoun. For example:

> Today our bank sank under the ice.
> The men have finished their fresh water.
> My legs ache.
> Shackleton described his plan.

Have students exchange sentences and check one another's use of possessive pronouns. Students may wish to add illustrations or use their sentences as the basis for a longer writing project. Then have them correct the Day 3 Daily Language Practice sentences.

Day 4

Practice/Homework Have students correct the Day 4 Daily Language Practice sentences. Then assign **Practice Book** page 107.

Day 5 Improving Your Writing

Proofreading for *its* and *it's* Display the two examples at the top of **Transparency 5–22.**

Have students compare *its* in the first sentence with *it's* in the second. Help them understand that *its* is a possessive pronoun meaning belonging to it, *it's* is a contraction for *it is*. Tell students that *its* and *it's* are two commonly confused words. Good writers always check these words when they proofread. Have students read each example and decide whether or not *its* or *it's* is used correctly.

Then have students review a piece of their own writing to see whether they can improve their use of *its* and *it's*.

Practice/Homework Have students correct the Day 5 Daily Language Practice sentences. Then assign **Practice Book** page 108.

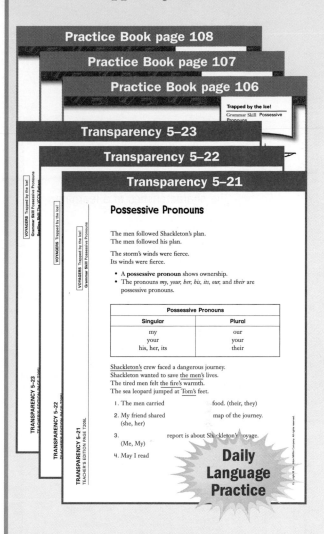

Practice Book page 108
Practice Book page 107
Practice Book page 106

Transparency 5–23
Transparency 5–22
Transparency 5–21

Possessive Pronouns

The men followed Shackleton's plan.
The men followed his plan.

The storm's winds were fierce.
Its winds were fierce.

- A **possessive pronoun** shows ownership.
- The pronouns *my, your, her, his, its, our,* and *their* are possessive pronouns.

Possessive Pronouns	
Singular	**Plural**
my	our
your	your
his, her, its	their

Shackleton's crew faced a dangerous journey.
Shackleton wanted to save the men's lives.
The tired men felt the fire's warmth.
The sea leopard jumped at Tom's feet.

1. The men carried _____ food. (their, they)
2. My friend shared _____ map of the journey. (she, her)
3. _____ report is about Shackleton's voyage. (Me, My)
4. May I read

Daily Language Practice

············· **Houghton Mifflin English** ···········
Correlated instruction and practice

Diagnostic Check

If...	→ You can ...
students need help using possessive pronouns,	use the Reteaching Lesson on page R22.

Writing Skills
Write a Learning Log Entry

▶ Teach

In *Trapped by the Ice!* students read about Shackleton's journey to Antarctica in the early 1900s. Students may have been surprised to learn that Shackleton and his entire crew survived the perilous journey. Shackleton and his crew learned a great deal about the Antarctic from their trip. A learning log is a tool students can use in their own learning. Explain to students that learning logs are a way for them to track what they have learned and to plan goals to work toward. Learning logs are tools for self-evaluation and discovery.

▶ Practice

Display **Transparency 5–24**. Have students read the self-evaluation paragraph. Ask:

■ What kinds of writing is the paragraph about? (a poem and a report)

■ What does the writer do well? (connects own experience to writing, relates topics to personal likes)

■ What does the writer not do very well? (spelling, proofreading)

■ What are the writer's future goals? (proofread more carefully, add to research report)

Then help students use the information in the paragraph to complete the following learning log graphic organizer..

Learning Log	
What I Learned:	**My Goals:**
_____	_____
_____	_____
_____	_____
_____	_____
_____	_____

Discuss with students the guidelines for writing a learning log entry.

 OBJECTIVES

Students

• identify the characteristics of a learning log entry

• write a learning log entry

• write dates and times

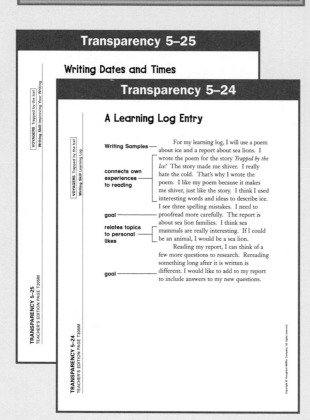

Transparency 5–25

Writing Dates and Times

Transparency 5–24

A Learning Log Entry

Writing Samples — For my learning log, I will use a poem about ice and a report about sea lions. I wrote the poem for the story *Trapped by the Ice!* The story made me shiver. I really hate the cold. That's why I wrote the poem. I like my poem because it makes me shiver, just like the story. I think I used interesting words and ideas to describe ice. I see three spelling mistakes. I need to proofread more carefully. The report is about sea lion families. I think sea mammals are really interesting. If I could be an animal, I would be a sea lion.

Reading my report, I can think of a few more questions to research. Rereading something long after it is written is different. I would like to add to my report to include answers to my new questions.

connects own experiences to reading

goal

relates topics to personal likes

goal

Type to Learn™

Students may use **Type to Learn™** to learn proper keyboarding technique.

©Sunburst Technology Corporation, a Houghton Mifflin Company. All Rights Reserved.

········ **Houghton Mifflin English** ········

Correlated instruction and practice

Portfolio Opportunity

Save students' learning logs as samples of their writing development.

Guidelines for
Writing a Learning Log Entry

- Select two different examples of your writing. They can be a story, a letter, a poem, or a report.
- Read your work carefully.
- List the things you have learned under *What I Learned*.
- List the areas that need improvement under *My Goals*.

Skill Finder

- More writing activities, pp. R23–R25

▶ Apply

Students can use **Practice Book** page 109 to help them plan and organize their writing. Have students use it to write a learning log entry for two writing samples from different times of the school year.

✓ Improving Your Writing
Writing Dates and Times

Teach Review with students that *Trapped by the Ice!* is written as a series of diary or journal entries that begin with dates. Explain that written dates begin with the month, followed by the number of the day, and then the year. Have students note that a comma separates the day and the year. Explain that September 19, 2003, in numerals is 9/19/03. Then have students find an entry that also includes the time. (pages 182 and 198) Review with students that *p.m.* stands for the Latin phrase *post meridiem*, meaning "after noon." Explain that p.m. goes from one minute after noon until midnight. Tell students that *a.m.* stands for the Latin phrase *ante meridiem*, meaning "before noon," and goes from one minute after midnight until noon.

Practice To model how to use dates and times display **Transparency 5–25**. Have students read the definitions and examples. Then work through the transparency together, writing the dates and times as directed.

Apply Assign **Practice Book** page 110. Have students review their logs.

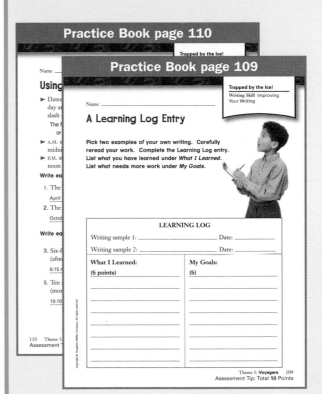

Practice Book page 110

Practice Book page 109

Trapped by the Ice!
Writing Skill Improving Your Writing

Name _____

A Learning Log Entry

Pick two examples of your own writing. Carefully reread your work. Complete the Learning Log entry. List what you have learned under *What I Learned*. List what needs more work under *My Goals*.

LEARNING LOG	
Writing sample 1: _____ Date: _____	
Writing sample 2: _____ Date: _____	
What I Learned: (5 points)	**My Goals:** (5)

Theme 5: **Voyagers** 109
Assessment Tip: Total **10** Points

Listening/Speaking/Viewing
Practice Group Problem Solving

▶ Teach

Remind students that Shackleton and his men need to solve some very serious problems in *Trapped by the Ice!* Explain that group problem solving helps them survive. After the *Endurance* sank, Shackleton, the leader of the expedition, meets with ship captain Frank Worsley and next-in-command Frankie Wild to work out a survival plan. Ask students to suggest reasons why a group might be better at finding a good solution to a problem than one person alone would be.

Reasons might include the following:

- More ideas will be suggested, and ideas that one person suggests may spark new ideas from other group members.

- Group members may have different areas of knowledge and expertise that they can contribute to the plan.

- A group can discuss the strengths and weaknesses of each idea; this can help them avoid mistakes.

Explain that groups usually work best when one person acts as leader. The leader makes sure that everyone has a chance to speak and that everyone's suggestions are respected. She or he also keeps the discussion on track.

▶ Practice

Divide the class into problem-solving groups. Ask each group to make a list of the three most difficult problems Shackleton and his men face. Tell them that they have five minutes to agree on what three things will be on their list. When the time is up, ask each group to present their list to the class. Then lead a discussion in which students reflect upon the group process. Did everyone in the group contribute to the plan? How did they agree on what to include on the list? How did they resolve their differences? How did they keep the discussion from straying off the topic?

▶ Apply

Divide students into new problem-solving groups. Present a problem such as the following:

Your group must survive for two days and one night in Antarctic conditions. You will have nothing with you except what you can carry for half a mile. You cannot make a trip back for more supplies. You will find no people or buildings, only rocks, ice, and wind.

Instruct each group to come up with a survival plan. Ask them to list the things they would bring and the procedures they would follow for survival in a cold, barren environment. Remind them that they must work as a group to solve the problem. After they have had time to develop their plans, have groups present their survival plans to the class.

Improving Listening Skills

Remind students that listening well to others' ideas is essential to group problem solving. Offer the following suggestions:

- For good listening, it is important that only one person speak at a time.

- It may be helpful to take notes, jotting down important words and phrases as you listen.

- If you are not certain that you understand another person's idea, repeat the idea in your own words and ask the speaker if your understanding is correct.

- Be respectful of the ideas others present. Remember that the goal is not to criticize or compete with one another, but to work together to find the best solution to a problem.

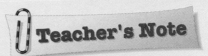

Teacher's Note

To introduce your students to more examples of real-world group problem solving, you may wish to bring in and read aloud magazine or newspaper articles that describe group problem-solving efforts, perhaps in response to an issue in a community or a school. Discuss with students how each group used group problem-solving skills. Talk with them about the planning that might have happened "behind" the headlines of and events in the articles.

Theme Assessment Wrap-Up

▶ Preparing for Testing

Remind students that they can use test-taking strategies to help them do well on important tests.

Writing an Answer to a Question Tell students that today they will learn strategies for writing an answer to a comprehension question. Have them read Taking Tests on Anthology pages 206–207.

Discuss the tips and the model student think aloud on Anthology pages 206–207 with students. Mention these points:

■ Plan your answer before you start to write.

■ Check to make sure you respond to what the question asks.

■ Write in complete sentences.

■ Even if you can only answer part of the question, write it down.

More Practice The **Practice Book,** pages 112–113, contains additional written-response comprehension questions for more practice.

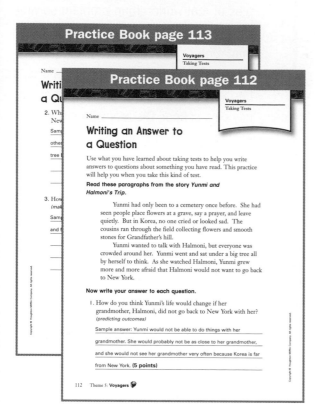

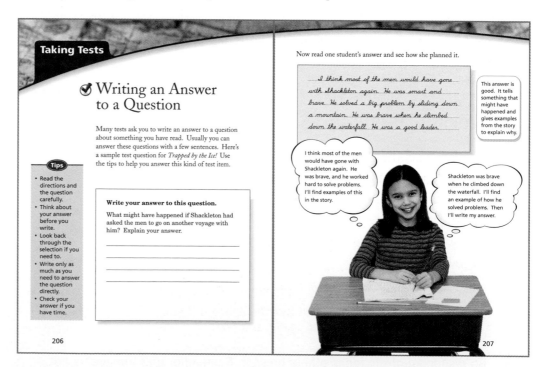

▶ Assessing Student Progress

Formal Assessment The **Integrated Theme Test** and the **Theme Skills Test** are formal group assessments used to evaluate student performance on theme objectives. The **Theme Skills Test** may be used as a pretest or may be administered following the theme.

The **Integrated Theme Test** assesses students' progress as readers and writers in a format that reflects instruction. Authentic literary passages test reading skills in context.

The **Theme Skills Test** assesses students' mastery of specific reading and language arts skills taught in the theme. Individual skill subtests can be administered separately.

■ Integrated test of reading and writing skills: Comprehension strategies and skills, word skills, spelling, grammar, and writing

■ Tests discrete skills: Comprehension skills, word skills, spelling, grammar, writing, and information and study skills

Spelling Review/Assessment

Practice Book
Practice Book: pp. 114–116 Take-Home Word Lists: Practice Book Handbook

5-Day Spelling Plan

See p. 137G

Review with students the Spelling Words and, if appropriate, the Challenge Words from the spelling lessons on pages 137G, 167G, and 205G. Have volunteers summarize each spelling principle and explain how the words in each lesson illustrate the principle.

Pretest/Test

1. The <u>cook</u> made the cookies so hard I broke a <u>tooth</u>!
2. "That mouse <u>ought</u> to be <u>caught</u>," said the cat.
3. On <u>Monday</u> there was a <u>sudden</u> rainstorm.
4. The strange plant <u>grew</u> in the shape of a spoon.
5. What will <u>happen</u> if the <u>balloon</u> gets a leak?
6. Is it true that my old <u>boot</u> <u>flew</u> a step or two?
7. That book in the store <u>window</u> costs one <u>dollar</u>.
8. The woman <u>taught</u> her <u>daughter</u> to play soccer.
9. I <u>brought</u> the new ball that I <u>bought</u> yesterday.
10. I <u>thought</u> I could <u>chew</u> the carrot, but it's too hard.
11. Don't <u>forget</u> that you have to work <u>until</u> five.
12. Mom will <u>order</u> me a <u>pretty</u> dress from the store.
13. It's always polite to say <u>hello</u> to people.

Challenge Words

14. The woman and her <u>granddaughter</u> waded in the <u>brook</u>.
15. Little children can <u>expect</u> to have <u>loose</u> teeth sometimes.
16. Are mules as <u>stubborn</u> as they are said to be?

MEETING INDIVIDUAL NEEDS

Challenge

Challenge Words Practice Have students use the Challenge Words from the Take-Home Word List to write a letter to a friend about a voyage they want to take some day.

Early Grade 3	79–110 words per min.
Mid-Grade 3	93–123 words per min.
Late Grade 3	114–142 words per min.

For some students in Grade 3, you may want to check the oral fluency rate four times during the year. For students who appear to be having difficulty learning to read, this assessment may need to be done more often. The rates above are approximate.

Decoding and comprehension should be considered together in evaluating students' reading development. For information on how to select appropriate text, administer fluency checks, and interpret results, see the **Teacher's Assessment Handbook.**

For more information on assessing fluency, also see the Back to School section of this **Teacher's Edition.**

▶ Assessing Student Progress (continued)

Assessing Fluency Oral reading fluency is a useful measure of a student's development of rapid automatic word recognition. Students who are reading on level in Grade 3 should be able to read, accurately and with expression, in appropriate level text at the approximate rates shown in the table to the left. In this theme, an appropriate selection to be used with most students is *Across the Wide Dark Sea.*

Using Multiple Measures Student progress is best evaluated through multiple measures, which can be collected in a portfolio. The portfolio provides a record of student progress over time and can be useful in conferencing with the student, parents, or other educators. In addition to the tests mentioned on page 207, portfolios might include the following:

- Observation Checklist from this theme
- Description writing from the Reading-Writing Workshop
- Other writing, projects, or artwork
- One or more items selected by the student

Using Assessment for Planning Instruction You can use the results of theme assessments to evaluate individual students' needs and to modify instruction during the next theme. For more detail, see the test manuals or the **Teacher's Assessment Handbook.**

Customizing Instruction

Student Performance Shows:	Modifications to Consider:
Difficulty with Decoding or Word Skills	**Emphasis:** Word skills, phonics, reading for fluency; check for phonemic awareness **Resources:** Teacher's Edition: *Phonics Review, Structural Analysis Reteaching lessons;* Phonics Screening Test; Lexia Quick Phonics Assessment CD-ROM; Lexia Phonics CD-ROM: Intermediate Intervention
Difficulty with Oral Fluency	**Emphasis:** Reading and rereading of independent level text; vocabulary development **Resources:** Teacher's Edition: *Leveled Books;* Reader's Library; Theme Paperbacks; Houghton Mifflin Classroom Bookshelf; Book Adventure Website
Difficulty with Comprehension	**Emphasis:** Oral comprehension; strategy development; story comprehension; vocabulary development **Resources:** Teacher's Edition: *Extra Support notes, Comprehension Reteaching lessons;* Get Set for Reading CD-ROM; SOAR to Success
Overall High Performance	**Emphasis:** Independent reading and writing; vocabulary development; critical thinking **Resources:** Teacher's Edition: *Think About the Selection questions, Challenge notes;* Theme Paperbacks; Houghton Mifflin Classroom Bookshelf; Book Adventure Website; Education Place Website; Challenge Handbook

Theme Resources

Theme Resources
Resources for Voyagers

Contents

Lesson Plans for Reader's Library

The Golden Land R2

Brother Are Forever R4

Iceberg Rescue R6

Reading

Reteaching Lessons for Comprehension Skills

Making Inferences R8

Predicting Outcomes R10

Text Organization R12

Challenge/Extension Activities for Comprehension Skills

Making Inferences R9

Predicting Outcomes R11

Text Organization R13

Word Work

Reteaching Lessons for Structural Analysis Skills

Suffixes: *-less, -ness* R14

Possessives, including s' .R16

VCCV Pattern R18

Challenge/Extension Activities for Vocabulary

Across the Wide Dark Sea R15

Yunmi and Halmoni's Trip R17

Trapped by the Ice! R19

Writing & Language

Reteaching Lessons for Grammar Skills

Subject Pronouns R20

Object Pronouns R21

Possessive Pronouns R22

Writing Activities for *Voyagers* R23

Cross-Curricular Activities R26

Technology Resources .R28

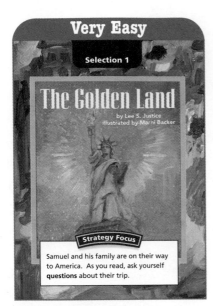

Very Easy

Selection 1

The Golden Land
by Lee S. Justice
illustrated by Marni Backer

Strategy Focus

Samuel and his family are on their way to America. As you read, ask yourself **questions** about their trip.

The Golden Land
by Lee S. Justice

Selection Summary

Papa has been in America for three years, earning money so that Mama, Myer, and Samuel can join him. The tickets arrive at last. Though sad to say good-bye to Grandmother, they are happy about going to "the golden land." They travel by wagon, train, and, finally, ship. At the end of their long journey, Mama, Myer, and Samuel are directed toward a stairway. It leads to the place where Papa is waiting—and America.

Key Vocabulary

port: a town or city where people board or leave ships

aboard: being on a ship

seasick: ill from up-and-down or jerking motions experienced on the water

gleaming: sparkling

The Golden Land

Reader's Library for Across the Wide Dark Sea: The Mayflower Journey

▶ Preparing to Read

Building Background Ask students what they know about moving from one country to another. After volunteers offer answers, point to Eastern Europe on a classroom map. Explain that many people from Eastern Europe immigrated, or moved, to the United States in the early 1900s. Many came from Russia, where they were badly treated because of their religious beliefs. Many were drawn by the promise of a more prosperous life in "the golden land" of America.

Developing Key Vocabulary Make sure students understand the meanings of the Key Vocabulary words listed at the left. Remind them to use the Phonics/Decoding Strategy when they come to a word that they do not know. For students who need more help with decoding, use the review on the next page.

▶ Strategy/Skill Focus

Refer students to the Strategy Poster. Review when and how to use the Question Strategy.

Making Inferences Remind students that they can often understand a story better by using story clues to make inferences. On the board, write this excerpt from *The Golden Land*. Point out the story clue *A wagon took the travelers to the train.*

> *A wagon took the travelers to the train. Samuel watched the family's house get smaller and smaller.*

Ask students where the wagon was taking travelers. (To the train) Guide students to infer what is happening here. (Samuel is leaving his home) Point out that the farther away the wagon got, the smaller the house looked to the travelers. Have volunteers to make an inference about how Samuel might feel at this moment.

▶ Guided Preview

Lead students in a picture walk through *The Golden Land*. Use words from the story as often as possible as you discuss the pictures. As students leaf through the book, ask them when they think the story takes place. (in the past) Ask what information the pictures give about the main character, Samuel, and his family.

▶ Guiding the Reading

Have students read silently or with a partner. If needed, use these prompts:

pages 4–9

- *Why did Papa go to America first?*

- *Why do Grandmother, Mama, Samuel, and even Myer cry when Mama and the boys leave for America?*

- *Describe Samuel's trip from the family's house to the port.*

pages 10–15

- *What does Myer infer about why all the travelers are checked for signs of sickness? Explain whether you think Myer's idea is correct.*

- *Does everyone on the ship speak the same language that Samuel does? How can you tell?*

- *Why does Mama hold Myer's head?*

pages 16–20

- *What questions must Mama answer? Why?*

- *How does the story fit the theme,* Voyagers?

- *Who meets Mama, Samuel, and Myer at the end of their voyage?*

▶ Responding

After students have finished reading *The Golden Land*, begin a discussion of the story by helping them answer the questions on page 21. Then have students refer to their completed charts as they discuss the inferences that they made from story clues.

Sample Answers **Questions 1)** Three years **2)** The people on the ship cheered and wept because they were so happy to have reached "the golden land" of America. **Chart:** Mama had been afraid that she and her sons would never reach the golden land; Papa had changed on the outside but stayed the same on the inside.

English Language Learners

Comparative Adjectives Point out the words *bumpier* and *noisier* on page 9. Explain that adjectives like *bumpier* and *noisier* compare two things. Point out that adjectives that compare two things often end in *-er*.

Strategy Review
Phonics/Decoding

Model usign the Phonics/Decoding Strategy. Write this excerpt on the board and point to the word *languages*:

> *On sunny days, Samuel played tag on the dock and listened to people talking. They spoke in all kinds of <u>languages</u>.*

Think Aloud

I look at the letters in this word from left to right to see if there are parts I already know. I know the sound that the final / –s / makes. I think I know how to say the first part, / l–a–n–g /. It might rhyme with "sang." But I don't have any idea about what the middle is. So, I'll have to use a dictionary, which is what I do. The dictionary says / LANG gwij / That means all the words that a community says and understands—like all the words in Spanish or Russian.

Diagnostic Check

If . . .	You can . . .
students need help with decoding,	use the lesson above to review the Phonics/Decoding Strategy.
students have difficulty making inferences,	use the Reteaching lesson on page R8.

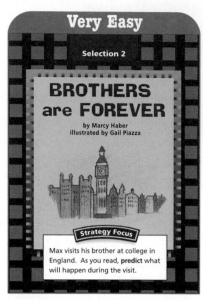

Very Easy

Selection 2

BROTHERS are FOREVER
by Marcy Haber
illustrated by Gail Piazza

Strategy Focus

Max visits his brother at college in England. As you read, **predict** what will happen during the visit.

Brothers Are Forever
by Marcy Haber

Selection Summary

Max is excited about seeing his big brother Russ at his college in London. But when he sees how Russ has changed—a new accent, new words—he is upset and unhappy with London. After Russ scores a goal at a football (soccer) game, he takes his family on a tour. He also re-establishes ties with his now-happy little brother.

Key Vocabulary

accent: way of speaking typical of a region or country

chums: British term for pals, friends

flatmate: British term for person sharing an apartment with another person

blurted out: said suddenly without thinking

MEETING INDIVIDUAL NEEDS

Brothers Are Forever

Reader's Library for Yunmi and Halmoni's Trip

▶ Preparing to Read

Building Background Ask students if they have ever visited a place that had different customs and ways of talking. Have volunteers share experiences. Locate London on a map. Explain that while British people speak English, the British sound to people from the U.S. as if they have an accent and they use different expressions from U.S. English.

Developing Key Vocabulary Make sure students understand the meanings of the Key Vocabulary words listed at the left. Remind them to use the Phonics/Decoding Strategy when they come to a word they don't know. For students who need more help with decoding, use the review on the next page.

▶ Strategy/Skill Focus

Refer students to the Strategy Poster. Review when and how to use the Predict/Infer Strategy.

Predicting Outcomes Remind students that they can predict what might happen to the characters in a story after the story ends by paying attention to the events in the story and what the characters do. Suggest that students also use the story details to make predictions about what will happen next as they read.

Invite volunteers to retell a story that all students will know, such as *Cinderella* or *Arthur's Pet Business*. Then discuss how you can predict what will happen to the main characters after the events of the story by hearing how they acted in the story.

▶ Guided Preview

Read the title to students and ask them to speculate about what it might mean. Then walk students through the illustrations, pointing out features (such as Big Ben) that place the story in London. Encourage students to use the art and the title to make predictions about the story.

➤ Guiding the Reading

Have students read silently or with a partner. If needed, use these prompts:

pages 22–27

- *Why do Max and his parents go to London?*

- *How does Max feel when he arrives? How does Russ feel?*

- *Max says the cows are smelly. How have his feelings changed?*

pages 28–33

- *What doesn't Max like about the "new" Russ? about England?*

- *What words confuse Max? How does he feel about this?*

- *What is Max afraid of? Do you think his prediction is correct? Explain.*

pages 34-38

- *What does Russ do with his family after the football game?*

- *Describe the talk the brothers have. Do they understand each other?*

- *What is Russ's plan? How does Max feel about this plan?*

➤ Responding

After students have finished reading *Brothers Are Forever,* begin a discussion of the story by helping them respond to the questions on page 39. Then have students think about clues they used to make predictions by filling in the web on page 39.

Sample Answers Questions **1)** to his college in London, England **2)** No. Russ has a new accent, uses strange words, and seems happy living in England. **Web** He says the cows are smelly. He thinks driving on the other side of the street is stupid. He says the English accent is different and stupid.

English Language Learners

Building Background Have volunteers share some experiences they had when they (or their relatives) first came to the U.S. What customs seemed strange? What words and expressions seemed funny to them?

Key Vocabulary Help students with these expressions and idioms: *yahoo, can't wait, under his breath,* and *not bad at it.*

Strategy Review
Phonics/Decoding

Model using the Phonics/Decoding Strategy. Write the sentence on the board and point to the word *college.*

> Max visits his brother at <u>college</u> in England.

Think Aloud

As I look at this word from left to right, I see / c-o-l-l / which might sound like "roll" or "doll." Then there's / e-g-e /, which I've never seen in a word before. I do know that when a word ends in a vowel plus / g-e /, the vowel has a long sound, the / g / has a soft sound and the / e / is silent — like in / page. / So, I'll try blending these sounds together in two ways: / KOHL eej / or / KAWL eej /. I don't recognize either pronunciation. I'll have to look this word up in a dictionary.

Diagnostic Check

If...	You can...
students need help with decoding,	use the lesson above to review the Phonics/Decoding Strategy.
students have difficulty predicting outcomes,	use the Reteaching lesson on page R10.

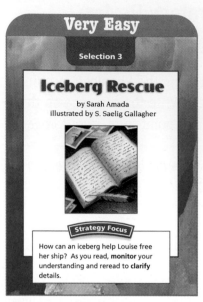

Very Easy

Selection 3

Iceberg Rescue
by Sarah Amada
illustrated by S. Saelig Gallagher

Strategy Focus

How can an iceberg help Louise free
her ship? As you read, **monitor** your
understanding and reread to **clarify**
details.

Iceberg Rescue

by Sarah Amada

Selection Summary

Explorer Louise Arner Boyd and her team
almost get stuck in the brutal winter of
Greenland. They are mapping the northeast
coast of that land, in 1933, when their ship,
the *Veslekari*, runs aground. When their initial
efforts to free the ship fail, Louise tries connecting the *Veslekari* to a nearby iceberg by
cable, and uses the ship's power to success-
fully lift the ship out of the mud. As the ship
pulls away, Louise is already contemplating
her return.

Key Vocabulary

glacier: giant body of ice

upright: right side up

iceberg: large, floating mass of ice that has
broken off a glacier

cable: very strong wire rope

Iceberg Rescue

Reader's Library for Trapped by Ice: Shackelton's Amazing Adventure

▶ Preparing to Read

Building Background Be sure students understand what an iceberg is.
Students may be interested to learn that Louise Arner Boyd (1887–1972) was a
Californian who used her personal fortune to explore the Arctic Ocean. She was
also the first woman to fly over the North Pole. Her expedition of 1933 was
sponsored by the American Geographical Society. In addition to studying the
fjords and glaciers of Greenland's northeastern coast, Boyd and her team used a
sonic device to measure offshore ocean depths.

Developing Key Vocabulary Make sure students understand the meanings of the
Key Vocabulary words listed at the left. Remind them to use the Phonics/Decoding
Strategy when they come to a word that they do not know. For students who need
more help with decoding, use the review on the next page.

▶ Strategy/Skill Focus

Refer students to the Strategy Poster. Review when and how to use the
Monitor/Clarify Strategy.

Text Organization Remind students that using text organizers can help them
learn and find information in a selection. On the board, write this excerpt from
Iceberg Rescue:

> *World of Ice*
> *It was the winter of 1933. Explorer Louise Arner Boyd and her team had
> been at sea for six weeks.*

Discuss how the heading helps visualize the setting. Point out that the heading
suggests Boyd and her team are in a bitterly cold region of ice and snow.

Guided Preview

Lead students in a picture walk through *Iceberg Rescue.* As students leaf
through the book, ask them what information the headings give about the
story problem. Ask what information the pictures give about the role of nature
in the story.

▶ Guiding the Reading

Have students read silently or with a partner. If needed, use these prompts:

pages 40–45

- *In what year and place does the story occur?*

- *What was Louise Arner Boyd's profession, or job?*

- *Do you think it is necessary for an explorer to notice and record details, as Louise Arner Boyd does? Why or why not?*

- *What is the problem the crew of the* Veslekari *faces?*

pages 46–51

- *Name three scary things that Louise knows about the situation she and her crew face.*

- *What did Louise and her team take off the* Veslekari?

- *Why did Louise and her team take so much off the* Veslekari?

pages 52–56

- *What is Louise's big idea?*

- *Do you think that Louise's idea will work? How did you decide your answer?*

- *What does the title* Iceberg Rescue *mean?*

- *What does Louise's plan to return to northeast Greenland show about her character?*

▶ Responding

After students have finished reading *Iceberg Rescue,* begin a discussion of the story by helping them answer the questions on page 57. Then have students refer to their completed charts as they discuss how headings organize the text.

Sample Answers Questions 1) Taking pictures and making maps 2) The headings can help you understand how *Iceberg Rescue* is organized. **Chart** Stuck!, Free!

English Language Learners

Key Vocabulary Be sure students understand the climate-related terms used in the selection, including the expressions *mountain of ice* and *broke through the ice.* Other unfamiliar terms may include *glacier* and *iceberg.*

Strategy Review
Phonics/Decoding

Model using the Phonics/Decoding Strategy. Write this sentence on the board and point to the word *dangerous:*

> *They were taking pictures and making maps of the wild and* <u>dangerous</u> *coast.*

Think Aloud

Looking at this word from left to right, I know how to say the last part /ous/, as in "famous." Next, I'll try breaking the word into chunks. I'll try three parts: / d–a–n /, / g–e–r /, and / o–u–s /. I guess that the first part sounds like the name "Dan" and that the second part sounds like the sound /grr/ at the end of "tiger." I'll try blending all the parts together / DAN / + / grr / + / ous /. That doesn't sound quite right, but it sounds like a word I know: dangerous. I'll change my pronunciation. The word is / DANE jeh res / — dangerous.

Diagnostic Check

If . . .	You can . . .
students need help with decoding,	use the lesson above to review the Phonics/Decoding Strategy.
students have difficulty uderstanding text organization,	use the Reteaching lesson on page R12.

Comprehension Skills: Making Inferences

Reteaching

OBJECTIVES

Students use their personal knowledge and understanding to make inferences.

Teach

Read the following story:

Jake stood on the riverbank. He cast his fishing line into the deep water. He had been trying to catch a fish for many hours. Alexandra and Zachary laughed as they watched Jake throw the line into the water one more time.

Ask, *What kind of person is Jake?* (patient, hard-working) *How do you think Alexandra and Zachary feel about Jake's efforts to catch a fish?* (They think he is wasting his time and will not catch anything.)

Explain that authors don't tell readers everything. Readers must fill in the information by using word clues and what they already know along with picture clues when they are present. Readers make inferences about the characters and events in the story.

Practice

Ask students, *What are the three types of clues you can use to make inferences?* (picture clues, word clues, and what we know clues) Make a chart like the one below on the chalkboard or on chart paper.

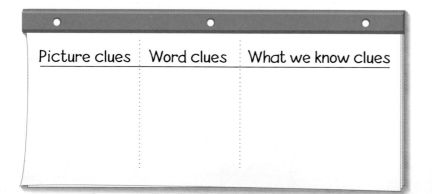

Picture clues	Word clues	What we know clues

Using the following examples from *Across the Wide Dark Sea* to fill in the chart.

Page 120 *"Tears streamed down my mother's face, yet she was smiling."*
How was mother feeling? (happy)
Word clues: *Land had been sighted. The trip was over. It had been difficult.*
What I know: *People sometimes cry when they are happy.*

Apply

Have students make inferences, with an eye to using picture clues, word clues and what they know as they read the **Reader's Library** selection *The Golden Land* by Lee S. Justice. Ask students to complete the questions and activity on the Responding Page.

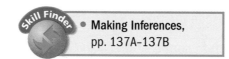

Skill Finder • Making Inferences, pp. 137A–137B

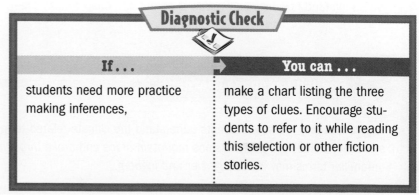

Diagnostic Check

If . . .	You can . . .
students need more practice making inferences,	make a chart listing the three types of clues. Encourage students to refer to it while reading this selection or other fiction stories.

Comprehension Skills: Making Inferences
Challenge/Extension

Social Studies
Plan a Trip

 Paired Activity Have students choose a place they would like to visit. Instruct them *not* to write where they would like to visit on their paper. Tell them to make a list of items they would need to bring, taking into account the weather, the kinds of activities they would want to engage in, and the length of time they would be there. Beneath their packing list, have them name the types of transportation they would need to reach their destination, such as plane, car, bus, boat, or horse-back. Have students exchange and read papers. Ask each student to try to guess where the other student would like to go, based on what they know and the word clues on the paper.

Challenge
Social Studies
Design an Experiment

 In the story, the settlers are planting seeds and crops that they have brought with them on the ship. Have students design an experiment to find out which native plants might be edible and which might be poisonous. Ask them to write a paragraph explaining how they would find out which plants are not poisonous. Remind them that they cannot test the plants by eating them, because the colony needs every member and cannot afford any additional sick members. Have students work alone, in pairs, or in small groups as their skills allow.

Listening/Speaking
Tell About a Voyage

Small Group Activity Have students bring in pictures or other souvenirs from a trip, family visit, or vacation they have taken. Ask them to tell what they liked best about the trip, and what they liked least about the trip. Ask classmates to think about the trips being described. Have them choose the trip they think would be the most exciting, and the one that would be the most fun. Have students explain why they chose each trip. Ask them to use the word clues they heard about each trip and what they know as they speak.

Reader's Library

Comprehension Skills: Predicting Outcomes

Reteaching

Teach

Ask students to think about the fable *The Tortoise and the Hare.* Ask, *What was the outcome of the story? How did it end?* (The tortoise won the race.) Ask, *Did any clues in the story lead you to think the tortoise would win the race?* (The tortoise kept going, and the hare took a nap.) Ask, *If the hare were to race against the tortoise again, what might happen?* Accept all reasonable suggestions, making sure one of the suggestions involves the hare acting in a way that is different from the original tale.

Use a Think-Aloud to model predicting outcomes:

Think Aloud

I use the details and events from the story and my prior knowledge to predict what will happen next or at the end of the story.

Explain to students that guessing what will happen next in a story and guessing how the story will end is called predicting outcomes. Tell students they can use story clues and their own knowledge to predict what will happen.

Practice

Ask, *What was the problem in the story* Yunmi and Halmoni's Trip? (Yunmi was afraid her grandmother would not return to New York.) Say, *What was the outcome of the story? How did it end?* (Halmoni said she would go back with Yunmi.)

Direct students to turn to page 153. Ask a student volunteer to read the text aloud. Ask, *How did Yunmi feel?* (worried and scared) Ask, *What was Yunmi worried about?* (She thought Halmoni might not want to leave Korea.) Tell students to look for story clues to help them predict what will happen.

Direct students to turn to page 159 and ask them to read the text. Ask, *What does Yunmi find out?* (Halmoni will go back to New York with her for another year.) Point out that the word "suddenly" in the last paragraph shows that a change is taking place. Ask, *How does Yunmi feel now?* (ashamed and selfish) Tell students to turn to pages 160–161. Ask them to look for clues in the text and picture that show how Yunmi's behavior changed. Call on volunteers to point out clues. (Yunmi is smiling; she is thinking about others instead of herself.)

Apply

Have students predict outcomes, with an eye to using story clues and their own knowledge, in the **Reader's Library** selection *Brothers Are Forever* by Marcy Haber. Ask students to complete the questions and activity on the Responding Page.

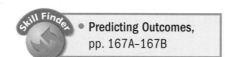

Skill Finder ● Predicting Outcomes, pp. 167A–167B

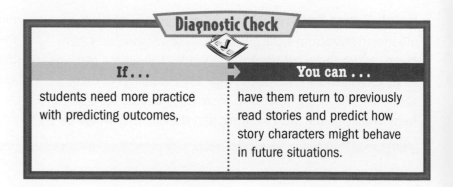

Diagnostic Check

If . . .	You can . . .
students need more practice with predicting outcomes,	have them return to previously read stories and predict how story characters might behave in future situations.

Comprehension Skills: Predicting Outcomes
Challenge/Extension

Listening/Speaking

Have students use story clues and personal knowledge to predict outcomes for characters they have read about. Ask them to discuss the following questions:

- What might Mulan say or do if the Emperor asked her to fight in another war?
- What do you think the Giant of Barletta would do if the townspeople asked him for help again?
- What might the little girl in *Raising Dragons* do if one of her eggs hatched a mean dragon instead of a nice one?

- Do you think Alan, from *The Garden of Abdul Gasazi*, would take Fritz for another walk? What might he do differently?
- What did Sonia learn about wildlife in the story *Two Days in May?* What might she do if some different animals wandered into her garden?

Challenge
Science

Paired Activity Have students perform a simple experiment with magnets. Before they begin their experiment, ask them to predict which materials will be attracted to the magnet and which will not. Have them draw a simple chart to demonstrate this. Give pairs of students a magnet and six objects: iron nail, thumb tack, cork, crayon, aluminum washer, eraser.

Have students test their predictions and note what happens. When they finish, have them share what they have found.

C	yes	no	C	yes	no
eraser			tack		
nail			crayon		
cork			washer		

Math

Paired Activity Explain that predicting outcomes is often used in mathematics. Tell students that this concept in math is called probability, and mathematicians use their prior knowledge and facts to predict how likely it is that an event will happen. Have students test this by flipping a coin 100 times. First, have each pair predict how many times the coin will land on heads, and how many times the coin will land on tails. Next, have them take turns flipping the coin. Ask them to make a simple chart and use hatch marks to record their results. When they are finished, discuss the results as a whole group. Ask, "Did your results match your prediction? Why or why not?" Discuss.

Reader's Library

Comprehension Skills: Text Organization

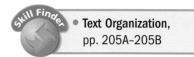

Reteaching

> **OBJECTIVES**
>
> Students identify how text is organized in a book or story.

Teach

Have chapter books on hand, including one that has numbers as chapter heads and one that has chapter titles. Have a newspaper on hand as well. Show students the chapter book that is separated into sections by numbers. Explain that dividing a book into chapters is one way of organizing the text in the story. Show them the chapter book with chapter titles. Explain that another way of organizing text is to label each chapter with a short title that tells something about that chapter.

Show students the newspaper. Ask, *How is the text organized in the newspaper?* (by subject) Ask, *What sections is this newspaper organized into?* (Answers will vary but may include world news, local news, sports, classifieds, and life or variety.)

Hold up the first section of the newspaper. Ask, *What kind of stories would you expect to find in this section?* (major news, world news) Repeat this procedure with the other sections of the newspaper. Explain that text organization can help us to locate specific information in a newspaper. Inform students that authors organize text to make information clear. Text headings help readers make sense of the information in a story.

Practice

Direct students back to page 172 of the story *Trapped by the Ice.* Ask students to identify how the text is organized on this page. (by date) List the date heading on the board. (October 27, 1915) Page through the story and locate some of the headings. List them on the board.

Discuss what is important about each heading. Ask students to tell how the headings help them understand what they read. Explain that text can be organized by dates, events, or main ideas.

Apply

Have students note how text is organized, with an eye to identifying chapters, heads, dates, and events, in the **Reader's Library** selection *Iceberg Rescue* by Sarah Amada. Ask students to complete the questions and activity on the Responding Page.

> **Skill Finder**
> • Text Organization, pp. 205A–205B

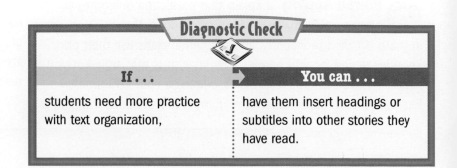

Diagnostic Check

If . . .	You can . . .
students need more practice with text organization,	have them insert headings or subtitles into other stories they have read.

Challenge/Extension

Math

 Independent Activity Have students use the date headings and other information in the story *Trapped by the Ice* to write and solve time problems. Have students write the problem and solution on their papers. You may want to have old calendars on hand for the students to use as counting tools. (Note: 1916 was a leap year, so students must remember to count Feb. 29.) Write the following questions on the board or create your own examples:

- How many days passed between the day the Endurance was trapped by the ice and the day she sank? (from October 27 to November 21; 25 days)
- How many days passed between the day the Endurance was trapped by the ice and the day Shackleton reached the whaling station? (from October 27, 1915 to May 20, 1916; 207 days)
- How many days passed between the day the men got the lifeboats to open water and the day they spotted Elephant Island? (from April 8 to April 15; 8 days)

Challenge
Social Studies

Small Group Activity Have students work in small groups to map out a voyage from their hometown to Antarctica. Gather atlases or world maps for the students to use. Direct them to travel through major or capital cities whenever possible. Demonstrate for students how to recognize a major city, a country name, and the name of a body of water on a world map. Direct students to travel by land and sea only. Have students discuss what types of transportation they will use and make a list of the major cities and countries they will pass through on their journey.

Art/Writing

Independent Activity Cut large construction paper into 11" x 9" strips. Give each student two paper strips. Have students glue strips together, overlapping them slightly. Have students make a timeline showing important dates in their lives, beginning with their birth. Ask them to write a date for each event. Direct students to include the year for each date. Have them write a title for each event. Next, have them illustrate each event or write a brief description about the event's importance. Suggest such milestones as birthdays, holidays, and trips. Encourage them to include activities such as learning to ride a bike, winning a ball game, and learning to play a musical instrument.

Structural Analysis Skills: Suffixes *-less* and *-ness*

Reteaching

OBJECTIVES

Students

- identify words that contain the suffixes *-less* and *-ness*
- define meanings for words containing the suffixes *-less* and *-ness*

Teach

Remind students that suffixes are word parts that are written after a base word. Give each student two index cards containing the suffixes *-less* or *-ness*. Tell students that they are going to use these suffixes to make new words from base words. Direct them to hold up their card (or cards) when they see a base word that their suffix will work with.

Write *hope* on the chalkboard or chart paper. Ask, *What word part can combine with hope to make a new word?* Wait for students holding the *-less* suffix to hold up their cards. Use colored chalk or marker to add the suffix *-less* to the base word *hope*. Ask, *What is this word?* Wait for a choral response.

Continue this procedure using the following words:

> *help* (helpless)
> *end* (endless)
> *sick* (sickness)
> *fearful* (fearfulness)
> *hopeful* (hopefulness)

Explain to students that the suffix *-less* means *without,* and the suffix *-ness* means *the state of being.* Have students define the words above, helping them as necessary.

Remind students that when we add suffixes, we change the meanings of the base words. Tell students they are going to use what they know to decode words having the suffixes *-less* and *-ness*.

Practice

Go back to the story *Across the Wide Dark Sea.* Reread the list of words above. Have the students find an example of when the people in the story might have experienced the feeling of helplessness. (during the storms) Continue through the other words in the list, having students locate one or more examples for each word.

Ask, *What does the suffix -less mean?* (without) Say, *Tell me some words containing -less.* Write the words on chart paper. Repeat the procedure with the meaning for *-ness* (the state of being) and words containing that suffix. Return to the words written on the chart paper. Point to a specific word and call on a volunteer to give a definition for that word. Continue until each student has had the opportunity to share an answer.

Apply

Have students write sentences using words with *-less* and *-ness.* Direct them to use words from the list you created together. Remind them to think about the meanings of the words as they write them. Have exchange papers and underline the words with the suffixes *-less* and *-ness.*

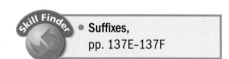

Skill Finder
- Suffixes, pp. 137E–137F

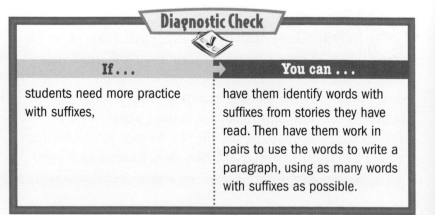

Diagnostic Check

If . . .	You can . . .
students need more practice with suffixes,	have them identify words with suffixes from stories they have read. Then have them work in pairs to use the words to write a paragraph, using as many words with suffixes as possible.

Voyagers
Vocabulary Activities

Challenge
Antonyms

Have students fold a piece of paper in half lengthwise. Next, have them fold the paper in half, widthwise, three times. When the paper is unfolded, they will have two columns, each with eight boxes. Direct students to write a word containing the suffix *-less* or *-ness* in each box in the left column. In the right column, have them write a word that is opposite in meaning of the word in the left column. Allow students to use a dictionary or thesaurus as needed.

Play a Word Game

Write the word *thoughtlessness* on the board. Instruct students that they are to make as many words as they can from the letters in this word. Tell them that the letters they use do not have to be in the same order as they are in the word *thoughtlessness* on the board, but they can only use as many letters as are in the original word. For example, there is only one "o" in thoughtlessness, so students can only use one "o" in any word they make. Tell them that they can reuse letters when they begin a new word.

> thoughtlessness
> ought
> guess
> nest

Vocabulary Expansion

Write the following words on the board: *madness, clueless, peacefulness, weightless, senseless.*

Ask students to tell you the meaning of each word, assisting them as needed or you might want students to use dictionaries to identify each word's meaning. Direct students to choose a word and write it in the center of a word web. Ask students to use as many words as they can to describe the center word, without using the center word in any form.

Structural Analysis Skills: Possessives

 **Reteaching**

OBJECTIVES

Students

- identify examples of possessives in a story
- use possessives in writing, including 's and s'

Teach

Write the following phrases on the board:

Point out the apostrophes in both sentences. Ask, *What does the apostrophe show us in these phrases?* (possession, belonging) Read the phrases aloud. Explain to students that we add an apostrophe and the letter *s* to singular nouns to show possession. Explain that since plural nouns usually end in s already, we just add the apostrophe.

One boy's jacket
The students' jackets

Write the following phrases on chart paper or on the board.

Have students add the apostrophe in each phrase. Help them to see that the apostrophe indicates possession—whether it precedes or follows the *s*. Work with students to help them understand how the apostrophe is used differently with singular and plural nouns.

dads jacket (dad's)
two girls lunches (girls')
teachers desk (teacher's)
Glorias pencil (Gloria's)
dogs tail (dog's)
elephants trunks (elephants')

Circle the apostrophe *s* or *s* apostrophe in each example. For each example, ask, *Who is showing possession? Who does the object belong to?* Encourage students to respond together.

Use the examples you have written to help students generate a rule about single nouns and a rule about plural nouns ending in *s.* Write the rules on chart paper for students to refer to. You may want to include rules similar to the following examples:

- If a noun is single, add an apostrophe *s* to the end of the noun.
- If a noun is plural and ends in *s,* just add an apostrophe.

Apply

Have students look at the illustrations from the story. For each picture, have students list a possessive phrase about an object they see. For example, on page 149 students could list Halmoni's house, Yunmi's cousins, or the house's steps. When they have completed their list, have students circle the apostrophe in each example.

- **Possessives,** pp. 167E–167F

Practice

Point out to students the apostrophe in the title of the story *Yunmi and Halmoni's Trip.* Invite students to explain the use of the apostrophe. Then work with them to find examples of possessives in the story. Write the examples on chart paper. You might want to include some of the following examples:

- p. 145 Grandfather's birthday celebration
  Yunmi's grandfather
- p. 146 foreigners' line
- p. 149 Halmoni's house
  Yunmi's cousins

Diagnostic Check

If . . .	You can . . .
students need more practice with possessives,	have them make a list of the items in a classmate's desk, using possessives. Then have them change it to indicate that the same items were in several students' desks.

Vocabulary Activities

Challenge
Synonyms

Write the following words from the story on the board: *died, promise, foreigner, broad, fluffy, sweet, roam, crowded, press, hurry.* Have students work in pairs using a dictionary or thesaurus to find synonyms for these words. Ask students to write each word and its synonym on their paper. Encourage them to identify both familiar and unfamiliar synonyms for their lists.

Have students describe an object or person from the story. Direct them not to list the object or person's name. Have them write the correct answer upside down on the back of their paper, at the bottom. Hang the descriptions on the board for classmates to guess, or compile them together in a book.

Possessives

Have students make a list of their classmates on a piece of paper. For each person, have students identify something the person is wearing, or an object the person owns, or a positive characteristic of that person and write the word on the paper next to the person's name. Remind students to use apostrophe *s* to describe possession. Write the following on the board as an example:

> Ross's red shirt
>
> Teresa's markers
>
> the teacher's stamp

Vocabulary Expansion

In this story, Yunmi experiences many feelings during her trip. Use the story to make a list of words related to feelings. Have students help you find examples of a variety of feelings in the story and, once identified, write them on chart paper. (excited, strange, happily, proud, worry, scared, surprised, ashamed, selfish.) Then direct them to fold a piece of paper into eight squares. In each square, have them write a

feeling word and draw a picture to express that word. Ask them to draw something that word makes them think of, or a person's face expressing that feeling.

Theme Resources

Word Work

Structural Analysis Skills: VCCV Pattern and Syllabication

 Reteaching

Teach

Write the word *happen* on the chalkboard or on chart paper. Under the word, write the letters VCCV, so the word appears like this:

happen
VCCV

Point out to students that the letters *appe* in the word *happen* are in a vowel-consonant-consonant-vowel pattern *(VCCV)*. Explain to students that we can use the patterns of letters in words to tell us several things. Tell them letter patterns can help us to know how to pronounce the word, how to divide the word into syllables, and how to spell the word.

Draw a vertical line between the two 'p's in happen. Tell students that when we divide this word into syllables, we divide it between the two consonants.

Say the word *happen* slowly, clapping each syllable. Explain that words with a VCCV pattern are usually divided between the two consonants. Ask, *What vowel sound do you hear in the beginning of happen?* (a) Ask, *Is this a long or short vowel sound?* (short) *What vowel sound do you hear in the second syllable of happen?* (e) *Is this a short or long vowel sound?* (short) Explain that words with a VCCV pattern often have short vowel sounds because the vowel is followed by a consonant.

Display the following words: *summer, winter, suffix, basket, market, target.* Have the students read the words with you. Explain that all of these words have VCCV patterns. Ask a volunteer to draw a line between the consonants in the word *summer.* Have the students clap the syllables in the word while saying it aloud. Continue through the other five words with other volunteers.

Remind students that knowing about and identifying the VCCV pattern can help us decode and pronounce unfamiliar words while we read. Finally, demonstrate for students that in most instances, we put the accent on the first syllable for words that contain a VCCV pattern.

Practice

Go back to the story *Trapped by the Ice.* Have students help you find words that have the VCCV letter pattern. Write each word on chart paper. Some words from the story are listed here: *person, lumber, skipper, possible, current, concern, hunters, danger, after.*

Have student volunteers use a marker to underline the letters forming the VCCV pattern. Using a different color marker, have volunteers divide the word into syllables. Repeat the words together, clapping the syllables.

Apply

Have students continue to look in the story for words with the VCCV pattern. Have each student make a list of words. Have students swap papers and circle the VCCV combinations in each other's lists. Have students exchange papers again and divide the words into syllables. When finished, ask each student to read the list of words, helping the student to see how understanding the VCCV pattern can help decode and pronounce words.

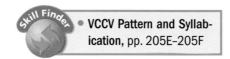

Skill Finder
- VCCV Pattern and Syllabication, pp. 205E–205F

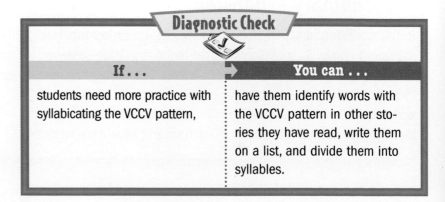

Diagnostic Check

If...	You can ...
students need more practice with syllabicating the VCCV pattern,	have them identify words with the VCCV pattern in other stories they have read, write them on a list, and divide them into syllables.

Vocabulary Activities

Word Mix-up

Give each student an even number of 3" x 3" pieces of construction paper (between 6 and 12 pieces). Ask students to make a list of two-syllable words that contain a VCCV pattern. Have students write the first syllable of the word on one piece of paper and the second syllable on another piece. Have students mix up their papers when they have finished writing. Direct each student to exchange papers with a partner. Have students take their new group of papers and make words out of the syllables. When they have matched all the syllables, have them read the words aloud to their partner. When the whole group has finished, switch again. After several repetitions, save the syllable cards and use for a center activity.

Challenge
Action Verb Game

Have students work in pairs. Direct each pair to look through the story *Trapped by the Ice* and make a list of action verbs. Some action verbs used in the story are *skiing, burst, lunged, slip, stalking, hunt, tripped, springing, cried, rushed, dropped.* Have each pair fold a blank piece of paper in half lengthwise twice, and then fold it in half widthwise, three times. The paper will show a total of 32 squares. Have the pair choose 16 action verbs and write them on the paper, one to a square, scattering them around the squares. Tell them that the words do not need to be in any kind of order or pattern. Ask them to fill in the remaining 16 squares with nouns.

Give each pair a number cube. Have one player roll the cube and move that number of spaces, from the top left to right. If the player lands on an action verb, he or she can roll again. If he or she lands on a noun, the other player takes a turn. Move from left to right until the end of a row, then drop down one square and continue from right to left. The game ends when one player has traveled to the bottom right corner of the paper. If time allows, have pairs switch papers and play again.

Vocabulary Expansion

Use the word Antarctica in a center circle for a word web. Brainstorm, with the whole class, as many words and phrases as possible to describe Antarctica. You may want to refer back to the story to look for descriptive words. After making a word web, direct students to write a cinquain. If students are unfamiliar with this style of poem, write the following on the board as an example:

> Antarctica
> Far away
> Cold, colder, coldest
> Ice, snow, frost, wind
> Seals, penguins, birds, walrus, fish

Grammar Skills: Subject Pronouns

 Reteaching

Teach

Write the following sentences:

> The girls play soccer.
>
> They play soccer.

Read each sentence aloud. Underline the word *they* in the second sentence. Explain to students that the word *they* is a pronoun that takes the place of the subject noun in the first sentence. Identify for students other
pronouns that can be used as subjects, for example, *I, you, she, he, it,* and *we.*

Have students work in pairs. Give each pair five index cards on which to write the subject pronouns *she, he, it, they,* and *we.* Tell students that you will say some sentences aloud. Ask them to listen carefully and identify the subject of the sentence. Tell each pair to hold up the index card that has the pronoun that can replace the subject. Read the following sentences aloud, or make up your own.

> *The boys rode bikes.* (They)
> *Hope and I watched TV.* (We)
> *The bird caught a worm.* (It)
> *Antonio wrote a poem.* (He)
> *Yolanda ate pizza.* (She)
> *The bug has green wings.* (It)

Practice

Repeat the activity above, using sentences from the story *Across the Wide Dark Sea.* Have the students follow along in the story with you. After each sentence you read, ask student pairs to hold up the index card with the pronoun that can replace the subject of the sentence. Some examples from the story include the following:

> Page 113 "My father was waving to friends on shore." (He)
> "Our family was luckier than most." (We were)
> Page 115 "My mother and brother were seasick down below." (They)
> Page 119 "Could our ship survive another storm?" (It)
> Page 120 "Our long journey was over." (It)

Summarize with students by asking the following questions: *What words are subject pronouns?* (I, you, he, she, they, we, it) *What does a subject pronoun do?* (replaces the subject noun in a sentence)

Apply

Have students write sentences of their own that contain the subject pronouns *I, he, she, we, they, it,* and *you.* When they are done, have students exchange papers. Students can then underline the subject pronouns in their partner's sentences. Then have them give the papers back so that each partner can check to see if the underlining is correct.

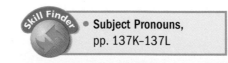
Skill Finder
- Subject Pronouns, pp. 137K–137L

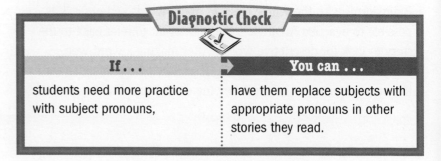

Diagnostic Check

If...	You can ...
students need more practice with subject pronouns,	have them replace subjects with appropriate pronouns in other stories they read.

Writing & Language   Theme Resources

Grammar Skills: Object Pronouns
Reteaching

Teach

Write the following sentences on the chalkboard:

> *Mary plays basketball with Lucy and Simon.*
> *Mary plays basketball with them.*

Read each sentence aloud. Underline the word *them* in the second sentence. Explain to students that the word *them* is a pronoun that replaces the proper nouns *Lucy* and *Simon* in the first sentence. Tell students that object pronouns include the following: *me, you, us, them, him, her,* and *it.*

Write the object pronouns on the chalkboard. Then give each pair of students five blank index cards. Tell them to write the object pronouns *us, them, him, her,* and *it* on their index cards. Explain that these can be used to replace a noun or nouns. Write the following sentences on the board with the noted underlines:

I like <u>Carla</u>. (her)

I went inline skating with <u>Luisa and Sheryl</u>. (them)

My mother danced with <u>my friend and me</u>. (us)

I bought the <u>comic book</u> for <u>Jared</u>. (it, him)

Josh loves to play cards with <u>Serena</u>. (her)

My big brother gave <u>his old TV</u> to <u>my sister and me</u>. (it, us)

The children read a <u>story</u>. (it)

Ask students to read the first sentence together. As you reread the sentence, have them hold up and say the object pronoun that can replace the underlined word. Follow the same procedure with each of the other sentences. You can use these sentences or create ones of your own.

Practice

Tell the students you are going to work together to identify object pronouns in the story *Yunmi and Halmoni's Trip.* Have the students follow along in the story with you. After you read each sentence, ask, *What noun or nouns did this pronoun replace?* The following are some examples of sentences from the story:

> Page 145 "She pulled out a thick bundle of photos of Yunmi's many relatives, and began to tell her about each of them." (Yunmi, Yunmi's relatives)
> Page 148 "Suddenly a huge crowd of people rushed toward them, waving and bowing." (Yunmi and Halmoni)
> Page 149 "A cat and a dog with a fluffy tail ran behind her." (Halmoni's sister) "Oh, I missed you, too," she said to him." (the dog)

When finished, review with students by asking: *What words are object pronouns?* (them, us, me, you, him, her, it) *What does an object pronoun do?* (replaces an object noun in a sentence)

Apply

Have students make up sentences containing the object pronouns *them, us, me, you, him, her,* and *it.* When they are finished writing their sentences, ask students to exchange papers and underline the object pronouns. Then have them return the papers and check their partner's underlining.

Skill Finder
- Object Pronouns, pp. 167K–167L

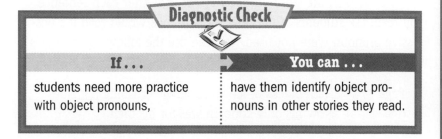

Diagnostic Check	
If . . .	**You can . . .**
students need more practice with object pronouns,	have them identify object pronouns in other stories they read.

Grammar Skills: Possessive Pronouns

 Reteaching

Teach

Write the following sentences on the board:

Read each sentence aloud. Underline the word *his* in the second sentence. Explain to students that the word *his* is a pronoun that shows possession.

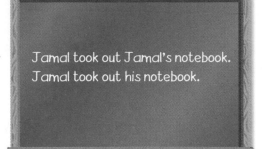

Jamal took out Jamal's notebook.
Jamal took out his notebook.

Suggest to students other pronouns that can be used to show possession, for example, *my, your, his, her, our, their,* and *its.* Explain that by using possessive pronouns, we avoid repeating the subject in the sentence, which sounds awkward.

Give each student an index card with a possessive pronoun written on it, excluding *my* and *your.* Tell students that you will be saying some sentences aloud. Ask them to listen carefully to each sentence. Tell them that if they are holding a card with the pronoun that can replace the possessive noun, they should hold it up. Then have all students read the sentences together, using the possessive pronouns. Read the following sentences aloud, or make up your own.

> Gina brought <u>Gina's</u> ball for the soccer game. (her)
> Stan brings <u>Stan's</u> lunch every day. (his)
> ou and I should take <u>your coat and my coat</u> off.
> (our coats)
> Jeff and Chantal forgot <u>Jeff and Chantal's</u> homework. (their)
> The cat licked the <u>cat's</u> paw. (its)

Practice

Tell the students you are going to work together to identify possessive pronouns in the story *Trapped by the Ice!* After each sentence you read, ask students to tell how the sentence would read if a possessive pronoun were not used. You can use the following examples from the story:

> Page 172 "Giant blocks of ice were slowly crushing <u>her</u> sides." (the ship's) "Now <u>his</u> only concern was for <u>his</u> men."

(Shackleton's) "The Endurance was a sad sight now, a useless hulk lying on <u>its</u> side." (Endurance's or hulk's)

Page 174 "Turning toward the ship's wreckage, they saw <u>her</u> stern rise slowly in the air, tremble, and slip quickly beneath the ice." (the ship's)

Page 176 "Executing <u>their</u> plan would be difficult." (the men's)

Page 180 "During <u>their</u> five and a half months on the ice they hadn't had a bath." (the men's)

Ask students: *What words are possessive pronouns?* (my, your, his, her, our, their, its) *What does a possessive pronoun do?* (replaces a possessive noun in a sentence)

Apply

Have students write sentences of their own that contain the possessive pronouns *my, your, his, her our, their,* and *its.* When they are done, have students exchange papers and underline the possessive pronouns. Then ask them to give the papers back and check their partner's underlining.

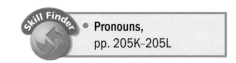

Skill Finder • Pronouns,
pp. 205K–205L

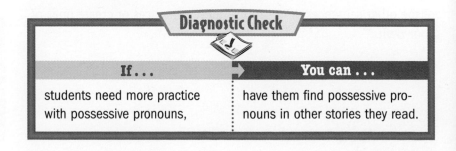

Diagnostic Check

If . . .	You can . . .
students need more practice with possessive pronouns,	have them find possessive pronouns in other stories they read.

Voyagers

Writing Activities

Write a Character Sketch

Tell the class that they are going to write a character sketch together. Have them brainstorm ideas about what a sailor's life on the *Mayflower* was like. Tell them they can use reference sources to look for word and picture clues. Write a word web that includes the qualities, feelings, and responsibilities of a sailor's life on the chalkboard. Have students use the web ideas to write a sketch describing a sailor of that time, as in the example shown.

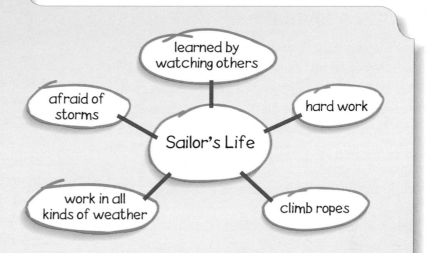

Challenge
Research Report

Have students research sailing and the lives of sailors in the 1600s. Have students use encyclopedias and other reference sources to gather information. Ask them to share their information and to write a group report. Invite them to present their report to the class.

Voyagers

Writing Activities

Write a Journal

Have students imagine what it might have been like to make a voyage across an ocean to live in a new land. Tell them to write journal entries as if they were part of the voyage, providing descriptive details. Direct students to write about the experience from the first-person perspective. Have them date the events and put them in order in their journals. Tell students to begin with their preparations for the trip and end with their arrival in a new land.

Read aloud the following example to the students:

June 21 We knew that we could only carry a few essential items. We chose to bring two long coats and other heavy clothing in the event of cold weather. We brought enough water and food to last several months for this long and unpredictable voyage.

June 28 We said goodbye to those we loved and they wished us well. We knew we would never see them again and this brought us tremendous sadness.

July 1 We arrived at our port. When we arrived, we found out that our voyage was delayed due to a problem with the sails that needed to be fixed before we left. This meant a delay for three days.

July 4 We left our port for America. We were filled with mixed emotions. We were excited but afraid. We were sad about leaving but happy about all of the new possibilities in this new land.

Writing Activities

Describe a Character Through Actions

Explain to students that authors often describe characters through their actions. You might ask students to provide some examples from stories they have previously read.

Have students choose someone to write about, especially an historical figure who took a voyage across an ocean, from one continent to another: for example, Christopher Columbus, Ferdinand Magellan, or Vasco da Gama. After reading about the historic figure, ask students to write a short biography about the person, using his or her actions or words whenever possible to describe the person to readers. Invite students to share what they have learned.

Write a Persuasive Paragraph

Tell students to imagine that a contest has been announced to find people to take a voyage into outer space. Tell each student to try to convince the judges that he or she would be the best person to go into outer space and the best civilian to manage the activities at a space station. Have students write a persuasive composition telling why they think they would be the best choice for such a position.

Portfolio Opportunity
Save responses to activities on these three pages for writing samples.

Voyagers

Cross-Curricular Activities

Science
Perform an Experiment

Have students test objects made of common materials to see if they sink or float. In pairs, have students place each object in a container of water and observe the result. As students work in small groups, ask them to record their answers on a simple chart. Objects might include craft sticks, cork, metal washers, aluminum foil, styrofoam, paper clips, pine cones, and bricks.

Ask students to write a paragraph describing their experiment and their findings.

Listening/Speaking
ABC Memory Game

Have students play a memory game. Use the following starter for the game: *I went on a trip across the sea, and into my suitcase I packed an apple.* Explain to students that as they go around their small or large group, each person will add a new item beginning with the next letter of the alphabet. Select a student volunteer to add an item beginning with the letter *B*. The story might then sound like this: *I went on a trip across the sea, and into my suitcase I packed an apple and a boomerang.* Have them continue around their group, selecting volunteers, until each letter of the alphabet has been used. If students have trouble remembering the list, allow the rest of the group help them before going on to the next letter.

Voyagers

Cross-Curricular Activities

Challenge
Math
Create a Budget

Bring in travel magazines, brochures, the travel section from the newspaper, hotel and motel guides, and any other transportation or vacation price guides available. Ask students to work in small groups to plan a trip for four. Have students select a destination and write a budget for a week's stay in the location of their choice. You may want to post a sample budget on the chalkboard for students to refer to. Ask students to include costs for the following:

Travel Budget

- transportation to and from destination
- lodging for six nights
- 3 meals per day for 4 people
- fees for recreational activities
- spending money for souvenirs

Social Studies
Research a Destination

Ask students to choose a city they would like to visit. Have students use newspapers, travel guides, magazines, and encyclopedias to find information about the city. Tell them to make a list of the things they would like to see and do in the city. Have them present the information to the class. Encourage them to show pictures to the class as they present their information.

You may want to have small groups write letters to the chamber of commerce of their city of choice, asking for more information.

Art
Design a Vehicle

Brainstorm a list of types of transportation on the chalkboard. Invite students to think about ways these vehicles could be improved. Suggest that they might be faster, more comfortable, quieter, or more fuel-efficient. Have each student design a vehicle and label their drawing with the improvements they made.

Technology Resources

American Melody
P. O. Box 270
Guilford, CT 06437
800-220-5557

Audio Bookshelf
174 Prescott Hill Road
Northport, ME 04849
800-234-1713

Baker & Taylor
100 Business Court Drive
Pittsburgh, PA 15205
800-775-2600

BDD Audio
1540 Broadway
New York, NY 10036
800-223-6834

Big Kids Productions
1606 Dwyer Ave.
Austin, TX 78704
800-477-7811
www.bigkidsvideo.com

Blackboard Entertainment
2647 International
Boulevard
Suite 853
Oakland, CA 94601
800-968-2261
www.blackboardkids.com

Books on Tape
P.O. Box 7900
Newport Beach, CA 92658
800-626-3333

Filmic Archives
The Cinema Center
Botsford, CT 06404
800-366-1920
www.filmicarchives.com

Great White Dog Picture Company
10 Toon Lane
Lee, NH 03824
800-397-7641
www.greatwhitedog.com

HarperAudio
10 E. 53rd St
New York, NY 10022
800-242-7737

Houghton Mifflin Company
222 Berkeley St.
Boston, MA 02116
800-225-3362

Informed Democracy
P.O. Box 67
Santa Cruz, CA 95063
831-426-3921

JEF Films
143 Hickory Hill Circle
Osterville, MA 02655
508-428-7198

Kimbo Educational
P. O. Box 477
Long Branch, NJ 07740
900-631-2187

The Learning Company (dist. for Broderbund)
1 Athenaeum St.
Cambridge, MA 02142
800-716-8506
www.learningco.com

Library Video Co.
P. O. Box 580
Wynnewood, PA 19096
800-843-3620

Listening Library
One Park Avenue
Old Greenwich, CT 06870
800-243-45047

Live Oak Media
P. O. Box 652
Pine Plains, NY 12567
800-788-1121
liveoak@taconic.net

Media Basics
Lighthouse Square
PO Box 449
Guilford, CT 06437
800-542-2505
www.mediabasicsvideo.com

Microsoft Corp.
One Microsoft Way
Redmond, WA 98052
800-426-9400
www.microsoft.com

National Geographic Society
1145 17th Street N. W.
Washington, D. C. 20036
800-368-2728
www.nationalgeographic.com

New Kid Home Video
1364 Palisades Beach Road
Santa Monica, CA 90401
310-451-5164

Puffin Books
345 Hudson Street
New York, NY 10014
212-366-2000

Rainbow Educational Media
4540 Preslyn Drive
Raleigh, NC 27616
800-331-4047

Random House Home Video
201 E. 50th St.
New York, NY 10022
212-940-7620

Recorded Books
270 Skipjack Road
Prince Frederick, MD 20678
800-638-1304
www.recordedbooks.com

Sony Wonder
Dist. by Professional Media
Service
19122 S. Vermont Ave
Gardena, CA 90248
800-223-7672

Spoken Arts
8 Lawn Avenue
P. O. Box 100
New Rochelle, NY 10802
800-326-4090

SRA Media
220 E. Danieldale Rd.
DeSoto, TX 75115
800-843-8855

Sunburst Communications
101 Castleton St.
P. O. Box 100
Pleasantville, NY 10570
800-321-7511
www.sunburst.com

SVE & Churchill Media
6677 North Northwest
Highway
Chicago, IL 60631
800-829-1900

Tom Snyder Productions
80 Coolidge Hill Road
Watertown, MA 02472
800-342-0236
www.tomsnyder.com

Troll Communications
100 Corporate Drive
Mahwah, NJ 07430
800-526-5289

Weston Woods
12 Oakwood Avenue
Norwalk, CT 06850-1318
800-243-5020
www.scholastic.com

Focus On Biographies

Focus On **Biographies**

Biography

OBJECTIVES

During this Focus on Biography, students

- identify and define *biographies*
- identify the elements of a biography
- compare and contrast biographies
- write a biography

Introducing the Genre

Read aloud the opening paragraph on page 209. Ask students why they think people like to read biographies. List on the board some reasons, such as they give information about interesting people and it is fun and helpful to learn about other people's lives. Invite students to think about these reasons as they read the biographies.

▶ Building Background

Invite volunteers to read the elements of biography. Have students tell what they think they will learn by reading a biography.

 Journal Writing Have students record their thoughts about reading biographies and what can be learned from them. Invite them to list people they might like to read or write about.

 Teacher's Note

Discuss with students that stories have always been told about heroes or people who were admired. Sometimes they were told using poems or songs. These early tales were the first biographies. Tell students that in a modern biography, the author only tells what is true and can be proven.

208

MEETING INDIVIDUAL NEEDS **Extra Support**

Ordering Events

Invite students to order what has happened in their day thus far. Remind them that in a biography, the author has to put events in the order in which they happened.

Focus on

Biography

Are you curious about real people and what happens in their lives? Then try reading a biography.

A BIOGRAPHY . . .
- is a true story about a person's life
- tells about a person who is living now or who lived earlier
- gives facts and important information about a person
- usually starts with the early years of a person's life and then moves on to later years.

Contents

Becoming a Champion:
The Babe Didrikson Story 210
   by Stephen Berman

Bill Meléndez: An Artist in Motion 216
   by Stephen Berman

Brave Bessie Coleman: Pioneer Aviator 222
   by Veronica Freeman Ellis

Hank Greenberg: All-Around All-Star 228
   by Becky Cheston

209

▶ Suggestions for Using *Focus on Biography*

- ■ Students note key elements of a biography.
- ■ Students study Writer's Craft.
- ■ Students practice implementation of various reading strategies.
- ■ Students gain a basis of comparison for writing their own biography.

▶ Genre Connection

Use **Practice Book** pages 117 and 118 to review and reinforce the biography genre. Students can complete the **Practice Book** pages after finishing the biographies. Use the **Practice Book** pages when students most need review and reinforcement.

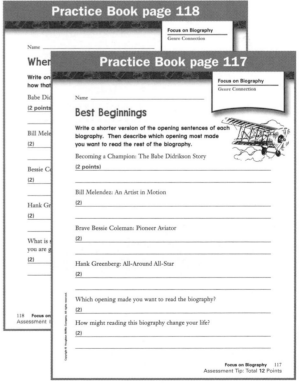

Reading "Becoming a Champion: The Babe Didrikson Story"

pages 210–215

▶ **Preparing to Read**

Have students look at the time line on pages 212–215.

■ Review the dates on the time line. Remind students that these are important dates in Babe Didrikson's life.

■ Point out the birth of Babe Didrikson on the time line. Explain that during much of Didrikson's life, women were not allowed to participate in many things. Didrikson opened many doors for other women.

■ Talk about why people who are first to do something make good or significant subjects for biographies.

▶ **Purpose Setting**

Have students read to identify important events in Babe Didrikson's life.

 Journal Writing Invite students to write two questions that they would like to ask a favorite athlete.

Vocabulary *(pages 210–211)*

athlete: someone who plays sports

competitive: working hard to win

cyclones: wind storms, such as tornadoes

BECOMING A CHAMPION

The Babe Didrikson Story
by Stephen Berman

1 BABE DIDRIKSON once announced that she wanted to be "the greatest athlete that ever lived." She didn't say "woman athlete." She didn't think that way, and she didn't want others to think that way either. Whenever she had the chance, she competed with boys and men. And she beat them too!

Didrikson was born in Port Arthur, Texas, in 1911. Her parents named her Mildred. She was athletic and competitive. She always played just as hard as the boys, if not harder. One day she hit five home runs in a neighborhood baseball game. That day, the players nicknamed her "Babe," after the great baseball star Babe Ruth. The nickname stayed with her for life.

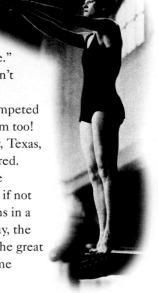

210

 English Language Learners

Listing Sports Expressions

Invite students to list sports expressions they know. They can keep this list and add to it as they read this biography.

Babe wasn't just good at baseball, though. Basketball, tennis, track, diving — even bowling — came easily to her. And she said she loved them all. "I sleep them, eat them, talk them, and try my level best to do them as they should be done," she said.

In high school, Babe was a basketball star. In 1930, the owner of a Dallas insurance company saw her play. He offered her a job. With the job came the chance to star on the company's basketball team, the Golden <u>Cyclones</u>.

Babe practices for a basketball game, January, 1933.

211

Revisiting the Text

Writer's Craft Lesson
Sequence of Events/Foreshadowing

OBJECTIVES

Students identify the sequence of events in a biography.

Talk briefly with students about where Didrikson is in her life when the biography begins. Was she a child or an adult when she said that she wanted to be the greatest athlete? (She probably said it as an adult.)

Ask students to name three significant events in the order in which they happened in Didrikson's life. (Answers may include the following: she was born in Port Arthur, Texas; she was a high school basketball star; she won Olympic gold medals in track and field; she won sixty-five golf tournaments.)

Point out that sometimes an author begins a biography with a special event that shows something important about the subject's character. This is called *foreshadowing:* presenting a suggestion to the reader beforehand.

Invite small groups of students to choose something from Babe Didrikson's biography that foreshadows her career. Allow time for students to share their work.

Cross-Curricular Connection

Social Studies Babe Didrikson was nicknamed after Babe Ruth (1895–1948), one of the greatest baseball players of all time. Yankee Stadium is referred to as "The House That Ruth Built" because of the enormous boost he gave to people's interest in baseball when he played there. Ruth was inducted into the Baseball Hall of Fame in 1936.

Reading "Becoming a Champion: The Babe Didrikson Story," continued
pages 210–215

▶ ## Supporting Comprehension

1 Reread the first sentence on page 210. Why do you think the author begins the biography in this way? (It catches the reader's attention; it makes the reader wonder if Didrickson became one of the greatest athletes ever.)

2 How does the author show how competitive Didrikson was? (Everything Didrikson says shows her great determination. For example, she wanted to be *"the greatest athlete that ever lived," "I sleep them [sports], eat them, talk them . . . ,"* and *"I trained and trained and trained."*)

3 Why does the author tell us that when Didrikson began playing golf, she practiced sixteen hours a day and bruised her hands? (to show Didrikson's determination)Why didn't the author simply say that Didrikson was determined? (Answers will vary.)

Vocabulary *(pages 212–213)*

excelled: did the best at something

tournaments: sports contests

As a Cyclone, Babe often scored thirty or more points a game. She led the team to the national women's basketball championships in 1930 and 1931. Other companies offered her higher pay, but Babe's company was starting a women's track-and-field team. She couldn't wait to try this new sport.

Once again, Babe excelled at something new. She was good at all three kinds of track-and-field events — running, jumping, and throwing. She decided to try out for the Olympics.

Babe jumps a hurdle.

1911
Born on June 26 in Port Arthur, Texas.

1930 – 1931
Joined the Golden Cyclones. Chosen as an All-American basketball player two years in a row.

1932
Won two gold medals (javelin and 80-meter hurdles) and a silver medal (high jump) at the Olympic Games in Los Angeles, California.

212

Challenge

Comparing Athletes

Invite students to compare Babe Didrikson to a modern athlete, telling how they are similar and different.

2 "I trained and trained and trained," she wrote to a friend. "I've been that way in every sport I've ever taken up." At the Olympic tryouts, she won five events and broke four world records. People called it the most amazing performance in track-and-field history — not just for a woman, but for anyone. Of course, she made the team too. And at the 1932 Olympic Games, Babe won three medals in track-and-field — one for every event she entered. At the end of the Olympics, she was as famous as Charles Lindbergh and Amelia Earhart.

3 Babe wasn't ready to rest, though. As a new challenge, she turned to golf. It turned out to be the greatest love of her life. She began practicing golf for up to sixteen hours a day. When her hands got sore and bruised from holding the clubs, she bandaged them and kept on playing.

Here's Babe warming up for the javelin throw.

1935	1945 – 1947	1948
Began playing golf; went on to win 65 <u>tournaments</u>.	Chosen "Woman Athlete of the Year" by the Associated Press three years in a row.	Won first U.S. Open golf tournament.

213

Extra Support

Listing Questions

As students read, encourage them to write questions in their journal about anything that isn't clear. They can ask them later or during reading.

Reading "Becoming a Champion: The Babe Didrikson Story," continued
pages 210–215

▶ **Supporting Comprehension**

4 What are some of the details that show what a fierce competitor Didrickson was in the sport of golf? (She always assumed she would be first, and she played golf after doctors told her she would never play again.)

Babe's humor and self-confidence brought her attention and friends wherever she went. Even male golfers had to laugh when she announced, "OK, now Babe's here! Now who's gonna finish second?"

Golf made Babe famous and wealthy. But she cared about more than her own success. She was also determined to help others succeed. Babe helped start the Ladies Professional Golf Association so that other women could pursue a career in golf. And her own powerful example showed others that women could and should be involved in sports.

Babe loved to entertain her fans with jokes and trick shots.

1949
Helped start the Ladies Professional Golf Association.

1950
Chosen "Woman Athlete of the Year" and "Woman Athlete of the Half Century" by the Associated Press. Won second U.S. Open golf tournament.

214

Challenge

Researching More Information

Have students choose one of Didrikson's sports and find out more about her involvement in it, using reference materials or the Internet.

Babe earned many honors. She won titles in basketball, track, and golf. She was named Woman Athlete of the Year six times. In 1950, sportswriters named her the greatest female athlete for the years 1900–1950. Babe decided she wanted to be the greatest in the next fifty years too.

Then in 1953, she became ill with cancer. Doctors told her she would never play golf again. They were wrong. "Babe was a very brave girl or she could never have become the person she was," a friend once said. Babe's bravery took her back to first place in less than a year.

4

Two years later, in 1956, Babe died. Finally, cancer was the one thing she couldn't beat. But she was a fierce competitor until the very end.

Babe signed autographs for fans of all ages.

1954	1956	1999
Chosen "Woman Athlete of the Year" by the Associated Press. Won third U.S. Open golf tournament.	Died on September 26 in Galveston, Texas.	Chosen as one of the top ten "Athletes of the Century" by ESPN.

215

Wrapping Up "Becoming a Champion: The Babe Didrikson Story"
pages 210–215

Comprehension/Critical Thinking

1 What lessons can a hard-working, determined person such as Babe Didrickson teach us? (to set goals, to work hard, to fight against the odds) **Drawing Conclusions**

2 How can the lessons of Babe Didrikson's life be used outside of sports? (Hard work and determination can be applied to anyone trying to reach a goal.) **Making Generalizations**

3 Compare Didrikson to another famous athlete or person of accomplishment. How is that person like Didrikson? (Answers will vary.) How is that person different? (Answers will vary.) **Compare and Contrast**

Reading "Bill Meléndez: An Artist in Motion"

pages 216–221

▶ Preparing to Read

Tell students they are going to read about Bill Meléndez, an animator of cartoons. Have students describe favorite cartoons from television or movies. Have a volunteer define *animator.* (An animator animates, or brings to life, drawings of characters.) Then ask if any students have ever drawn cartoons. If so, have them explain why they like to draw cartoons.

▶ Purpose Setting

Ask students to read to identify when and why Bill Meléndez became an animator.

 Journal Writing Before reading, have students write a note entitled "What I Know About Animation."

Vocabulary *(page 216)*

doodled: drew while thinking about something else

animators: people who draw cartoons for television or movies

Focus on
Biography

Bill Meléndez
An Artist in Motion

by Stephen Berman

5

Bill Meléndez

Bill Meléndez wasn't born with a crayon in his hand, but it wasn't long before he picked one up. As a boy, he doodled on every scrap of paper he could find. As an adult, he turned his love of drawing into his career. Today, he is one of the world's most successful animators.

Meléndez was born in Mexico in 1916. His parents named him José. When his family moved to the United States, everyone began calling him Bill. Meléndez already spoke Spanish. In his new home, he quickly learned English as well. He went to high school and then to college in Los Angeles, California.

216

As a young man, Meléndez worked at all kinds of jobs. Then in 1938, he found his first job as an artist. The Walt Disney studios hired him to work as an animator. It was the perfect job for him. As an animator, Meléndez had to draw, draw, draw, all day long. And he loved it.

Meléndez has animated many famous cartoon characters, including Bugs Bunny.

Revisiting the Text

Writer's Craft Lesson
Researching a Subject

OBJECTIVES

Students identify which key events in a person's life they should research in order to write an accurate biography.

Remind students that a biography must present true information and events in the subject's life. Ask students how an author can learn these facts. Discuss the ways in which an author researches, using reference books, magazine articles, personal interviews, and the Internet.

Share some biographical information about a well-known person with students. Have small groups of students identify two key facts about that person. Allow time for students to share their work.

Journal Writing Invite students to list sources they could use when writing their own biography.

Reading "Bill Meléndez: An Artist in Motion," *continued*
pages 216–221

▶ **Supporting Comprehension**

5 Reread the first sentence on page 216. Does the author really believe that some people are born holding a crayon? Why does he say that? (It's an exaggeration meant to emphasize the fact that Bill Meléndez started drawing when he was very young.)

6 How does the author show that Bill Meléndez loves his job? (Meléndez says, "What a fun job!")

Vocabulary *(page 219)*

<u>waddle:</u> walk like a duck

<u>stroll:</u> walk at a slow place

An animator brings cartoon characters to life by making them appear to move. To show this movement, animators must create thousands of drawings. Each drawing is a little bit different from the one before it. These drawings show the beginning and ending of each movement, and all the steps in between.

Today, many animators use computers. But when Meléndez first started animating, every drawing had to be created by hand. Some people might think this sounds boring, but not Meléndez. "Animators don't think of it as drawing one drawing after another after another. We think of it as illustrating action," he says. The joy of his job, he explains, is that "with a light and fun touch, you can create the feeling that these are real people."

218

Meléndez soon began animating many famous cartoon characters, including Schroeder and Lucy from *Peanuts* (above).

Meléndez started working at Disney when Mickey Mouse cartoons were first becoming popular. Disney needed lots of animators — and fast. "They were hiring anybody who could draw a straight line!" Meléndez says. "Now, I had never really studied art, but in school I was always doodling. I was drawing, drawing, drawing, just for the fun of it, all the time. So, when I was hired by Disney I thought, 'What a fun job!'"

6

At Disney, Meléndez made Donald Duck and Mickey Mouse <u>waddle</u> and <u>stroll</u> across the screen. He made their beaks and mouths move so that they seemed to talk. He made Mickey hold his belly when he laughed. Meléndez also worked on the famous Disney animated movies *Pinocchio, Fantasia, Dumbo,* and *Bambi*.

219

Genre Lesson
Biography

OBJECTIVES

Students identify the elements of a biography.

Review the elements of a biography. Have students locate some examples in these first two biographies.

A biography

- is the true story of someone who lived in the past or is living now

- usually starts with the early years of a person's life and then moves on to their later years

- presents facts and important information about a person's life

Point out that by reading biographies of people whose lives began before ours, we can learn about the past. Talk about ways in which both biographers show us how life years ago was different from the way it is now. Talk as well about ways in which they show us how people from previous times are similar to people today.

MEETING INDIVIDUAL NEEDS
Challenge

Researching Animation

Remind students that some well-known animation studios produce movies and television shows. Have students talk about their favorites. They can then use the Web to research interesting facts about these companies and what they are working on. Have volunteers tell the class what they find out.

Reading "Bill Meléndez: An Artist in Motion," *continued*
pages 216–221

▶ ## Supporting Comprehension

7 How does the author show that Meléndez's first love of drawing has continued through-out his life? (He became an animator and has continued drawing all his life.)

8 Why does the author name many of the cartoon characters that Bill Meléndez has worked on over the years? (He probably wants to show that Meléndez keeps his job interesting by working on a variety of characters.)

 Journal Writing Have students begin a list of people who could be subjects for their own biography.

Vocabulary *(pages 220–221)*
sound effects: in cartoons, the voices and sounds that are recorded to go with the drawings

feedback: other people's opinions

In 1941, Meléndez went to work for a company called Warner Brothers. There he animated other well-known cartoon characters, such as Bugs Bunny, Daffy Duck, and Porky Pig.

But Meléndez may be most famous as the animator of the "Peanuts" characters — Snoopy, Charlie Brown, Lucy, and the rest of the gang. Meléndez first animated some of these characters for television commercials. Then he began working with the creator of "Peanuts," Charles Schulz, to make movies and TV specials, such as **7** *A Charlie Brown Christmas.* He's even created some of the <u>sound effects</u> for the movies. "I do Snoopy's growls, grunts, and howls," he says. **8** "AAOOOOOO! Recognize that howl?"

220

 English Language Learners

Repeating Favorite Expressions

Have students tell each other or the whole class about their current favorite animated movie or television show. Ask them to tell any words or expressions a favorite character uses again and again.

Meléndez started his own animation studio, Bill Meléndez Productions, in 1964. He likes working with other people much more than he likes drawing by himself. "I tried working at home — it just made me nervous!" he says. "At the studio there's a team of us, a whole bunch of people laughing over this and that, giving each other feedback. It makes work fun and easier."

Animation is always hard work. Still, Meléndez would never trade it for making movies and TV shows with real, live actors. "The best animation does what can't be done in live action," he says. "Nothing is impossible in animation. That's the magic of it!"

Meléndez helped bring the whole *Peanuts* gang to life.

221

Wrapping Up "Bill Meléndez: An Artist in Motion"

Comprehension/Critical Thinking

1 What are some things about Bill Meléndez's life that would make people want to read about him? (his interesting work; how his childhood interests led to his work as an animator) **Making Generalizations**

2 What do you think the subtitle *An Artist in Motion* means? (The artist is active as he draws and the drawings he makes look as though they move.) **Drawing Conclusions**

3 Meléndez says he prefers working at a studio rather than at home alone. What do you think the differences would be? Which would you prefer? (quiet at home, no distractions; people at the studio with whom to exchange ideas and to laugh) **Compare and Contrast**

4 Why do you think Meléndez says that animation is always hard work? (Animation requires attention to small detail, repetition, and sometimes meeting tight deadlines.) **Making Inferences**

Reading "Brave Bessie Coleman: Pioneer Aviator"

pages 222–227

▶ Preparing to Read

■ Ask students to describe experiences they have had with airplanes, such as watching them at an airport, riding in one, or attending an air show.

■ Talk about the meaning of the words *pioneer* ("someone who is the first to do something or who leads the way") and *aviator* ("someone who flies a plane; an airplane pilot"). Then discuss how an aviator might be a pioneer.

▶ Purpose Setting

Have students read to find out the ways in which Bessie Coleman was brave, and to see how the biographer shows she was a pioneer.

Vocabulary *(pages 222–223)*

stunt plane: a plane that does tricks

spectators: people watching an event

license: a special card that gives you permission to do something

flocking: gathering in a crowd

 Journal Writing Ask students to write down the names of other pioneers.

Focus on
Biography

BRAVE Bessie Coleman

Pioneer Aviator

by Veronica Freeman Ellis

On October 15, 1922, at an air show in Chicago, Illinois, all eyes were on the sky. A crowd watched a small stunt plane high above begin to dive at top speed. Would it crash? Suddenly, at the last minute, the plane swooped up, shot over the heads of the spectators, and climbed back up into the air. The crowd applauded and cheered!

222

 Extra Support

Being First

Remind students that this is another biography of a woman who did many "firsts." Invite students to tell why being first in something is both hard and rewarding.

Coleman with her first airplane, a Curtiss JN-4, also called a Jenny.

Flying the plane was Bessie Coleman, the first African American to earn a pilot's <u>license</u>. Two years before, Coleman had left Chicago to follow her dreams of flight. Airplanes were still new inventions. In 1903, the Wright brothers had flown the first powered airplane. By 1922, large audiences were <u>flocking</u> to air shows to enjoy the amazing sight of "barnstormers," stunt pilots who flew in loops and spins through the air. Coleman had returned to Chicago to show her family and friends that she, too, could soar across the sky like a bird.

223

English Language Learners

Reading Captions

Point out that captions help tell part of the story. Remind students that they can use the photos and captions to help them understand this biography.

Revisiting the Text

Writer's Craft Lesson
Drawing Conclusions

 OBJECTIVES

Students identify ideas and information they learn by "reading between the lines."

Have students read the first two paragraphs of the biography. Ask if they think Bessie Coleman had ever seen real barnstormers when she decided to be a pilot. Help students see that she probably did, but nowhere is that stated exactly. Refer students to sections of the text that provide information that helps students to "read between the lines" to answer the following questions:

1 How do you know that the opinion of friends and family was important to Coleman? (She returned to Chicago to show her family and friends that she could fly.)

2 How did you know that Coleman would be successful? (The first paragraph tells of a crowd watching her fly an airplane.)

Remind students that many writers of biographies allow readers to "read between the lines" to draw conclusions. They can use this lesson as a model for creating text that allows the reader to "read between the lines" in their own biography.

 Journal Writing Have students write some conclusions that they have drawn by reading between the lines.

Reading "Brave Bessie Coleman: Pioneer Aviator," *continued*
pages 222–227

▶ **Supporting Comprehension**

9 Why does the author tell us that Coleman cared for her sisters, picked cotton, and studied hard as a child? What does that have to do with being a pilot? (The author wants the reader to know that Coleman was a hard worker from childhood on.)

Vocabulary *(pages 224–225)*

cockpit: the place in a plane where the pilot sits

spirals: circles

plunged: dropped downward suddenly

fascinated: very interested

A plane flying over the Chicago airfield during an air show in August, 1911.

Coleman looked brave when she waved to the crowd from the open <u>cockpit</u> of her plane. And she really looked brave when her plane flipped upside down, swirled in <u>spirals</u>, or <u>plunged</u> toward the ground and streaked back upward! But Coleman's bravest actions took place long before she ever learned to fly. During her lifetime, many people didn't believe that women could do something as difficult and dangerous as piloting a plane. African Americans like Coleman were not allowed to attend the same schools, work at the same jobs, or live in the same neighborhoods as white people. But Coleman refused to let these problems get in her way. She set the highest goals for herself and reached them — against enormous odds.

Coleman was born in 1892. She grew up in Waxahachie, Texas. While her mother worked as a maid, Coleman cared for her sisters, earned money by working in the cotton fields,

224

 Challenge

MEETING INDIVIDUAL NEEDS

Finding Out About Barnstormers

Ask students to locate information about barnstormers, where their name comes from, who they were, and what they did.

A plane performing an upside-down roll in the early 1920s.

Journal Writing Invite students to write down the most important events in their own lives so far, in sequence.

and still found time to do her schoolwork. After high school, **9**
she went to Langston College in Oklahoma. She could only
afford to attend classes for one year. But by that time, she
had already set her sights on the sky.

Coleman discovered that in 1911, Harriet Quimby had
become the first American woman to receive a pilot's license.
Coleman was <u>fascinated.</u> She thought it must be wonderful
to fly. After leaving college, Coleman moved to Chicago.
There, as she looked in libraries and newspapers for more
information, she decided that she wanted to go to flying
school. However, few aviation schools in the United States
were willing to train women. None of the schools would train
an African American woman.

225

Focus on
Biography

Reading "Brave Bessie Coleman: Pioneer Aviator," continued
pages 222–227

▶ ## Supporting Comprehension

10 What examples of bravery does the author give in this biography? (Bessie Coleman traveled to a foreign country to learn to fly; she took up the dangerous career of barnstormer; she protested the bad treatment of people of color.)

11 The author sums up Bessie Coleman's life in one sentence at the end. What is that sentence and what does it mean? (*When you face obstacles, just fly right over them.* There is no obstacle you can't get around if you use your talents and determination.)

Vocabulary (pages 226–227)

daring: brave; willing to do something dangerous

rehearsing: practicing

obstacles: things that get in your way

Coleman wrote many letters to set up her air shows. Her writing paper (above) showed some of her stunts.

Coleman remained determined. She decided to travel to France, where women and people of color had better opportunities. There, she attended one of the best aviation schools in the country. In 1921, she earned her pilot's license.

When Coleman returned to the United States, no one would hire her as a pilot because she was African American and a woman. To make a living, she became a barnstormer. Coleman was one of the most <u>daring</u> barnstormers of them all! Her thrilling stunts earned her the nicknames "Queen Bess" and "Brave Bessie."

Coleman used her talent to fight for her beliefs. She would not perform at air shows unless African Americans

226

 Extra Support

Writing Final Sentences

Remind students that the final sentence of a biography often sums up the person's whole life. Work with students to write some final sentences that sum up the lives of the people in these biographies.

Bessie Coleman
World's first black aviator,
breaking down racial barriers.

In 1995, the United States Postal Service issued a stamp honoring Coleman.

were allowed to attend. In Waxahachie, she refused to fly until people of color were allowed to enter through the same gate as white people. She visited schools and churches all over the United States to encourage African Americans to follow their own dreams — and to learn to fly. **10**

More than anything, Coleman wanted to start a school to train African American aviators. Sadly, on April 30, 1926, Coleman was <u>rehearsing</u> for an air show when the gears on her plane jammed. The plane spun out of control and crashed. Coleman died doing what she loved most. But her shining example will always live on: When you face <u>obstacles</u>, just fly right over them. **11**

227

Wrapping Up "Brave Bessie Coleman: Pioneer Aviator"
pages 222–227

Comprehension/Critical Thinking

1 How do you think Bessie Coleman felt when no flying school in the United States would train an African American woman? (She probably felt frustrated and angry and determined to get around this problem.) **Making Inferences**

2 What was brave about Bessie's going to live in France? (It was far away, a country where people speak a different language, and most Americans had not traveled to foreign countries at that time.) **Making Judgments**

3 In your opinion, what is the bravest thing Bessie Coleman did? Why do you think so? (Answers will vary.) **Making Judgments**

 Journal Writing Have students add to their list of possible subjects for a biography. Some may wish to share their lists with the rest of the class and tell why they are considering writing about these people.

 English Language Learners

Illustrating the Biography

Have students use a drawing they have made or a paper airplane to describe the way Bessie flew in air shows. Invite individuals to use the props to show the whole class.

Reading "Hank Greenberg: All-Around All-Star"

pages 228–233

....

▶ Preparing to Read

Have students tell what they know and like about baseball. Ask any baseball fans what Babe Ruth, Mark McGwire, and Sammy Sosa have in common. (They are all record-breaking home-run hitters.)

....

▶ Purpose Setting

Tell students that they are going to read the biography of Hank Greenberg who became a baseball star as famous in his day as Ruth, McGwire, and Sosa. Have them read to find out how he became a star off the baseball field as well.

> ### Vocabulary *(pages 228–229)*
> **slugger:** hitter, batter
>
> **valuable:** important
>
> **natural:** born with a talent to do something

Focus on

Hank Greenberg

All-Around All-Star

by Becky Cheston

Hank Greenberg

First big league home run:
May 6, 1933

American League MVP:
1935 and 1940

All-Star Team: 1938 and 1940

Elected to Hall of Fame:
January 25, 1956

Going for the record: In 1938, Greenberg hit 58 home runs, almost beating Babe Ruth's record of 60.

It was July 1, 1945. It had been four years, one month, and twenty-four days since Hank Greenberg had last thrilled fans with a home run. Now, back from World War II, he was again up at bat. A cheering crowd waited to see what the star <u>slugger</u> for the Detroit Tigers would do.

Before the war, Greenberg had twice been voted the American League's Most <u>Valuable</u> Player. And in 1938, before Mark McGwire and Sammy Sosa were even born, Greenberg gave baseball fans a summer to

228

 Extra Support

Baseball Rules

To help those who don't know much about baseball, have students who follow baseball share the rules of the game with the class. Then have them tell which their favorite teams are and why.

remember when he almost wiped out Babe Ruth's home run record. But on that day in 1945, fans must have been wondering — did Greenberg still have what it takes to be an all-star? The answer was in his actions. Greenberg smacked a homer into the left-field seats.

The secret to Greenberg's success as a ball player was hard work and determination. Even when people said he was too tall, or called him names because he was Jewish, Greenberg always held on to his dream of playing in the big leagues. "I wasn't a <u>natural</u> ball player like Babe Ruth or Willie Mays, but if you practice the way I did — all day long, day after day — you're bound to get pretty good," Greenberg said.

12

Greenberg jumps high to catch a long fly ball during spring training for the Detroit Tigers.

229

Writer's Craft Lesson
Choosing a Quotation

OBJECTIVES

Students identify quotations in a biography and tell why they are useful.

Point out the quotations in this biography. (Greenberg's own comments and the poem on page 231) Explain that including quotations from others or quotations from the subject in a biography tells the reader more about that person.

They also help readers hear for themselves what the person was really like. Discuss different ways authors of biographies obtain direct quotations. (interviews, speeches, things the person has written)

Have small groups look through the biographies to find quotations. Allow them time to share their work.

 Journal Writing Invite students to write a quotation that they would like someone to write or say about themselves.

 Extra Support

MEETING INDIVIDUAL NEEDS

Punctuating a Quotation

Point out the punctuation used at the beginning and end of a quotation. (quotation marks) Remind students that punctuation helps the reader identify a quotation.

Reading "Hank Greenberg: All-Around All-Star," continued

pages 228–233

. . . .

▶ ## Supporting Comprehension

12 Why do you think the author includes this quotation from Greenberg: *"I wasn't a natural ballplayer like Babe Ruth or Willie Mays, but if you practice ... all day long, day after day, you're bound to get pretty good."* (to emphasize how determined and hard-working Greenberg was and that not every successful person is born with talent)

13 What does Greenberg's refusal to play baseball on a Jewish holiday show about his character? (Some things were more important to Greenberg than baseball; he valued his religion and traditions.)

14 Why do you think the author includes this poem by Edgar Guest? (to show how respected and popular Greenberg was; to show that Greenberg inspired people)

Vocabulary *(pages 230–231)*

professional: paid to do something

pennants: championships

synagogue: a building where Jewish people worship

As a child, Greenberg rushed home every day after school, grabbed his bat, glove, and ball, and dashed to the ballpark. To work on his hitting, he asked friends to pitch to him. To improve his fielding, he asked friends to hit the ball to him, while he counted how many he could catch in a row.

In 1929, Greenberg was invited to play baseball for several professional teams. He joined the Detroit Tigers. In 1930, he started training in the minor leagues. He spent three long years in the minors, watching, practicing, and learning.

Finally, in 1933, Greenberg got his chance. In his first major league start with the Tigers, Greenberg smashed the ball out of the park — a home run!

Playing baseball wasn't always fun for Greenberg, though. Whenever he went up to bat, some of the fans and players would call him names because he was Jewish. But over time, as he led the Tigers to win four pennants and two World Series, he earned the respect of those around him.

Greenberg at the plate, ready to hit the ball for his team.

230

 ## Cross-Curricular Connection

Social Studies Yom Kippur is the most important Jewish holy day. In the Jewish calendar, it falls on the tenth day of the first month, Tishri. On this day, religious Jews fast, do no work, and go to services at a synagogue or temple. Religious Jews also abstain from working on the Sabbath, the day of rest, which begins every week at sunset on Friday evening and lasts until sunset on Saturday.

In the last game of the 1945 season, Greenberg hit a grand-slam home run in the ninth inning. His homer won the American League pennant for the Detroit Tigers.

In the summer of 1934, Greenberg did something else that made people admire him. The Tigers were in a race to win the American League pennant. Every game mattered. But one game was scheduled on Yom Kippur, an important Jewish holiday. Greenberg decided not to play. **13**

Everyone was talking about it. Edgar Guest, a famous poet, even wrote about Greenberg:

We shall miss him on the infield and shall miss him at the bat,
But he's true to his religion — and I honor him for that! **14**

When Greenberg entered his <u>synagogue</u> that day, everyone applauded. Greenberg had become a hero.

231

Reading "Hank Greenberg: All-Around All-Star," *continued*
pages 228–233

....

▶ ## Supporting Comprehension

15 What facts does the author use to back up her statement that *"Greenberg was also a good team player"*? (He was asked to give up the position of first base to a new player who couldn't play anything else.)

16 How does the author's use of descriptive words, such as *thrilled, slugger, smacked, rushed, dashed,* and *stormed,* make this biography more interesting? (Descriptive words provide a better mental picture of what is going on as well as make the writing livelier.)

17 What two things does the author highlight that show that what Greenberg did in childhood, he also did as an adult? (overcoming teasing for being Jewish and asking others to play ball with him)

Greenberg was also a good team player. In 1940, the Tigers had a new hitter. The only position on the field he could play was first base — Greenberg's job. The Tigers asked Greenberg to play in the outfield. Some players might have stormed off in anger, but not Greenberg. Instead, he agreed to switch. At first he had trouble playing left field. But he practiced long hours before and after games. He even got the peanut vendors and kids who hung around the ballpark to hit to him!

Greenberg (at right) was named to the All-Star team twice. Another famous first baseman, Lou Gehrig (at left), was on the team too.

232

 ## Cross-Curricular Connection

Social Studies The National Baseball Hall of Fame in Cooperstown, New York, elects new players every year. In order to be elected, players must have been retired for at least five years and have played in the major leagues for at least ten years.

During World War II, Greenberg was the first baseball star to join the Armed Forces. He left baseball, a job that paid him $11,000 a month, to earn $21 a month as a soldier. "My country comes first," Greenberg said. Once again, people admired Greenberg for more than his baseball talent.

In 1947, Greenberg retired from playing baseball, but he never really left the game behind. He worked as a team manager and an owner. In 1956, he received baseball's highest honor when he was elected to the Hall of Fame. He was the first Jewish player to be elected. Greenberg died on September 5, 1986. He will always be remembered as an all-star — both on and off the playing field.

Greenberg (left) with Joe DiMaggio, September 3, 1939.

Greenberg's plaque at the National Baseball Hall of Fame in Cooperstown, New York.

233

Wrapping Up

Comparing and Contrasting Biographies

1 All the people in these biographies overcame odds and showed determination. What other qualities did they show? (Answers might include courage, hard work, and intelligence.) **Making Generalizations**

2 Which person whom you read about would you most wish to be like? What do you admire about that person? (Answers will vary.) **Making Judgments**

3 Why do people read biographies? (Answers will vary.) **Making Generalizations**

4 How can reading biographies help you with your own life? (Answers will vary.) **Drawing Conclusions**

Journal Writing Invite students to write about their favorite biography, explaining why it is their favorite. They can use this biography as a model for the one they write.

Extending

Before students begin writing their own biography, you can teach the following brief writing lesson.

Writing Skill Lesson
Writing a Biography

OBJECTIVES

Students apply the elements of a biography.

Have students review the biographies, their notes and journals, and other work from this unit. Then review the elements of a biography:

■ It is a true story about a person's life.

■ It tells about a person who is living now or who lived earlier.

■ It gives facts and important information about a person.

■ It usually starts with the early years of a person's life and then moves on to later years.

Have students select the person they would like to write about. Give them time to research their subject's life. Have students follow the stages of the writing process as they write their biography. Give students time to brainstorm, draft, edit, rewrite, and finish their writing. As students write, have them consider the following:

■ Have they put events in the correct order?

■ Do they have a good opening sentence that will "hook" the reader?

■ Do they have a strong conclusion that tells why this person's life makes a good biography?

Extending
Biography

Informing

Write a Biography

Find out more about a person you are curious about. The person could be a president, an explorer, or a musician. Look up facts about the person in books, in magazines, in the encyclopedia, or on the Internet. Write a biography of the person.

Tips

• Start the biography with an important event or a special fact about the person.

• In the main part of the biography, write about the person's early life first. Then tell about the person's later years.

• Write an exciting title that will get a reader's attention.

Martin Luther King, Jr.

Louisa May Alcott

Michelle Kwan

Neil Armstrong

234

MEETING INDIVIDUAL NEEDS

English Language Learners

Remembering Heroes from Home

Some students may be reminded of a hero from the country in which they were born. Encourage them to tell a small group what is so admirable about that person and then to write a short biography.

Meet More Real People

Maya Lin: Architect
by Lynn Yokoe (Modern Curriculum)
Maya Lin's work brings people together in simple but powerful ways.

Five Brave Explorers
by Wade Hudson (Scholastic)
Learn about five courageous journeys — on land, on the sea, across the ice, and into space — and the black explorers who made them.

Eleanor Everywhere
by Monica Kulling (Random)
A shy girl grew up to become one of the bravest and most famous first ladies of the United States.

Sammy Sosa
by Laura Driscoll (Grosset)
Sammy Sosa's race for the home-run record gave baseball fans a reason to smile.

235

Presentation Activities

Use one or more of these activities to extend the *Focus on Biography*.

Fact-Finding

Invite students to find new and interesting information about any of the four biography subjects. Encourage them to use libraries, the Internet, and magazine and newspaper articles, and, if relevant, to interview family members or friends who can recall the people.

This Is the Ballad of...

Let pairs of students write a ballad (a song or poem that tells a story) about one of their heroes. They can use an old song as the basis for their new ballad, writing new words. Encourage them to share their song with the class, reading or singing the words.

Dramatization

Invite students to choose a particular event from the life of one of the biographical subjects and to dramatize it.

Glossary

Glossary

This glossary contains meanings and pronunciations for some of the words in this book. The Full Pronunciation Key shows how to pronounce each consonant and vowel in a special spelling. At the bottom of the glossary pages is a shortened form of the full key.

Full Pronunciation Key

Consonant Sounds

b	**bib**, ca**bb**age	kw	**ch**oir, **qu**ick	t	**t**ight, s**t**opped
ch	**ch**urch, sti**tch**	l	**l**id, need**l**e, ta**ll**	th	ba**th**, **th**in
d	**d**ee**d**, mai**l**ed, pu**dd**le	m	a**m**, **m**an, du**mb**	th	ba**th**e, **th**is
		n	**n**o, su**dd**en	v	ca**v**e, **v**al**v**e, **v**ine
f	**f**ast, **f**i**f**e, o**ff**, **ph**rase, rough	ng	thi**ng**, i**nk**	w	**w**ith, **w**olf
g	**g**a**g**, **g**et, fin**g**er	p	**p**o**p**, ha**pp**y	y	**y**es, **y**olk, on**i**on
h	**h**at, **wh**o	r	**r**oar, **rh**yme	z	ro**s**e, **s**ize, **x**ylophone, **z**ebra
hw	**wh**ich, **wh**ere	s	mi**ss**, **s**auce, **sc**ene, **s**ee	zh	gara**g**e, plea**s**ure, vi**s**ion
j	**j**u**dg**e, **g**em	sh	**d**i**sh**, **sh**ip, **s**ugar, ti**ss**ue		
k	**c**at, **k**i**ck**, s**ch**ool				

Vowel Sounds

ă	p**a**t, l**au**gh	ŏ	h**o**rrible, p**o**t	ŭ	c**u**t, fl**oo**d, r**ou**gh, s**o**me
ā	**a**pe, **ai**d, p**ay**	ō	g**o**, r**ow**, t**oe**, th**ou**gh		
â	**ai**r, c**a**re, w**ear**	ô	**a**ll, c**augh**t, f**o**r, p**aw**	û	c**i**rcle, f**u**r, h**ear**d, t**er**m, t**ur**n, **ur**ge, w**or**d
ä	f**a**ther, k**o**ala, y**ar**d	oi	b**oy**, n**oi**se, **oi**l		
ĕ	p**e**t, pl**ea**sure, **a**ny	ou	c**ow**, **ou**t	yōō	c**u**re
ē	b**e**, b**ee**, **ea**sy, p**ia**no	ŏŏ	f**u**ll, b**oo**k, w**o**lf	yōō	**a**b**u**se, **u**se
ĭ	**i**f, p**i**t, b**u**sy	ōō	b**oo**t, r**u**de, fr**ui**t, fl**ew**	ə	**a**go, sil**e**nt, penc**i**l, lem**o**n, circ**u**s
ī	r**i**de, b**y**, p**ie**, h**igh**				
î	d**ear**, d**ee**r, f**ier**ce, m**ere**				

Stress Marks

Primary Stress ´: bi·ol·o·gy [bī **ŏl´** ə jē]
Secondary Stress ´: bi·o·log·i·cal [bī´ ə **lŏj´** ĭ kəl]

Pronunciation key and definitions © 1998 by Houghton Mifflin Company. Adapted and reprinted by permission from *The American Heritage Children's Dictionary.*

342

A

an·chor (**ăng´** kər) *noun* A heavy metal object, attached to a ship, that is dropped overboard to keep the ship in place: *We dropped the **anchor** so that our sailboat wouldn't crash onto the rocky shore.*

ap·pre·ci·ate (ə **prē´** shē āt´) *verb* To enjoy and understand: *Max could **appreciate** that having a dog was a big responsibility.*

a·shore (ə **shôr´**) *adverb* On or to the shore: *The seal came **ashore** and then went back into the water.*

B

bar·ren (**băr´** ən) *adjective* Not able to produce growing plants or crops: *Because the country's land was **barren**, food had to be shipped in from other places.*

bask (băsk) *verb* To rest in a pleasant warmth: *Rochelle enjoyed the summer weather as she **basked** in the warm sun.*

buf·fet (**bŭf´** ĭt) *verb* To strike against powerfully: *Luis held his kite tightly as it was **buffeted** by the strong wind.*

bur·row (**bûr´** ō) *noun* A hole or tunnel small animals use as an underground nest.

bus·tling (**bŭs´** lĭng) *adjective* Full of activity; busy: *The **bustling** mall was full of people shopping for holiday gifts.*

C

cease·less (**sēs´** lĭs) *adjective* Continuing without end: *Kim played indoors all day because of the **ceaseless** rain.*

com·pan·ion·a·ble (kəm **păn´** yən ə bəl) *adjective* Friendly: *María talked to a **companionable** girl who was sitting next to her on the train.*

cramped (krămpt) *adjective* So small as to prevent free movement: *The travelers could not stretch out their legs in the plane's **cramped** space.*

cre·vasse (krĭ **văs´**) *noun* A deep opening or crack: *A **crevasse** appeared in the iceberg before it broke apart.*

cus·tom (**kŭs´** təm) *noun* Something that the members of a group usually do: *It is an American **custom** to eat turkey on Thanksgiving.*

burrow

Companionable
Companionable comes from the Latin word *companio*. *Com-* means "together" and *panis* means "food." Friends who share activities and sometimes eat together are companions.

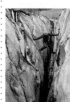

crevasse

ōō **boot** / ou **out** / ŭ **cut** / û **fur** / hw **which** / th **thin** / *th* **this** / zh **vision** / ə **ago**, **silent**, **pencil**, **lemon**, **circus**

343

D

floe

de·sert·ed (dĭ **zûrt´** ĕd) *adjective* Not lived in; having few or no people: *No one has lived in the **deserted** house for many years.*

dis·cour·aged (dĭ **skûr´** ĭjd) *adjective* Less hopeful or enthusiastic: *Instead of being **discouraged** by his poor grade on the test, Matt decided to study more for the next one.*

dis·mal (**dĭz´** məl) *adjective* Causing, feeling, or showing gloom or sadness: *It was a **dismal** day for Yoshiko when her best friend moved away.*

drape (drāp) *verb* To hang in loose folds: *Ellie's long skirt **draped** to the floor.*

drear·y (**drîr´** ē) *adjective* Gloomy; dismal; without cheer: *We decided not to let the **dreary** weather ruin our vacation.*

E

en·chi·la·da (ĕn´ chə **lä´** da) *noun* A tortilla that is folded around a meat filling and covered with a spicy tomato sauce: *Greg learned to make delicious chicken **enchiladas** in cooking class.*

ex·haust·ed (ĭg **zôst´** əd) *adjective* Worn out; tired: *Tina was **exhausted** after carrying the heavy boxes.*

graze

F

fab·ric (**făb´** rĭk) *noun* Material that is produced by weaving threads, or fibers, together; cloth: *Kelly's shirt was made of a cotton **fabric**.*

floe (flō) *noun* A large, flat mass of floating ice: *The polar bear dove off the ice **floe** into the freezing water.*

for·eign·er (**fôr´** ə nər) *noun* A person from a different country or place: *Americans are **foreigners** in Europe.*

G

graze (grāz) *verb* To feed on growing plants: *The cows were **grazing** on grass near the barn.*

gru·el·ing (**grōō´** ə lĭng) *adjective* Extremely tiring: *Hannah went to sleep early after running the **grueling** ten-mile race.*

H

hem (hĕm) *verb* To fold back and sew down the edge of: *I will have to **hem** my new skirt because it is too long.*

ă **rat** / ā **pay** / â **care** / ä **father** / ĕ **pet** / ē **be** / ĭ **pit** / ī **pie** / î **fierce** / ŏ **pot** / ô **go** / ô **paw**, **for** / oi **oil** / ōō **book**

344

---

ho·ri·zon (hə **rī´** zən) *noun* The line along which the earth and the sky appear to meet: *Jack watched the setting sun until it disappeared below the **horizon**.*

I

im·pass·a·ble (ĭm **păs´** ə bəl) *adjective* Impossible to travel across or through: *The mountains were **impassable**, so we had to drive around them.*

in·stinc·tive·ly (ĭn **stĭngk´** tĭv lē) *adverb* Acting on an inner feeling that is not learned: *Most dogs **instinctively** try to protect their owners.*

J

jour·ney (**jûr´** nē) *noun* Movement from one place to another; a trip: *The astronauts traveled in a spaceship during their **journey** to the moon.*

L

lan·guage (**lăng´** gwĭj) *noun* Spoken or written human speech: *Jessica took a class to learn the Russian **language**.*

M

mend (mĕnd) *verb* To put back into good condition; repair: *Koji couldn't wear the shirt until the rip on the sleeve was **mended**.*

P

pass·port (**păs´** pôrt) *noun* A government document that gives a person permission to travel in foreign countries: *Alicia needed a **passport** to travel to Brazil.*

pat·tern (**păt´** ərn) *noun* An artistic design used for decoration: *The curtains have a blue striped **pattern**.*

pelt (pĕlt) *verb* To strike or beat against again and again: *During the storm, Tomás listened to the rain **pelting** down on the roof.*

per·il·ous (**pĕr´** ə ləs) *adjective* Dangerous: *The icy steps were **perilous** to walk on.*

launch (lônch) *verb* To send forcefully upwards like a rocket: *The swimmer pushed off the diving board before **launching** into the air high above the pool.*

horizon

Language
Language comes from the Latin word *lingua*, which means "tongue."

Mend
Mend is a shortened form of the word *amend*, which means "to improve."

ōō **boot** / ou **out** / ŭ **cut** / û **fur** / hw **which** / th **thin** / *th* **this** / zh **vision** / ə **ago**, **silent**, **pencil**, **lemon**, **circus**

345

quay

skyscraper

Skyscraper
The highest sails on a ship used to be called skyscrapers. When the world's first ten-story building was built, writers called it a skyscraper, naming it after those high sails.

Strand
Strand comes from an Old English word that meant "seashore."

plaid (plăd) *adjective* Having a pattern formed by stripes of different widths and colors that cross each other at right angles: *Gus put on his plaid scarf before he went out into the cold.*

pop·u·la·tion (pŏp´ yə lā´ shən) *noun* The total number of plants, animals, or people living in a certain place: *Our class did a population survey to learn about the people who live in our town.*

Q

quay (kē) *noun* A dock where ships are loaded or unloaded: *The boy stood on the quay watching supplies being loaded onto the ships.*

R

rus·tling (rŭs´ lĭng) *noun* A soft fluttering sound: *Deb heard the rustling of the leaves in the wind.*

S

sal·sa (säl´ sə) *noun* A spicy sauce made of tomatoes, onions, and peppers: *We dipped our chips in the spicy salsa.*

seep (sēp) *verb* To pass slowly through small openings; ooze: *We stuffed a towel in the crack under the door to keep the cold air from seeping in.*

set·tle·ment (sĕt´l mənt) *noun* A small community in a new place: *When they reached the new land, the pioneers built a settlement to live in.*

sight·see·ing (sīt´ sē´ ĭng) *verb* The act of touring interesting places: *When Marc took his visitors sightseeing in Washington, D.C., they went to the Washington Monument.*

sky·scra·per (skī´ skrā pər) *noun* A very tall building: *The Empire State Building is one of the tallest skyscrapers in New York City.*

Span·ish (spăn´ ĭsh) *noun* The language of Spain, Mexico, and most of Central America and South America: *My cousin grew up in Mexico and speaks Spanish.*

starve (stärv) *verb* To suffer or die from lack of food: *We put seeds in the feeder so the birds wouldn't starve in the winter.*

strand·ed (strănd´ əd) *adjective* In a difficult or helpless position: *When our car ran out of gas, we were stranded on the side of the road.*

à rat / ā pay / â care / ä father / ĕ pet / ē be / ĭ pit / ī pie / î fierce / ŏ pot /
ô go / ô paw, for / oi oil / ōō book

---

sul·len·ly (sŭl´ ən lē) *adverb* Angrily or unhappily: *When his parents wouldn't let him have a cookie, the little boy sullenly refused to eat dinner.*

surf (sûrf) *verb* To ride on waves, often on a surfboard: *During summer vacation, Doug surfed at the beach.*
—*noun* The waves of the sea as they break on a shore or reef: *Lucy swam in the surf.*

sur·round·ing (sə roun´ dĭng) *adjective* On all sides of: *The surrounding trees shaded the house from the sun.*

sur·vive (sər vīv´) *verb* To stay alive or continue to exist: *A whale cannot survive out of water.*

swell (swĕl) *noun* A long rolling wave in open water: *The swimmer was lifted gently by the ocean swell.*

swoop (swōōp) *verb* To move with a sudden sweeping motion: *The seagull swooped down to catch a fish.*

T

ta·co (tä´ kō) *noun* A tortilla that is folded around a filling, such as ground meat or cheese: *We added lettuce and tomato to our tacos.*

ta·ma·le (tə mä´ lē) *noun* A steamed cornhusk that is wrapped around a meat filling made with red peppers and cornmeal: *When I go to my favorite Mexican restaurant, I love to order tamales.*

ter·rain (tə rān´) *noun* Any piece of land; ground, soil, earth: *It was difficult to hike across the rocky terrain.*

ter·ri·to·ry (tĕr´ ĭ tôr´ ē) *noun* An area of land; region: *Bears roam their territory in search of food.*

tor·til·la (tôr tē´ yə) *noun* A round, flat bread made from cornmeal and water and baked on a grill: *My grandmother showed me how to make a tortilla.*

U

un·in·hab·i·ted (ŭn´ ĭn hăb´ ə tĭd) *adjective* Having no people living there: *The explorer was the first person to visit the uninhabited island.*

V

vend·or (vĕn´ dər) *noun* A person who sells something: *In Chicago, Carl bought a hot dog from a street vendor.*

surf

Terrain
Terrain comes from the Latin word *terra*, which means "earth." Other words that come from *terra* are *territory*, *terrace*, and *terrier*.

vendor

ōō boot / ou out / ŭ cut / û fur / hw which / th thin / th this / zh vision /
ə ago, silent, pencil, lemon, circus

venture

ven·ture (vĕn´ chər) *verb* To do something in spite of risk: *We decided to venture out to the edge of the cliff.*

W

wan·der (wŏn´ dər) *verb* To move from place to place without a special purpose or goal: *People in shopping malls often wander from store to store.*

wea·ry (wîr´ ē) *adjective* Needing rest; tired: *After climbing the mountain, the weary hikers took a nap.*

à rat / ā pay / â care / ä father / ĕ pet / ē be / ĭ pit / ī pie / î fierce / ŏ pot /
ô go / ô paw, for / oi oil / ōō book

Acknowledgments

Main Literature Selections

Across the Wide Dark Sea, by Jean Van Leeuwen, illustrated by Thomas B. Allen. Text copyright © 1995 by Jean Van Leeuwen. Illustrations copyright © 1995 by Thomas B. Allen. Reprinted by permission of Dial Books for Young Readers, a division of Penguin Putnam Inc.

Nights of the Pufflings, by Bruce McMillan. Copyright © 1995 by Bruce McMillan. Reprinted by permission of Houghton Mifflin Company.

Pepita Talks Twice/Pepita habla dos veces, by Ofelia Dumas Lachtman and illustrated by Alex Pardo DeLange. Text copyright © 1995 by Ofelia Dumas Lachtman. Reprinted by permission of the publisher, Arte Público Press – University of Houston.

Poppa's New Pants, by Angela Shelf Medearis, illustrated by John Ward. Text copyright © 1995 by Angela Shelf Medearis. Illustrations copyright © 1995 by John Ward. All rights reserved. Reprinted by permission of Holiday House, Inc.

"*Rainy Sunday,*" from *Ramona Quimby, Age 8,* by Beverly Cleary, illustrated by Alan Tiegreen. Copyright © 1981 by Beverly Cleary. Reprinted by permission of HarperCollins Publishers.

Seal Surfer, by Michael Foreman. Copyright © 1996 by Michael Foreman. Reprinted by permission of Harcourt Inc.

Trapped by the Ice! Shackleton's Amazing Antarctic Adventure, by Michael McCurdy. Copyright © 1997 by Michael McCurdy. Reprinted by permission of Walker & Co.

Two Days in May, by Harriet Peck Taylor, illustrated by Leyla Torres. Text copyright © 1999 by Harriet Peck Taylor. Illustrations copyright © 1999 by Leyla Torres. Reprinted by permission of Farrar, Straus and Giroux, LLC.

Yunmi and Halmoni's Trip, by Sook Nyul Choi, illustrated by Karen Dugan. Text copyright © 1997 by Sook Nyul Choi. Illustrations copyright © 1997 by Karen Dugan. Reprinted by permission of Houghton Mifflin Company.

Links and Theme Openers

"*Big-Apple Birding,*" by Radha Permaul, with Arthur Morris, from the March 1992 issue of *Ranger Rick* magazine. Copyright © 1992 by the National Wildlife Federation. Reprinted by permission of the publisher, the National Wildlife Federation.

"*Henry and Ramona,*" based on the books by Beverly Cleary, dramatized by Cynthia J. McGean. Copyright © 1996 by Cynthia J. McGean and Beverly Cleary. Reprinted by permission of HarperCollins Publishers.

"*I Like to Ride My Bike/Me gusta montar mi bicicleta,*" by Lori Marie Carlson, from *Sol a Sol: Bilingual Poems Written and Selected by Lori Marie Carlson.* Copyright © 1998 by Lori Marie Carlson. Reprinted by permission of Henry Holt and Company, LLC.

"*I Work in the Ocean,*" by Kristin Ingram, appeared in the January 1998 issue of *Spider, the Magazine for Children.* Copyright © by Kristin Ingram. Reprinted by permission of the author. All rights reserved.

"*January Deer,*" from *Turtle in July,* by Marilyn Singer. Copyright © 1989 by Marilyn Singer. Reprinted by permission of Atheneum Books for Young Readers, an imprint of Simon & Schuster's Children's Publishing Division.

"*Little Piece of Prickly Pear/Pedacito de nopal,*" from *My Mexico/México mío,* by Tony Johnston, illustrated by F. John Sierra. Text copyright © 1996 by Tony Johnston. Reprinted by permission of G. P. Putnam's Sons, a division of Penguin Putnam Inc.

"*My Grandma's Songs/Las canciones de mi abuela,*" from *Laughing Tomatoes and Other Spring Poems,* by Francisco X. Alarcón. Poems copyright © 1997 by Francisco X. Alarcón. Illustrations copyright © 1997 by Maya Christina Gonzalez. Reprinted by permission of Children's Book Press. All rights reserved.

"*No Problem!*" comprised of the following:
1) "*Foxtrot comic strip,*" from *Foxtrot,* by Bill Amend. Copyright © by Bill Amend. Reprinted by permission of the Universal Press Syndicate. All rights reserved.

G2   **Glossary**

2) "Peanuts." Two untitled comic strips by Charles M. Schulz. PEANUTS © United Feature Syndicate, Inc. Reprinted by permission of United Feature Syndicate, Inc.
3) "Let's go, Calvin. Time for . . .," and "Oh no, I lost my quarter! . . ." comic strips from Calvin and Hobbes, by Bill Watterson. Copyright © by Bill Watterson. Reprinted by permission of the Universal Press Syndicate. All rights reserved.

"Puffin-Stuff," by Joan Peronto, from Ladybug magazine, June 1996, Vol. 6, No. 10. Copyright © 1996 by Joan Peronto. Reprinted by permission of the publisher.

"Seal," from Laughing Time: Collected Nonsense, by William Jay Smith. Copyright © 1990 by William Jay Smith. Reprinted by permission of Farrar, Straus and Giroux, LLC.

"Travellers," by Arthur St. John Adcock. Copyright by Arthur St. John Adcock. Reprinted by permission of Hodder & Stoughton Ltd.

"Under the Trees," from In the Woods, In the Meadow, In the Sky, by Aileen Fisher. Copyright © 1965, 1993 by Aileen Fisher. Reprinted by permission of Marian Reiner for the author.

"The Ways of Living Things," from The Random House Book of Poetry for Children, selected and introduced by Jack Prelutsky. Poem copyright © 1983 by Jack Prelutsky. Reprinted by permission of Random House Children's Books, a division of Random House Inc.

"Young Voyagers: A Pilgrim Childhood." Grateful acknowledgment is given to the Plimoth Plantation for the printed resource materials that were provided for informational purposes.

Additional Acknowledgments

Special thanks to the following teachers whose students' compositions appear as Student Writing Models: Cindy Cheatwood, Florida; Diana Davis, North Carolina; Kathy Driscoll, Massachusetts; Linda Evers, Florida; Heidi Harrison, Michigan; Eileen Hoffman, Massachusetts; Linda Evers, Florida; Bonnie Lewison, Florida; Kanetha McCord, Michigan.

Credits

Photography

Cover (bkgd) John Elk/Tony Stone Images. **3** Arthur C. Smith III/Grant Heilman. **5** (br) Superstock. **7** AP/Wide World Photos. **10** (snowflake) Artville. **10–11** ©Michio Hoshino/Minden Pictures. **16–17** (bkgd) ©Hubert Stadler/Corbis. **17** (t) ©Sigurgeir Jonasson. (b) ©James P. Rowan. **18** (tc) Benner McGee, ©1995 Bruce McMillan. **19–33** ©Bruce McMillan. **35** (br) Arthur C. Smith III/Grant Heilman. **36–9** (all) ©Arthur Morris/BIRDS AS ART. **40** ©Kit Kittle/CORBIS. **41** ©Clem Haagner; Gallo Images/CORBIS. **42** ©Lynda Richardson/CORBIS. **43** (t) ©James L. Amos/CORBIS. **44** (starfish) image Copyright ©2000 PhotoDisc Inc. (c) ©Tony Stone Images/Rick Rusing. (bl) ©Roger Tidman/CORBIS. **44–5** ©Bill Ross/CORBIS. **45** (cl) ©Art Wolfe. (br) ©Phil Schermeister/CORBIS. **46** ©Ron Sutherland. **65** (br) A.K.G., Berlin/Superstock. **66–9** (all) ©Norbert Wu. **70** (banner) ©W. Cody/CORBIS. (bl) ©Erwin and Peggy Bauer. **70–1** ©Daniel J. Cox/Natural Exposures. **71** (inset) ©Daniel J. Cox/Natural Exposures. **72** (bkgd) W. Cody/CORBIS. **93** (bl) John Crispin/Mercury Pictures. (tr) Eric Bakke/Mercury Pictures. **102** (banner) ©Ken Reid/FPG International. **102–3** ©James Randklev/Tony Stone Images. **108** (bl) Courtesy of the Pilgrim Society, Plymouth, Massachusetts. **109** (t) Photo by Bert Lane/Plimoth Plantation. (b) Courtesy of the Pilgrim Society, Plymouth, Massachusetts. **110** (tl) Photo by David Gavril from Growing Ideas published by Richard C. Owens Publishers, Inc., Katonah, NY 10536. (tr) Courtesy, Thomas B. Allen. **133** (br) Superstock. **136** (tl) Photo by Ted Curtain/Plimoth Plantation. (b) Photo by Ted Avery/Plimoth Plantation. **137** (t) ©Dorothy Littell Greco/Stock Boston. (c) (b) ©Russ Kendall. **140** (b) ©Wolfgang Kaehler/CORBIS. **141** (bl) (br) ©Kevin R. Morris/CORBIS. **142** (t) Jesse Nemerofsky/Mercury Pictures (b)Courtesy, Karen Dugan. **164** Geese in Flight, Leila T. Bauman, Gift of Edgar William and Bernice Chrystler Garbisch, ©2000 Board of Trustees, National Gallery of Art, Washington. **165** Giraudon/Art Resource, New York. **166** Erich Lessing/Art Resource, New York. **167** (t) Scala/Art Resource, New York. **168** (banner) G. Ryan & S. Beyer/Tony Stone Images. (tr) Scott Polar Research Institute, Cambridge, England. **169** ©Galen Rowell/Mountain Light. **170** Courtesy, Michael McCurdy. **171** (bkgd) G. Ryan & S. Beyer/Tony Stone Images. **200** (bl) image Copyright ©2000 PhotoDisc Inc. **201** (bl) Superstock. **202** (tr) Scott Polar Research Institute, Cambridge, England. (b) ©Royal Geographical Society, London. **203** Scott Polar Research Institute, Cambridge, England. **204** (tl) ©Royal Geographical Society, London. (cl) ©Royal Geographical Society, London. **204–5** (b) ©Royal Geographical Society, Cambridge, England. (t) Scott Polar Research Institute, Cambridge, England. **205** (c) ©Royal Geographical Society, London. **208–9** AP/Wide World Photos. **210** Corbis/Bettmann. **211** Corbis/Bettmann. **212** Corbis/Bettmann. **213** (t) Corbis/Bettmann. (b) Underwood & Underwood/CORBIS. **214** (tr) AP/Wide World Photos. (b) Corbis/Bettmann. **215** Zaharias Collection, Special Collections/Mary & John Gray Library/Lamar University, Beaumont, Texas. **216** Jeff Arnold/Bill Melendez Productions. **217** Photofest. **218** image Copyright ©2000 PhotoDisc, Inc. **219** Photofest. **220** Photofest. **221** Everett Collection. **222** Underwood & Underwood/CORBIS. **223** Security Pacific Collection/Los Angeles Public Library. **224** CORBIS. **225** Museum of Flight/CORBIS. **226** The Lilly Library, Indiana University, Bloomington. **227** USPS. **228** Corbis/Bettmann. **229** AP/New York Times Pictures. **230** Corbis/Bettmann. **231** AP/New York Times Pictures. **232** AP Wide World Photos. **233** (t) Corbis/Bettmann. (b) AP/Wide World Photos. **234** (l) AFP/Corbis. (cl) Flip Schulke/CORBIS. (cr) NASA/CORBIS. (r) Corbis/Bettmann. **242** (b) Power Photos. **243** (cl) ©Eric and David Hosking/CORBIS. (bl) Corbis Royalty Free. (br) image Copyright ©2000 PhotoDisc, Inc. **244** (tl) Michael Justice/Mercury Pictures. (tr) Courtesy, Mike Reed. **282** (tr) Andrew Yates/Mercury Pictures. (b) ©Tom Sciacca. **310** (t) Alan McEwen, 1999. (r) M. W. Thomas. **343** (t) ©Kevin Schafer/CORBIS. (b) ©Lowell Georgia/CORBIS. **344** (t) ©Dan Guravich/CORBIS. (b) ©Darrell Gulin/CORBIS. **345** ©Gary Braasch/CORBIS. **346** (t) ©Judy Griesedieck/CORBIS. (b) ©Kit Kittle/CORBIS. **347** (t) ©Tony Arruza/CORBIS. (b) ©Catherine Karnow/CORBIS. **348** ©Kevin R. Morris/CORBIS.

Assignment Photography

243 (tl) Banta Digital Group. **280–1, 308–9, 337–9** Joel Benjamin. **34** (bl), **35** (ml), **64** (bl), **65** (ml), **95** (ml), **132** (b), **133** (ml), **163** (ml, mr), **201** (mr), **273** (tr), **303** (ml, mr), **334** (bl) Jack Holtel. **101, 207, 243** (i) **341** Tony Scarpetta.

Illustration

47 (i), **48–63** Michael Foreman. **72** (i), **73–92** Leyla Torres. . **93** (ml), (tr) Dick Cole. **96–99** Normand Cousineau. **108–109, 134–135, 136–137** (bkgd) Luigi Galante. **111** (i), **112–131** Thomas B. Allen. **143** (i), **144–161** Karen Dugan. **171** (i), **173–199** Michael McCurdy. **236–237** Alfred Schrier. **245** (i) Alex Pardo DeLange. **246–271** Mike Reed. **274–275** Karen Blessen. **276–277** Maya Christina Gonzalez. **282** (bkgd) Dick Cole. **283** (inset) **284–301** John Ward. **312, 317, 319, 323, 325–329, 331, 333** Alan Tiegreen. **304, 307** Charles M. Schulz. **305** Bill Amend. **306** Bill Watterson. **311** (i), **312–333** Alan Tiegreen. **319** (i), **320–341** Elise Primavera. **351** (i), **352–367, 371** Chris Van Allsburg.

Index

Boldface page references indicate formal strategy and skill instruction.

A

Acquiring English, students. *See* English Language Learners.

Activating prior knowledge. *See* Background, building.

Art activities. *See* Cross-curricular links.

Assessment, planning for, *102G–102H*
Benchmark Test, *102G*
Comprehension, *102G*
Diagnostic Check, *119, 131, 137B, 137F, 137J, 153, 161, 167B, 167F, 167L, 183, 199, 205B, 205F, 205L, R3, R5, R7, R8, R10, R12, R14, R16, R18, R20, R21, R22*
Diagnostic Planning, *102G*
End-of-Selection Assessment, *133, 163, 201*
End-of-Theme Assessment, *102G*
Informal Assessment, *102G*
Integrated Theme Test, *102G*
National Test Correlation, *102H*
Ongoing Assessment, *102G*
Periodic Progress Assessment, *102G*
Portfolio Opportunity, *137N, 167N, 205N, R25*
Self-Assessment, *133, 163, 201*
Theme Skills Test, *102G*
Writing, *102G*

Audio visual resources, *R28–R29*

Author's craft. *See* Writer's craft.

Authors of selections in Anthology
Choi, Sook Nyul, *102A, 142*
McCurdy, Michael, *102A, 170*
Van Leeuwen, Jean, *102A, 110*

Author's viewpoint. *See* Comprehension skills.

Automatic recognition of words. *See* Spelling; Vocabulary, selection.

B

Background, building
biographies, *F208, F210, F216, F222, F228*
concept development, *108A–109A, 139I, 139K, 139M, 140A–141A, 168A–169A, R2, R4, R6*
prior knowledge, activating, *106A, 139S, 167U*
Reader's Library selections, *R2, R4, R6*
theme paperbacks, *139I, 139K, 139M*
See also English Language Learners; Previewing.

Bibliography, *102C–102D*

Biography, Focus on, *F208–F234,* **F211, F217, F219, F223, F229, F233**

Books for independent reading. *See* Reader's Library; Theme paperbacks.

C

Cause-effect relationships. *See* Comprehension skills.

Challenge. *See* Individual needs, meeting.

Characters, making inferences about. *See* Inferences, making.

Classroom management, *102E–102F*
individuals, *110–111, 142–143, 170–171*
whole class, *134, 164, 202*
See also Suggested daily routines.

Coherence in narrative text. *See* Comprehension skills, story structure.

Communication activities
nonverbal skills, **1670–167P**
See also Listening activities; Speaking activities; Viewing activities.

Community-school interactions. *See* Home/Community Connections book.

Compare/contrast. *See* Comprehension skills.

Comparing. *See* Connections.

Comprehension skills
cause and effect, *153,* **159,** *162, 183*
compare and contrast, *132, 137, 139V, 162, 167, 167X, 200, 205, F215, F221, F232*
conclusions, drawing, *162, 167, 200, 205, F215, F221, F232*
details, noting, *119, 132, 165*
generalizations, making, *132, 137,* **151,** *167, F215, F221, F232*
inferences, making, *106A, 107A–107C, 109B,* **109C,** *119,* **129,** *131, 132, 135, 137,* **137A–137B,** *153, 162, 167, 200, F221, F227, R2, R8–R9*
See also Inferences, making.
judgments, making, **125,** *137, 161, 162, 183, 199, 200, 205, F227, F232*
main idea, identifying, *131, 135*
outcomes, predicting, *139S–139V, 141B,* **141C, 157,** *162,* **167A–167B,** *R4, R10–R11*
problem solving, *132*
sequence of events, **175**
story structure, **113,** *161*
text organization, *137, 167U–167X, 169B,* **169C, 187,** *199, 205,* **205A–205B,** *R6, R12–R13*
topic/main idea and supporting details, **177**

See also Lessons, specific; Strategies, reading.

Comprehension strategies. *See* Strategies, reading.

Computer activities. *See* Technology resources.

Concepts of print
    punctuation of quotation, **F229**

Connections
    between art works, *164–167*
    between individuals/story characters, *162, 167X*
    between literature and life experience, *107C*
    between narrative selections, *137, 139V, 200*
    between photo essay and narrative selection, *205*
    cross-curricular. *See* Cross-curricular links.
    genre, *F209*
    theme connections, *106A, 108A, 139S, 140A, 167U, 168A*

Constructing meaning from text. *See* Comprehension skills; Decoding skills; Phonics; Strategies, reading.

Content areas, reading in the. *See* Cross-curricular activities; Cross-curricular links.

Context clues. *See* Decoding skills; Vocabulary.

Conventions of language. *See* Grammar and usage; Mechanics, language; Speech, parts of.

Cooperative reading. *See* Reading modes.

Creative dramatics
    biographical subject, *F234*
    guiding a tour, *163*

Creative response. *See* Responding to literature, options for.

Critical thinking, *119, 131, 132, 137, 153, 161, 162, 167, 183, 199, 200, 205, F215, F221, F227*

Cross-curricular activities, *R26–R27*
    art, *R13, R27*
    listening/speaking, *R9, R11*
    math, *133, R11, R13, R27*
    science, *201, R11, R26*
    social studies, *163, 201, R9, R13, R27*
    writing, *R13*

Cross-curricular links
    art, *164–167*
    media, *202–205*
    social studies, *116, 128, 134–137, 144, 156, 174, F211, F230, F231*

Cue systems. *See* Phonics; Structural analysis.

Daily language practice, *137K–137L, 167K–167L, 205K–205L*

Decoding skills
    longer words, **137E–137F, 167E–167F, 205E–205F**
    phonics/decoding strategy, **109A, 117, 123, 137F, 141A, 148, 167F, 169A, 197, 205F, R3, R5, R7**
    See also Phonics; Structural analysis; Vocabulary, selection.

Details, noting important, related, and sufficient. *See* Comprehension skills.

Diagrams. *See* Graphic information, interpreting.

Diaries and journals. *See* Journal.

Dictionary skills
    syllables, **137I–137J**

Drafting. *See* Reading-Writing Workshop, steps of.

Drama. *See* Creative dramatics.

Drawing conclusions. *See* Comprehension skills.

Editing. *See* Reading-Writing Workshop, steps of, proofreading.

English Language Learners, activities especially helpful for, *108A, 110, 121, 132, 133, 136, 137J, 140A, 142, 151, 162, 163, 166, 167P, 168A, 170, 183, 189, 201, 204, 205J, 205O*
    background, building, *R5*
    biography, writing, *F233*
    captions, reading, *F223*
    comparative adjectives, *R3*
    expressions, repeating favorite, *F220*
    illustrating a biography, *F227*
    language development, *153, 159*
    sports expressions, listing, *F210*
    vocabulary terms, *R5, R7*
    with theme paperbacks, *139J, 139L, 139N*

Evaluating writing. *See* Reading-Writing Workshop.

Evaluation. *See* Assessment, planning for.

Expanding literacy. *See* Skills links.

Fiction. *See* Literary genres; Selections in Anthology.

Fluency
    English Language Learners, *108A, 110, 132, 133, 140A, 142, 151, 153, 162, 163, 168A, 170, 183, 189, 201, 205O*
    reading fluency, *123, 147, 195*

Focus on Biography, *F208–F234, **F211, F217, F219, F223, F229, F233***

Generalizations, making. *See* Comprehension skills.

Genre. *See* Literary genres.

Get Set to Read
"Exploring Antarctica," *168A*
"Journey of the Pilgrims," *108A*
"Visiting Another Country," *140A*

Glossary in Student Anthology, *G1–G3*

Grammar and usage
speech, parts of. *See* Speech, parts of.
usage
object pronouns, **167K–167L,** *R21*
possessive pronouns, **205K–205L,**
R22
subject pronouns, **137K–137L,** *R20*

Graphic information, interpreting
diagrams, *134, 135*

Graphic organizers
art chart, *165, 167*
character chart, *141C, 153*
inference chart, *109B,* **109C**
phone message form, **167M**
SQRR, **167C–167D**
text organization chart, *169B,* **169C**
visual details chart, *203, 205*

Graphophonemic/graphophonic cues.
See Phonics.

Guided reading. *See* Reading modes.

Home-community connection. *See*
Home/Community Connections book.

Home connection. *See* Home/
Community Connections book.

Home-school connection. *See* Home/
Community Connections book.

Homework. *See* Home/Community
Connections book.

Illustrators of selections in Anthology
Allen, Thomas B., *102A, 110*
Dugan, Karen, *102A, 142*
McCurdy, Michael, *102A, 170*

Illustrator's craft
picture details, **155**

**Independent and recreational reading,
suggestions for.** *See* Reader's Library;
Reading modes; Suggested daily routines;
Theme paperbacks.

Individual needs, meeting, *102I–102J*
Challenge, *110, 113, 118, 125, 130,
137, 137H, 142, 149, 152, 155,
160, 167, 167H, 170, 178, 182,
187, 198, 205, 205H, F214,
F219, F224, R9, R11, R13, R15,
R17, R19, R23, R27*
Challenge/Extension activities
comprehension, *R9, R11, R13*
vocabulary, *R15, R17, R19*
Classroom management, *110, 134,
142, 164, 170–171, 202*
English Language Learners, *108A,
110, 121, 132, 133, 136, 137J,
139J, 139L, 139N, 140A, 142,
151, 153, 159, 162, 163, 166,
167P, 168A, 170, 183, 189, 201,
204, 205J, 205O, F210, F220,
F223, F227, F233, R3, R5, R7*
Extra Support, *111, 115, 117, 118,
120, 122, 123, 130, 135, 137B,
137G, 143, 147, 148, 152, 154,
157, 160, 165, 167B, 167G, 171,
175, 182, 184, 188, 197, 198,
203, 205B, 205G, F208, F222,
F226, F228, F229*
On Level Students, *110, 118, 125,
130, 142, 152, 160, 170, 182, 198*
Reader's Library. *See* Reader's Library
titles.
Reteaching
comprehension, *R8, R10, R12*
grammar, *R20, R21, R22*
structural analysis, *R14, R16, R18*
Strategy Review, *109A, 141A, 169A,
R3, R5, R7*

Inferences, making
about characters' actions and feelings,
106A, 107A–107C, 109B, **109C,**
119, **129,** *131, 132, 137,*
*137A–137B, 153, 162, 167, 200,
F227*
by drawing conclusions, *F221*
main idea, *135*
Reader's Library, *R2*
reteaching, *R8*

Informational selection, structure of.
See Comprehension skills, text
organization.

Information links. *See* Information
skills.

Information skills
graphic organizers, using, **167C–167D**
selecting multimedia resources,
137C–137D
time lines, using, **205C–205D**
See also Reference and study skills.

Interviewing. *See* Speaking activities.

Journal, *111, 120, 143, 154, 171, 184,
F208, F210, F216, F217, F220, F223,
F225, F227, F229, F232, R24*

Judgments, making. *See* Comprehension skills.

Knowledge, activating prior. *See*
Background, building.

Language and usage. *See* Grammar
and usage.

Language concepts and skills
development, by English Language
Learners, *153, 159*
primary language activities. *See*
English Language Learners.
See also Vocabulary, expanding.

Language mechanics. *See* Mechanics,
language.

Learning styles, activities employing alternate modalities to meet individual. *See* Individual needs, meeting.

Lessons, specific

comprehension, **109C, 113, 125, 127, 137A–137B, 141C, 151, 157, 159, 167A–167B, 169C, 175, 177, 187, 205A–205B**

decoding, **137E–137F, 167E–167F, 205E–205F**

dictionary, **137I–137J**

grammar, **137K–137L, 167K–167L, 205K–205L**

listening, speaking, viewing, **137O–137P, 167O–167P, 205O–205P**

literary genre, **117, 197, F219**

phonics, **137F, 167F, 205F**

Reader's Library, **R2–R7**

reading strategies, **109B, 141B, 169B**

spelling, **137G–137H, 167G–167H, 205G–205H**

study skills, **137C–137D, 167C–167D, 205C–205D**

visual literacy, **155**

vocabulary expansion, **137J, 167J, 205J**

writer's craft, **115, 193, F211, F217, F223, F229**

writing, **137M–137N, 167M–167N, 205M–205N, F233**

Leveled books

Houghton Mifflin Classroom bookshelf, *139H*

Reader's Library, *139H*, **R2–R7**

Theme Paperbacks, **139H–139N**

Library, using. *See* Information skills; Reference and study skills.

Limited English proficient students. See English Language Learners.

Linking literature. *See* Connections; Cross-curricular activities.

Listening activities

ABC memory game, *R26*

group problem solving, **205O–205P**

purpose

to think aloud. *See* Think Aloud.

to a read aloud. *See* Reading modes.

to creative dramatics. *See* Creative dramatics.

to literature discussion. *See* Responding to literature, options for.

to oral reading. *See* Reading modes; Rereading.

See also Dictionary skills; Vocabulary, expanding; Vocabulary, selection.

Listening comprehension

inferences, making, *106A, 107A–107C*

outcomes, predicting, *139S–139V*

text organization, *167U–167X*

Literacy, expanding. *See* Skills links.

Literary analysis. *See* Literary genres.

Literary devices

foreshadowing, *F211*

point of view

third person, *178*

quotation, *F229*

Literary genres, characteristics of

biography, *F208–F234*, **F219**

historical fiction, **117**

narrative nonfiction, **197**

See also Selections in Anthology.

Literary skills. *See* Literary devices; Story elements.

Literature

comparing. *See* Connections.

discussion. *See* Responding to literature, options for.

literary devices. *See* Literary devices.

responding to. *See* Responding to literature, options for.

story elements. *See* Story elements.

Locating information. *See* Information skills; Reference and study skills.

Main idea and supporting details, identifying. *See* Comprehension skills.

Management, special needs of students, meeting. *See* Classroom management; Individual needs, meeting.

Managing

assessment. *See* Assessment, planning for.

instruction. *See* Classroom management; Suggested daily routines.

program materials. *See* Classroom management; Suggested daily routines.

Mathematics activities. *See* Cross-curricular activities.

Meaning, constructing from text. *See* Comprehension skills; Decoding skills; Phonics; Strategies, reading.

Mechanics, language

punctuation of quotation, **F229**

Media

animation, researching, *F219*

multimedia report, creating, **137C–137D**

photo essay, reading, *202–205*

resources, *R28–R29*

Metacognition. *See* Lessons, specific; Strategies, reading; Think Aloud.

Modeling

monitor/clarify strategy, *175, 188*

phonics/decoding, *109A, 117, 123, 141A, 148, 169A, 197*

predict/infer strategy, *147, 157*

question strategy, *115, 122*

student, *116, 119, 124, 131, 152, 153, 156, 161, 176, 183, 186, 199*

teacher, *116, 137A, 137C, 152, 176*

think aloud. *See* Think Aloud.

Monitoring comprehension. *See* Strategies, reading.

Morphemes. *See* Decoding skills.

Morphology. *See* Decoding skills; Phonics; Structural analysis.

Movement. *See* Cross-curricular activities.

Music
    ballad writing, *F234*

N

National Test Correlation. *See* Assessment, planning for.

Newsletters. *See* Home/Community Connections book.

Nonfiction. *See* Literary genres; Selections in Anthology.

Nouns. *See* Speech, parts of.

O

Options for Reading
    Deciding About Support, *110, 142, 170*
    Meeting Individual Needs, *110, 142, 170*
    Reading in Segments, *110, 142, 170*
    Theme Paperbacks, *139H*

Oral composition. *See* Speaking activities.

Oral presentations. *See* Speaking activities.

Oral reading. *See* Reading modes; Rereading.

Oral reading fluency. *See* Fluency, reading.

Oral reports. *See* Speaking activities.

Oral summary. *See* Summarizing.

P

Parent conferences. *See* Home/Community Connections book.

Parent involvement. *See* Home/Community Connections book.

Peer conferences. *See* Reading-Writing Workshop, conferencing.

Peer evaluation. *See* Reading-Writing Workshop, conferencing.

Personal response. *See* Responding to literature, options for.

Phonics
    consonants
        double, **205F**
    vowel sounds
        in *bought,* **167F**
        in *tooth* and *cook,* **137F**
    See also Decoding skills; Spelling.

Planning for assessment. *See* Assessment, planning for.

Poems in the Anthology
    "Travellers," *102K*

Poets in the Anthology
    Adcock, Arthur St. John, *102K*

Point of view. *See* Literary devices.

Predicting outcomes. *See* Comprehension skills.

Predictions, making and checking
    reviewing, *119, 131, 153, 161, 183, 199*
    while reading, *156*

Presentation skills
    biography-related, *F234*
    nonverbal communication, **167P**
    oral reports, **137O–137P**
    using multimedia sources, **137C–137D**

Previewing
    extra support for, *111, 120, 143, 154, 171, 184*
    Reader's Library selections, *R2, R4, R6*
    strategy/skill, **109B–109C, 141B–141C, 169B–169C**
    theme paperbacks, *139I, 139K, 139M*

Prewriting. *See* Reading-Writing Workshop, steps of; Writing skills.

Prior knowledge. *See* Background, building.

Problem-solving and decision making. *See* Comprehension skills.

Process writing. *See* Reading-Writing Workshop, steps of; Writing skills.

Proofreading. *See* Reading-Writing Workshop, steps of.

Publishing. *See* Reading-Writing Workshop, steps of.

Punctuation. *See* Mechanics, language.

Purpose setting
    fine art, *165*
    for reading
        Across the Wide Dark Sea, 111, 120
        Becoming a Champion: The Babe Didrikson Story, F210
        Bill Meléndez: An Artist in Motion, F216
        Brave Bessie Coleman: Pioneer Aviator, F222
        Hank Greenberg: All-Around All-Star, F228
        "Shackleton's Real-Life Voyage," 203
        Trapped by the Ice!, 171, 184
        "Young Voyagers: A Pilgrim Childhood," 135
        Yunmi and Halmoni's Trip, 143, 154

Q

Quotations
    punctuating, **F229**

R

Reader's Library titles
    Brothers Are Forever by Marcy Haber, *167B,* **R4–R5**
    The Golden Land by Lee S. Justice, *137B,* **R2–R3**
    Iceberg Rescue by Sarah Amada, *205B,* **R6–R7**

Reading across the curriculum. *See* Cross-curricular activities; Cross-curricular links.

Reading fluency. *See* Fluency.

Reading log. *See* Journal.

Reading modes
> guided reading
>> Reader's Library selections, *R3, R5, R7*
>> theme paperbacks, *139I, 139K, 139M*
> teacher read aloud, *106A, 107A–107C, 139S–139V, 167U–167X*

Reading strategies. *See* Strategies, reading.

Reading-Writing Workshop (process writing), 138–139, 139A–139G
> steps of, **139A–139G**
>> conferencing, **139E**
>> drafting, **139C–139D**
>> evaluating, **139G**
>> prewriting, **139A–139B**
>> proofreading, **139F**
>> publishing, **139G**
>> revising, **139E**

Reads on and rereads. *See* Strategies, reading, monitor/clarify.

Reference and study skills
> graphic sources. *See* Graphic information, interpreting.
> information, gathering
>> for multimedia report, **137C–137D**
>> *See also* Information skills.
> reference resources
>> primary sources, *203*
>> *See also* Graphic information, interpreting.
> study strategies
>> research skills, *137,* **F217,** *F219*
>> SQRR, **167C–167D**
>> time lines, using, **205C–205D**
> *See also* Research activities.

Rereading
> for fluency, *123, 147, 195*

Research activities, *137, F214*
> animation, researching, *F219*
> writer's craft lesson, **F217**

Responding to literature, options for
> discussion
>> of *Across the Wide Dark Sea, 118, 119, 130, 131, 132*
>> of Reader's Library selections, *R3, R5, R7*
>> of theme paperbacks, *139J, 139L, 139N*
>> of Teacher Read Alouds, *107C, 139V, 167X*
>> of *Trapped by the Ice!, 182, 183, 198, 199, 200*
>> of *Yunmi and Halmoni's Trip, 152, 153, 160, 161, 162*
> personal response
>> to *Across the Wide Dark Sea, 133*
>> to Reader's Library selections, *R3, R5, R7*
>> to theme paperbacks, *139J, 139L, 139N*
>> to Teacher Read Alouds, *107C, 139V, 167X*
>> to *Trapped by the Ice!, 201*
>> to *Yunmi and Halmoni's Trip, 163*
> writing
>> *Across the Wide Dark Sea* and, *132*
>> *Trapped by the Ice!* and, *200*
>> *Yunmi and Halmoni's Trip* and, *162*

Reteaching. *See* Individual needs, meeting, reteaching.

Revising. *See* Reading-Writing Workshop, steps of.

S

Science activities. *See* Cross-curricular activities.

Selecting books. *See* Reader's Library; Theme paperbacks.

Selections in Anthology
> art
>> "Journeys Through Art," *164–167*
> biography
>> *Becoming a Champion: The Babe Didrikson Story, F210–F215*
>> *Bill Meléndez: An Artist in Motion, F216–F221*
>> *Brave Bessie Coleman: Pioneer Aviator, F222–F227*
>> *Hank Greenberg: All-Around All-Star, F228–F233*
> fiction
>> *Yunmi and Halmoni's Trip, 143–163*
> historical fiction
>> *Across the Wide Dark Sea, 111–133*
> narrative nonfiction
>> *Trapped by the Ice!, 171–201*
> nonfiction
>> "Young Voyagers: A Pilgrim Childhood," *134–137*
> photo essay
>> "Shackleton's Real-Life Voyage," *202–205*

Self-assessment. *See* Assessment, planning for.

Self-correcting reading strategy. *See* Strategies, reading, monitor/clarify.

Semantic cues. *See* Decoding skills; Vocabulary skills.

Sequence of events, noting. *See* Comprehension skills.

Setting. *See* Story elements.

Skills links
> diagram, reading, *134–135*
> fine art, how to look at, *164–167*
> photo essay, reading, *202–205*

Social studies activities. *See* Cross-curricular activities.

Sounding out words. *See* Decoding skills.

Sound-spelling patterns. *See* Phonics; Spelling.

Speaking activities
ABC memory game, *R26*
dramatics. *See* Creative dramatics.
giving oral reports, **137O–137P**
group problem solving, **205O–205P**
role-play. *See* Creative dramatics.
writing conferences. *See* Reading-Writing Workshop, conferencing.
See also Creative dramatics; Fluency; Reading modes; Rereading.

Speech, parts of
object pronouns, **167K–167L**
possessive pronouns, **205K–205L**
subject pronouns, **137K–137L**
See also Grammar and usage.

Spelling
assessment, **137H, 167H, 205H**
games, *137H, 167H, 205H*
integrating grammar and, **137K–137L, 167K–167L, 205K–205L**
patterns
VCCV, **205G–205H**
vowel sounds
in *bought*, **167G**
in *tooth* and *cook*, **137G–137H**

Spelling-grammar connection, 137E–137F, 137K–137L, 167E–167F, 167K–167L, 205E–205F

Story elements
setting, **193**
structure, **113**
See also Comprehension skills.

Storytelling. *See* Speaking activities.

Strategic reading. *See* Strategies, reading.

Strategies, reading
Monitor/Clarify, **169B**, *175, 176, 186, 188*
Phonics/Decoding, **109A**, *117, 123,* **137F, 141A**, *148,* **167F, 169A**, *197,* **205F**, *R3, R5, R7*
Predict/Infer, **141B**, *152, 156, 157*

Question, **109B**, *115, 116, 122, 124*
Summarize, *107C, 119, 131, 139V, 153, 161, 167X, 183, 199*

Strategies, writing. *See* Reading-Writing Workshop.

Structural analysis
possessives, **167E**, *R16*
suffixes
-less and *-ness*, **137E**, *R14*
VCCV pattern, **205E**
syllabication and, *R18*
See also Decoding skills; Vocabulary, expanding; Vocabulary, selection.

Student self-assessment. *See* Assessment, planning for.

Study skills. *See* Reference and study skills.

Study strategies. *See* Reference and study skills.

Suffixes. See Structural analysis.

Suggested daily planning. See Suggested daily routines.

Suggested daily routines
Across the Wide Dark Sea, *104A–105A*
reading instruction, *106A*
word work instruction, *137E*
writing and language instruction, *137K*
Trapped by the Ice!, *167S–167T*
reading instruction, *167U*
word work instruction, *205E*
writing and language instruction, *205K*
Yunmi and Halmoni's Trip, *139Q–139R*
reading instruction, *139S*
word work instruction, *167E*
writing and language instruction, *167K*

Summaries
of Anthology selections
Across the Wide Dark Sea, 103C

Trapped by the Ice!, 167R
Yunmi and Halmoni's Trip, 139P
of Reader's Library selections
Brothers Are Forever, R4
The Golden Land, R2
Iceberg Rescue, R6
of theme paperbacks
Balto and the Great Race, 139M
A Child's Glacier Bay, 139K
The Josefina Story Quilt, 139I

Summarizing
reading selection, *107C, 119, 131, 132, 139V, 153, 161, 167X, 183, 199*

Syntactic cues. *See* Structural analysis.

Syntax. *See* Decoding skills.

T

Teacher-guided reading. *See* Reading modes.

Teacher's Note, *107A, 109B, 137D, 137J, 139U, 141B, 167D, 167J, 167P, 167V, 167W, 169B, 205P, F208*

Teaching across the curriculum. *See* Cross-curricular activities; Cross-curricular links.

Teaching and management. *See* Classroom management; Individual needs, meeting.

Technology resources, *R28–R29*
Get Set for Reading CD-ROM, *108A, 140A, 168A*
Spelling Spree!™ CD-ROM, *137H, 167H, 205H*
Student Writing Center, *R25*
Type to Learn™, *137N, 167N, 205N*
Wacky Web Tales, *137K, 167K, 205K*

Text organization and structure. *See* Comprehension skills.

Theme Assessment Wrap-Up, *206–207, 207A*

Theme at a Glance, *102E–102F*

Theme concept. *See* Theme at a Glance.

Theme, Launching the, *102K, 103A*

Theme paperbacks, *139H–139N*
  Balto and the Great Race by Elizabeth Cody Kimmel, *139M–139N*
  A Child's Glacier Bay by Kimberly Corral, *139K–139L*
  The Josefina Story Quilt by Eleanor Coerr, *139I–139J*

Theme resources, *R1–R29*

Themes
  Animal Habitats. *See* Theme 4.
  Celebrating Traditions. *See* Theme 2.
  Incredible Stories. *See* Theme 3.
  Off to Adventure! *See* Theme 1.
  Smart Solutions. *See* Theme 6.
  Voyagers. *See* this theme.

Think Aloud, *109A, 109B, 137B, 137D, 137E, 137F, 137I, 141A, 141B, 167B, 167D, 167E, 167F, 167I, 169A, 169B, 205B, 205C, 205E, 205F, 205I, R3, R5, R7, R10*
  See also Modeling, teacher.

Thinking. *See* Critical thinking.

Topic, main idea and supporting details. *See* Comprehension skills.

Topics, selecting. *See* Reading-Writing Workshop, prewriting; Research activities.

Usage. *See* Grammar and usage.

Viewing activities
  nonverbal communication, **167O–167P**

Visual literacy
  cubism, *166*
  details chart, *203, 205*

photography, *204*
scene, picturing, **155**
selection in Anthology "Journeys Through Art," *164–167*

Vocabulary, expanding
  action verb, *R19*
  antonyms, *R15*
  family words, **167J**
  feeling words, *R17*
  -less or *-ness,* words ending in, *R15*
  opposites. *See* Vocabulary, expanding: antonyms.
  possessives, *R17*
  ship parts, words for, *133,* **137J**
  ships, words used on, *133,* **205J**
  synonyms, *149, R17*
  word web, *R19*
  See also Language concepts and skills.

Vocabulary, selection
  key words, *107A, 109A, 112, 114, 116, 118, 120, 122, 124, 126, 130, 133, 134, 136, 139T, 139U, 140A, 141A, 144, 146, 148, 150, 152, 154, 158, 163, 167V, 167W, 168A, 169A, 172, 174, 176, 178, 180, 182, 184, 186, 188, 190, 192, 194, 196, 204, F12, F214, F216, F218, F220, F222, F224, F226, F228, F230, F231, R2, R4, R6*
  theme paperbacks, *139I, 139K, 139M*
  spelling words, **137G, 167G, 205G**
  See also Daily language practice; Decoding skills.

Vocabulary skills
  analogies, **167I–167J**
  antonyms, *R15*
  homophones, **205I–205J**
  language games, *R15, R19*
  possessives, *R17*
  syllables, **137I–137J**
  synonyms, *R17*
  word web, *R19*

Vowels. *See* Decoding skills; Spelling.

Word analysis. *See* Structural analysis; Vocabulary, expanding; Vocabulary, selection.

Writer's craft
  conclusions, drawing, **F223**
  descriptive language, **115**
  foreshadowing, **F211**
  quotations, choosing, **F229**
  researching a subject, **F217**
  sequence of events, **F211**
  setting, **193**

Writer's log. *See* Journal.

Writing, activities and types
  ballad, *F234*
  character sketch, *R23, R25*
  journal. *See* Journal.
  personal narrative, *162*
  persuasive paragraph, *R25*
  research report, *R23*
  speech, *200*
  summary. *See* Summaries.
  theme resources, *R23–R25*
  See also Reading-Writing Workshop; Writer's craft.

Writing as a process. *See* Reading-Writing Workshop.

Writing conferences. *See* Reading-Writing Workshop.

Writing skills
  biography, writing, **F233**
  computer tools, using. *See* Technology resources.
  drafting skills
    dates and times, **205N**
    exclamations, using, **137N**
    final sentences, *F226*
    information, complete, **167N**
    learning log entries, **205M–205N**
    messages, writing, **167M–167N**
    play, writing, **137M–137N**
    proofreading for *its* and *it's,* **205L**

subject pronouns, sentence combining with, *137J*

verb forms, correct, *167L*

formats. *See* Writing, activities and types.

process writing, steps of. *See* Reading-Writing Workshop.

See also Reading-Writing Workshop; Writer's craft.